T0097611

Monopoly and King Mob

Monopoly and King Mob

Edited by
Anthony Comegna

CATO INSTITUTE
WASHINGTON, D.C.

ISBN: 978-1-944424-56-5
eISBN: 978-1-944424-57-2

Printed in Canada.
Library of Congress Cataloging-in-Publication Data available.

TABLE OF CONTENTS

Introduction: American History,
Above and Below 1

Part One: Feudalism to Corporatism 17

1. Early New English Charters 19

2. New Netherland Company Charter 29

3. Thomas Morton's New English Canaan 45

4. The Saga of Pirate Captain John Gow. 93

5. Slavery & Empire: The Destruction of
Whydah by Dahomey. 111

6. Slavery's Defenders versus the First Abolitionists 123

7. "Their Voyage to Hell": Piracy, Thick and Thin 133

Part Two: The Revolutionary Nineteenth Century 147

8. Walker's Appeal 149

9. The Equal Rights or Locofoco Party
Declaration of Principles 167

10. Theodore Sedgwick, Monarchy vs. Democracy 175

11. Leggett, The Restraining Law, and the Street
of the Palaces. 183

12. O'Sullivan, Introduction to the
Democratic Review 191

13. Leggett and Spooner, Abolishing Slavery
without the State. 205

14. The Autobiography of Ferret Snapp
    Newcraft, Esquire 215

15. Extracts from the Private Diary of
    a Certain Bank Director 235

16. O'Sullivan's Great Nation of Futurity 255

17. Whipple, Memoirs of Elleanor Eldridge 263

18. Gemmel, Two Years in Van Dieman's Land. 275

19. Ann Parlin, Great Meeting in Relation to Rhode
    Island (Speech at the New York Shakespeare Hotel) 285

20. Levi Slamm, Battling the Empire 295

21. Abram D. Smith, *In Re Booth* 315

22. Spooner, Abolition Plan/To the Non-Slaveholders
    of the South. 335

Part Three: The Century of Statism and Beyond 347

23. American Reactions to Italian Fascism, 1922 349

24. Smedley Butler and the "Business Plot" (1934) 363

25. Eisenhower, Farewell Address 389

26. Barry Goldwater, Acceptance Speech (1964 Republican
    National Convention) 399

Conclusion: *The New Necromancers: Technology,
Democracy, and Individualism* 413

Notes 441

Introduction: American History, Above and Below

Historians today possess a wide and constantly developing array of methodological perspectives and research methods to assist them in understanding how our world became the way it is. In a previous reader volume,[1] we surveyed classical liberal and libertarian theories of history: interpersonal conflict arose when some individuals chose to exercise power to curtail the liberties of others. In this volume, we turn from theory to method. In *Monopoly & King Mob*, our documents will take us through American history from the dawn of the early modern era to the Cold War. We will expand on the liberal theory of history by showing how different historical methods of reconstructing the past yield different narratives about what exactly happened and what we do with our knowledge.

History is what economist Ludwig von Mises termed "thymology" because it deals with the psychology *preceding* human action.

History is in the domain of human motivations, and it does not describe the mechanics or logic of human action. History is not about necessary causes and effects, and it is not a hard science explaining the facts of nature. It is about the ideas according to which people made their decisions, and as such there is no practical end to the amount and types of evidence historians might muster. Every fact in someone's personal history may come to bear on the choices they make, though the law of supply and demand may never change. Any general theories of history, therefore, must follow from our observations of what motivates behavior. The economist may demonstrate the law of comparative advantage without referencing individual psychologies, but the historian must amass evidence to explain why people choose to cooperate when they do. Although economics is primarily a theoretical discipline that uses the stuff of history to illustrate theory, history must be a vigorously and rigorously empirical discipline that builds theories on mountains of evidence. Historians can then hand their gargantuan haul of data about human motivations to the economist to speculate about how individuals might best achieve their goals. The thymologist tags in the praxeologist, and the liberal or libertarian social sciences have a powerful combination of disciplines.[2]

The historian's craft, then, demands especially careful attention to research methods and the collection, analysis, and presentation of evidence. Historical research methods are numerous and diverse, ranging from the straightforward and well known (such as oral history) to the obscure but highly useful (such as prosopography). Although many research methods do not necessarily come with any ideological baggage attached and they may not change the resulting narrative of events dramatically, sometimes the tools we choose during research deeply affect the facts we find. Although most students of history are aware of the problems of source bias, the researcher's selection bias, and the various limitations of methods, too few students spend serious time considering how one's theoretical understanding of human action influences one's collection and presentation of data. If, for example, the historian in question believes that only individuals act, she is more likely to practice "history from below." If the historian believes that collective entities are the most important agents in human decision making, she will be more likely to practice "history from above."

History from above is the reconstruction of past events as the deeds of Great Men and their Great Books, Great Laws, and Great Works; the influence of Big Institutions, Big Forces, and Big Ideas. Very often, history from above is the story written *specifically to justify the world as it is*. It tends to serve the interests of those in power and explain how virtually everything good in the world is the result of those in power.

History from below is the history of average people, common people, working people; racial, ethnic, religious, and political minorities; women; children; and any other socially, economically, politically, or culturally marginalized people. The perspective "from below" demands a far different set of source materials from that of history from above. To learn what powerless people thought and did, we must trudge through unpublished and uncollected letters and manuscripts; we must dig away in archaeological sites; we must practice a variety of interdisciplinary methods, from anthropology to linguistics; and we must diligently trace the lives of individuals *as individuals*, because history is built from the millions of choices each of us makes on a daily basis.

Should one construct American history from above, it usually would end up sounding like the time-worn and too-familiar story about American exceptionalism and Manifest Destiny coupled with the steadily growing and centralizing national government led by quasi-deified Great Chieftain presidents. In that version, American history has been the project of early settlers in desperate search of freedom and a subsequent "natural aristocracy" of "Founding Fathers." The Founders brilliantly managed to harmonize popular liberty with centralized power in the New World without constant civil wars or foreign imperialism. The American Revolution delivered the world promised to European immigrants during the 17th and 18th centuries of British rule, and over time the Revolutionary promise gradually blessed more and more of the population. As Great Men like Lincoln exercised good will toward all (even martyring himself in the cause), Americans vicariously cleansed themselves of any wrongdoing and progressed clear-souled into the limitless future.

So long as we continue paying due deference to our (divinely inspired?) Constitution and every year do our supreme democratic duty to vote, we will march right along and fulfill history's dictates. More often than not, history from above produces a narrative in which The People constitute a stupid and unfortunate influence on American life. Their only saving grace is in the election of Great Leaders. According to the perspective from above, the great things have been accomplished by an exceedingly small number of great individuals leading huge, impersonal collectivities.

Although much history from above has been explicitly orchestrated for the purposes of defending one regime or another, legitimate and essentially disinterested histories can indeed be written from above and very often have been. In many branches of historical study—such as political and intellectual history—the standard approach to the subject has always been from above. The sources one has in abundance are, after all, those handed down by the ruling classes and their (typically) loyal intelligentsia. Those historians who wish to tell the stories of ruling elites and philosophers almost *have* to write history perched on high; therefore, histories of policy, politics, and ideas tend to be written from the perspective of those who wielded power. Although that fact does not necessarily weaken the historical arguments in question, readers should always be aware that change may come from outside the status quo or ruling class as often as from within.[3]

In other cases of history from above, the historian's methodological perspective allows for collective action, and individual agency is dissolved into the vast socioeconomic soup. Those historians subsume individual actions to the behavior of groups, and narratives of nations or markets replace narratives of real human beings. Methodological collectivism produces history from above—and far more problematically so than does the method of studying elites' documents. Although the historian in question may not *intend* to serve the status quo, the nature of the evidence tends to do so without the craftsman having much of a say in the final product. Since the inception of professional history in the early 19th century, practitioners have periodically striven to perch themselves as far as possible above the realm of daily lived experience. From the lofty heights of quantitative history, they glory in the gargantuan forms of gross domestic product, interest rates, average wages, and aggregate prices. Statistical evidence undoubtedly has much to offer—it is, after all, very often representative of human activity writ large—but statistics do not interpret themselves. In the process of explaining data, the historian often projects his own preconceived notions onto the evidence. Aggregated data—absent a from-below picture of human motivations—can actually explain very little about the past, and even that is entirely uninteresting. Statistics can provide us with details to the narrative, but to understand individual action, we have to study individual thought and circumstance.[4]

It must be said, though, that history from above is still necessarily a corollary to history from below. To explain as much of the human experience as possible, we must account for the fundamental social forces that cause change over time. One of those major social forces is the tension established between those individuals who use their power to infringe on the liberties of others. Although most of human history has been dominated by Power's self-serving narratives, historians have recently begun correcting for that imbalance. Yet the balance is important, and we should be careful to always tell the *whole* story of the past. We should tell the stories of the exploiters as well as the exploited. We should be aware that biographies of presidents are important, but we should also recognize that without the necessary corrective in perspective from below, we risk reducing the past to the activities of a few, with the remaining population spoken for by aggregated figures. We should know that traditional political and intellectual history has an important place in the human story, but politics and academic philosophy are emphatically *not* the daily lived experiences of most human beings.

Should one conduct American history from below, the familiar narrative from grade school is seriously disrupted—often disturbingly so. History from below tends to yield a narrative in which European and African aristocrats violently drove great masses of their populations into servitude or slavery for New World colonial masters.[5] Rather few immigrants to pre-Revolutionary British North America were truly free and voluntary, and the United States was certainly no experiment in historical exceptionalism. In fact, say the historians-from-below, in American history we see the periodic rise and fall of a "mushroom aristocracy" (a phrase borrowed from Jacksonian America). The mushroom aristocrats derived their powers in the New World from the history of the Old: through corporate charters, medieval and early modern monarchs outsourced the duties of kingship to private entities. The colonies themselves, of course, were corporations with charters, and those fundamentally medieval devices for public-private partnership became entrenched as the basis of American law. Far from being an exceptional break with the Old World and its history, the United States became its most successful and direct heir. Mushroom aristocrats took the place of warlord and landlord aristocrats, and the richest and most powerful in American life constitute an entrenched and corrupting influence.[6]

In the from-below narrative, the great masses of people have struggled against power, sometimes themselves becoming powerful in the process. Liberal historians-from-below may emphasize the individual's multivariate battles against oppressive political and social forces of all sorts, from local, state, and national governments to patriarchal households and mob censorship. Marxist historians may choose instead to emphasize the battles of the poor and working classes against capitalist factory owners or landlords. Postmodernists and others may opt instead to explore the history of material or popular culture; they may probe the intellectual history of democratic majorities and the many groups clustered at the margins; or they may use scattered, bare, and aggregated evidence to reconstruct daily life in distant ages. Although their theories may differ and their analyses diverge, historians-from-below tend to agree that what progress may have been attained over the ages has come with great struggle and cost to average and marginalized people. If indeed our world is preferable to the world of the past, it is only because innumerable average and unstoried people have fought and labored to make it better, and the mushroom aristocracy has at best begrudgingly accepted it over time (if at all).[7]

It is my contention that a classical liberal theory of history compels one to adopt methods both from above and from below. The liberal theory of history provides a holistic vision of change both through consensus and through conflict in American history. It offers a narrative of American exceptionalism that provides room for the idea that North America was (for a short time) somewhere that marginalized people could actually live freely and without concentrated social power infringing on their lifestyles.

That liberated starting position was almost immediately compromised by nearby models of colonial governance, and it was nearly stamped out entirely during the reign of New England Puritans and Virginia land barons in the late 17th and early 18th centuries. As Part One shows, the early colonial powers established themselves in the New World via the corporate charter. That innovative new method of funding and operating state projects developed out of the medieval period, in which feudal lords possessed absolute rights over their personal domains. After the Great Plague and an ensuing spike in wages, European aristocrats found themselves in a somewhat frantic search for a way out of declining incomes. By offloading the long host of medieval rights and privileges they possessed to the burgeoning commercial classes, monarchs and noblemen offset financial losses and provided for the origins of modern corporate capitalism. The new species of corporations took an unending variety of forms, including colonial companies scattered across the globe. Colonial corporations represented and enriched their mother governments in exchange for exclusive trading rights, product monopolies, regulatory bonanzas, and a slew of other public–private partnership spoils.

Chapters 1 and 2 explore history from above through the corporate device in New England and New Netherland, and we find that from its inception, colonial North America was a theater for Old World powers to further aggrandize themselves. Also from the earliest days of European settlements, however, were outcasts from polite society who wished to live as freely as possible. Chapter 3 explores history from below through the saga of Thomas Morton and Merrymount, a settlement founded by Morton in which an early modern "rainbow coalition" carved space for liberty on the frontiers of imperialism. Their Puritan neighbors, however, had a very different vision of frontier life than Morton and his consociates. The Puritan armies destroyed the fledgling settlement and almost permanently stunted the libertarian impulse in American life. Throughout the late colonial period and even the Revolutionary era, Americans consistently failed to pick up the libertarian mantle from where Thomas Morton and antinomians like Anne Hutchinson had left it. The rebel colonists smashed the idea of monarchy, but they maintained the king's corporations. The colonial corporations became states and the charters became constitutions. Chapter 4 (also history from below) presents John Gow, who murdered his captain and turned pirate in the early 18th century. Gow's story illustrates the sharp, stark class divisions that ripped apart rulers and the ruled during the height of early modern imperialism. Chapters 5, 6, and 7 continue the theme but once again present history from above. Slave ship captain William Snelgrave's accounts of West Africa and the Middle Passage remind us that whether the perspective comes from above or below, early modern Atlantic history quickly became exceptional for its unmatched level of systematized violence, brutality, and inhumanity. In many ways we do not often consider, the New World was more of a frontier for torture and exploitation than it was a haven for liberty.

Historian Carl Becker argued that the American Revolution addressed two important questions, only one of which was actually settled by the war's end: Shall there be home rule? and Who shall rule at home? The people may have won their war for independence (for the time being), but once acquired, would the same old class of colonial elites go on ruling over their corporations, with little to no feedback from the "stockholders"? Those who tell the story from above argue that in fact, Americans are united from far and wide in a vast and all-encompassing ideological consensus that obviates such questions. The narrative from above presents the elite as a natural aristocracy of Great Leaders diligently and nobly doing the People's work. The elite become the agents of history by virtue of their institutional representation of the popular will; the historians' politics pushes them to aggregate popular opinion into one great mass. Even bitter partisan politicking is therefore not representative of fundamental conflict in American life—rather, it is indicative of our deep and abiding faith in representative democracy, the hopeful historian's darling baby.

Only the perspective from below truly addresses Becker's two questions in satisfying and accurate ways. The Revolution was a moment of popular and elite resistance to a common enemy, but once the British were removed from American governing institutions, the fundamental conflict remained between those who wield power and those whose liberties were infringed by the exercise of that power. American aristocrats essentially led a *coup d'état* against the Articles of Confederation government because it was thought incapable of defending the interests of the new status quo elites. Only 6–8 percent of Americans ever actually voted in favor of the Constitution, and, as Lysander Spooner so hotly and brilliantly noted, *no individual ever signed that contract.* Although American history from above generally treats the U.S.

Constitution as the culmination of consensus thought—the most ingenious and inspired governing system ever devised and the natural state of American life—the perspective from below demands that we ask, Exactly whose law is it, anyway?

In Part Two, we leap to the late 1820s, a period in which a variety of technological, economic, and political factors converged to prompt Americans to once again seriously question the existence of Old World institutions on this side of the Atlantic. In Chapter 8, David Walker implores his fellow African Americans to seize their freedom as a matter of individual right, no matter what the powers from above did to resist it. And resist it, they did. After Nat Turner's rebellion in 1831, fewer and fewer southerners seriously considered emancipation either possible or desirable. While American slaves suffered under the artificial claims of some to the labors of (powerless) others, northern radicals steadily connected several disparate intellectual threads into the philosophy we might call "locofocoism." Chapter 9 introduces the Locofoco, or Equal Rights, Party, an organization whose associated intellectuals linked the monopoly rights of slavemasters with the artificial rights of corporations. Both species of artificial rights had their origins in political power, and as Theodore Sedgwick and William Leggett argue in Chapters 10 and 11, the creation of any such rights and privileges necessarily divides the population into factions with antagonistic interests. Sedgwick and Leggett joined contemporaries such as Chapter 12's John L. O'Sullivan and Chapter 13's Lysander Spooner in advocating both a radical interpretation of democracy (in their view, only properly exercised as voluntary governance) and absolute commitments to individual rights.

To the most hopeful and, arguably, naive of those 19th-century thinkers from below, the American Revolution may not have perfected institutions, but it did indeed unleash a set of ideas about the natural world and social order that could not be constrained. Once average individuals discovered the truth of their freedom, dreamers such as O'Sullivan hoped, they would join in the great Democratic effort to root out any Old World institutions the Revolution may have missed. O'Sullivan's mission throughout life, in fact, was to prepare the cultural way for this mass Democratic revelation. Chapters 14 and 15 are fictional histories from above written for O'Sullivan's *Democratic Review* that provide readers insight into the minds of those who rule American life. Chapter 16 then presents O'Sullivan's own vision for American Manifest Destiny (a term he coined), in which the New World would finally become the haven for liberty it promised to be from the start: "The Great Nation of Futurity."

Many of his contemporaries in radical politics shared O'Sullivan's optimism, although they believed greatness did not come from creating one's own version of democratic mythology. In Chapter 17, Frances Whipple suggests that before we can correct failed institutions, we must be better individuals. In Chapter 18, reformed filibuster James Gemmel regrets his involvement in the 1837–1839 Canadian rebellions against British corporatism and imperialism, believing after the fact that Americans' greatest contribution to liberty is simply living freely. Others, such as Rhode Island's Ann Parlin, determined that if the corporate creatures—including chartered holdout institutions such as her own state government—would not relinquish their ill-begotten rights and privileges, it is the duty of the current and successive generations to root them out. Journalist and Locofoco activist Levi Slamm (Chapter 20) pivoted from attacking Rhode Island's British charter to stalking Victoria's growing empire at every turn. From the Hawaiian Islands to Afghanistan, Slamm follows the proliferation of British power by relating the stories from below of those ground under the imperial wheel. Abram D. Smith (who was also a filibuster in Canada and was even elected president of the Republic of Canada, although he was in Ohio at the time) managed to combine a penchant for territorial expansionism, anti-slavery, and anti-corporatism into a single worldview. The main effect of that explosive brew was Smith's nullification of the Fugitive Slave Act on the basis that government did not exist to serve the interests of a special, privileged class; rather, state officials owed each citizen respect for their universal, equal rights. If the government's legitimacy really does come from below, Smith reasoned, then he was bound to nullify such a law in operation against his state. Finally, we conclude the 19th century with Lysander Spooner's own version of nullifying slavery: simply ignore the state's grant that *some* may own *others*, invade the South, and free those held in bondage. Although Spooner believed that the United States government possessed no more legitimate authority than Queen Victoria's government, the great masses of his contemporaries did not agree. What was more, they flocked to Civil War killing fields to protect the interests of sectional elites. By the latter part of the century, little remained of Americans' traditional rights and liberties; most of them were conquered by corporatism and imperialism.

We turn, therefore (albeit briefly), to the 20th century on a distinctly melancholy note. Part III begins with a selection of American reactions to Mussolini's regime in Italy. Some 60 years after the Civil War, Americans were quite comfortable thinking of the world from above. The First World War left the United States the planet's most productive economy and perhaps the single most powerful military power as well. Yet the days of Thomas Morton's rainbow frontier were so far gone and the corporatist triumph so complete during the Progressive Era that many Americans positively craved a bit of fascism. As we can observe in General Smedley Butler's "Business Plot" testimony in Chapter 24, the handful of shadowy figures who hoped to oust Franklin Delano Roosevelt seemed to consider themselves the defenders of traditional American democracy—corporatism from above and civic-religious devotionals from below. The dangers of such a formula for state legitimacy in the modern era, however, are fantastic and horrifying. In Chapter 25, President Dwight D. Eisenhower bids farewell to the nation at the close of his terms and earnestly warns against once again granting immense powers to an elite and self-interested few. Chapter 26 expands on the point as Senator Barry Goldwater accepts his presidential nomination and declares the virtues of extremism in defense of liberty. Thirty years after the Cold War hard-liner announced his libertarian extremism, the communist threat had vanished, but the American empire remained.

The post–Civil War leviathan state has found little to no opposition able to stray the beast from its course, but we stand forever at the crest of history. We do know that we are in fact free, and that realization seems unlikely to disappear entirely from our thought and culture. We can—if we so choose—recover what Morton and countless nameless, faceless millions of others have lost or died for, but we can do so only when armed with a clear perspective on the exercise of power from above, and the very real potential to match and exceed that power from below.

Part One:

Feudalism to Corporatism

1

Early New English Charters

What the monarch giveth, the monarch may taketh away—such was the way of the world before the modern era, and perhaps it remains true despite the proliferation of nominally democratic regimes over the past few centuries. The transition from the feudal to the Early Modern period was marked by cessions of royal prerogatives, rights, and privileges to legally incorporated bodies of individuals. Those new corporations pooled capital to perform the task of governing the realm in a far more efficient, cost-effective, and transformative way than one king ever could. Having opened so much of the world to greater degrees of competition and free exchange, monarchs emptied a veritable Pandora's box of social, economic, cultural, and political changes that eroded the very foundations of monarchy over successive centuries. The exchange of royal rights for corporate money benefited both parties in the short and medium terms, but in the long run it was capital that dominated over kingship.

The struggle took a particularly violent and generative tone in England. Although English monarchs had dispensed corporate charters for some centuries, by the early 1600s, colonial projects were becoming increasingly more important for state expansion. The Stuart monarchs James I and Charles I followed their Tudor predecessor Elizabeth I in granting corporate charters to colonial companies, which promised to expand England's military and trading reach while directly contributing to the kings' coffers. The corporate-monarch relationship became especially important as Charles I crusaded against his own parliament, seeking money wherever he could to fight the Thirty Years' War on the continent. Parliament refused to tax the people so that Charles could build his ships and pay his mercenaries. The contest between king and parliament forced a renewal of the ancient battle between Saxon liberties and continental (monarchical) power. In the following selection of New World corporate charters, we witness the contest between Charles and his parliament reflected in New World political structures.

The first document shows the thoroughness with which kings granted away their right to rule over their lands. Virtually all aspects of economic life in the Swanckadocke country were batch granted as the personal property of Thomas Lewis and Richard Bonighton, so long as they paid 20 percent of all gold and silver discovered there to the Crown and 20 percent to shareholders. In the second item, the Council for New England petitioned the crown to dissolve its charter and reconstitute the colony as a Crown settlement. With a new royal charter in place, the king appointed Sir Ferdinando Gorges governor of the colony in 1637.

Gorges was by then one of the most important and long-standing figures in the history of English colonization, and, although a staunch royalist, he and his son Robert (a former governor-general for New England) wished the colonies to remain under private control. For all the work and wealth emptied into the colonies from private capitalists and their precious few colonists, a king would apparently strip them of their rights at will if his pocketbook or honor demanded as much. For both the growing class of powerful capitalists and the religious dissenters planning God's Kingdom in the New World, the monarch's continued power and presence seemed to threaten the entire early modern project. For the children to succeed, they would have to dethrone their great English father. He would have been lucky, in fact, to receive a simple dethroning. When the battle between capital and Crown developed to the fullest, Charles lost his head and England lost much of its mind.

Grant of Land North of the Saco River to Thomas Lewis and Richard Bonighton by the Council for New England; February 12, 1629

Whereas King James . . . by his Highness' letters patent and royal grant . . . did absolutely give, grant, and confirm to the said Council for the affairs of New England in America, and their successors forever, all the land of New England lying and being from forty to forty-eight degrees of northerly latitude and in length by all that breadth aforesaid from sea to sea throughout the main land, together with all the woods, waters, rivers, soils, havens, harbors, islands, and other commodities whatsoever thereunto belonging, with diverse other privileges, preeminences, profits, and liberties by sea and land, as by the said letters patents among other things contained. . . . For the good of his Majesty's realms and dominions and for the propagation of Christian religion among those infidels, and in consideration also that the said Thomas Lewis together with Captain Richard Bonighton, and also with their associates and company, have undertaken at their own proper costs and charges to transport fifty persons there within seven years next ensuing to plant and inhabit there to the advancement of the general plantation of that country and the strength and safety thereof among the natives or any other invaders, also for the encouragement of the said Thomas Lewis and Captain Richard Bonighton, and other considerations the said council thereunto moving, have given, granted, enfeoffed, and confirmed, and by this present writing do fully, clearly, and absolutely give, grant, enfeof, and confirm to the said Thomas Lewis and Captain Richard Bonighton, their heirs and assigns for ever, all that part of the main land in New England in America, aforesaid, commonly called or known by the name of Swanckadocke. . . . To have and to hold all and singular the said lands and premises with all and singular the woods, quarries, marshes, waters, rivers, lakes, fishings, fowlings, hawkings, huntings, mines, minerals, of what kind or nature soever, privileges, rights, jurisdictions, liberties, royalties, and all other profits, commodities, emoluments, and hereditaments whatsoever before in and by these presents given and granted, or herein meant, mentioned, or intended, to be hereby given, or granted with their and every of their appurtenances and every part and parcel thereof. . . . Yielding and paying to our sovereign lord the King, one-fifth part of gold and silver ore, and another fifth part to the council aforesaid and their successors, to be holden of the said council and their successors by the rent hereafter in these presents reserved.

Declaration for Resignation of the Charter by the Council for New England; April 25, 1635

Forasmuch as we have found by a long experience that the faithful endeavors of some of us that have sought the advancement of the plantation of New England have not been without frequent and inevitable troubles of companions to our undertakings from our first discovery of that coast to the present by great charges and necessary expenses, but also depriving us of diverse of our friends and faithful servants employed in that work abroad while we at home were assaulted with sharp litigious questions before the lords of his Majesty's most honorable Privy Council, by the Virginia Company, and that in the very infancy thereof, who finding they could not prevail in that way they failed not to prosecute the same in the House of Parliament, pretending our said plantation to be a grievance to the Commonwealth, and for such presented it to King James of blessed memory, who, although his justice and royal nature could not so relish it, but was otherwise pleased to give his gracious encouragement for prosecution thereof, yet such was the times, as the affections of the multitude were thereby disheartened. . . . [After a renewed parliamentary commitment to settler colonies,] Captain Robert Gorges . . . who, being made governor of those parts, went in person and took an absolute seizure and actual possession of that country by a settled plantation he made in the Massachusetts Bay, which afterwards he left to the charge and custody of his servants and certain other undertakers and tenants belonging to some of us, who were thrust out by those intenders that had exorbitantly bounded their grant from east to west . . . three thousand miles in length. . . . But herewith not yet content, they labored and obtained unknown to us a confirmation of all this from his Majesty, and unwitting thereof by which means they did not only enlarge their first extents to the west limits spoken of, but wholly excluded themselves from the public government of the council authorized for those affairs, and made themselves a free people, and for such hold themselves at the present. Whereby they did rend in pieces the first foundation of the building and so framed to themselves both new laws and new conceits of matters of religion and forms of ecclesiastical and temporal orders and government, punishing diverse that would not approve thereof, some by whipping, others by burning their houses over their heads, and some by banishing and the like, and all this partly under other pretences, though indeed for no other cause save only to make themselves absolute masters of the country, and unconscionable in your new laws. So as those complaints posting first to ourselves that had no sufficient means to redress or give satisfaction to the persons aggrieved, they were at last of necessity petitioners to his Majesty who, pitying their cases, referred them to the lords to examine the truth thereof, and to consider of the means of reformation, who calling some of us to give account by what authority or by whose means these people were sent over, and conceiving some of us to be guilty thereof, we were called for from our houses far remote in the country at unseasonable times to our great charge and trouble. But as innocence is confident, so we easily made it appear that we had no share in the evils committed, and wholly disclaimed having any hand therein, humbly referring to your lordships to do what might best sort with your wisdoms who found matters in so desperate a case as that they saw a necessity for his Majesty to take the whole business into his own hands, as otherwise we could not undertake to rectify what was brought to ruin. But, finding it a task too great for us to perform, we rather chose to resign all into his Majesty's hands to do therein as he pleased, to whom we conceived it did principally belong to have care of a business of so high a consequence as it is now found to be.

After all these troubles and upon these considerations, it is now resolved that the patent shall be surrendered to his Majesty with reservation of all such lawful rights as any is or has been seized with either before or since the patent granted to those of the Bay of Massachusetts. And that it may please his Majesty to pass particular grants to us of such proportions of lands as we have mutually agreed upon and are recorded before in this book that we, having his Majesty's grants of the same under a settled government, may the more cheerfully proceed in the planting of our several provinces, and with the better courage and assurance prosecute the same to a full settling of the state of those countries, and a dutiful obedience of all such as shall come under us to his Majesty's laws and ordinances there to be established and put in execution by such his Majesty's lieutenants or governors as shall be employed for those services to the glory of Almighty God, the honor of his Majesty, and public good of his faithful subjects. And thus much we have thought fit to be recorded and, in convenient time, published that posterity may know the reasons and necessities moving us to quit ourselves of these inconveniences and dangers that might have fallen upon the plantations for want of power in us to reform the same.

Commission to Sir Ferdinando Gorges as Governor of New England by Charles; July 23, 1637

Manifesting our royal pleasure for the establishing a general government in our territories of New England for prevention of those evils that otherwise might ensue for default thereof, forasmuch as we have understood and been credibly informed of the many inconveniences and mischiefs that have grown and are like more and more to arise amongst our subjects already planted in the parts of New England by reason of the several opinions, differing humors, and many other differences springing up between them and daily like to increase, and for that it rested not in the power of the Council of New England by our gracious father's royal charter established for those affairs to redress the same, without we take the whole managing thereof into our own hands and apply thereunto our immediate power and authority, which being perceived by the principal undertakers of those businesses, they have humbly resigned the said charter unto us, that thereby there may be a speedy order taken for reformation of the aforesaid errors and mischiefs. And knowing it to be a duty proper to our royal justice not to suffer such numbers of our people to run to ruin and so religious and good intents to languish for want of timely remedy and sovereign assistance, we have, therefore, graciously accepted of the said resignation and do approve of their good affections to a service so acceptable to God and us. And we have seriously advised with our Council both of the way of reformation and of a person meet and able for that employment by whose gravity, moderation, and experience we have hopes to repair what is amiss and settlement of those affairs to the good of our people and honour of our government. And for that purpose we have resolved with ourself to employ our servant Ferdinando Gorges, Knight, as well for that our gracious father of blessed memory as we have had for a long time good experience of his fidelity, circumspection, and knowledge of his government in martial and civil affairs, besides his understanding of the state of those countries wherein he has been an immediate mover and a principal actor to the great prejudice of his estate, long troubles, and the loss of many of his good friends and servants in making the first discovery of those coasts, and taking the first seizure thereof, as of right belongs to us our Crown and dignity, and is still resolved according to our gracious pleasure to prosecute the same in his own person, which resolution and most commendable affection of his to serve us therein as we highly approve, so we hold it properly of our princely care to second him with our royal and ample authority, such as shall be meet for an employment so eminent and the performance of our service therein. Whereof, we have thought it fit to make public declaration of our said pleasure, that thereby it may appear to our good subjects the resolution we have graciously to provide for the peace and future good of those whose affection leads them to any such undertaking, and withall to signify that our further will and pleasure is that none be permitted to go into any those parts to plant or inhabit but that they first acquaint our said governor therewith, or such other as shall be deputed for that purpose during his abode here in England, and who are to receive from him or them allowance to pass with his or their further directions where to set down most for their particular commodities and public good of our service, saving and reserving to all those that have joined in the surrender of the great Charter of New England and have grants immediately to be holden of us for their several plantations in the said country free liberty at all times hereafter to go themselves and also to send such numbers of people to their plantations as by themselves shall be thought convenient. Hereby strictly charging and commanding all our officers and others to whom it shall or may pertain, to take notice of this our pleasure and to be careful the same be firmly observed as they or any of them shall answer the same at their utmost peril.

2

New Netherland Company Charter

The turn of European history from the medieval to the early modern period consisted partly of monarchs shedding themselves of various feudal burdens. As they granted an endless series of state powers to private, chartered, incorporated entities, monarchs entered into league with a new class of capitalist-monopolists (and although they possessed no real theory of economics to speak of, those of this interest group are generally referred to as the "mercantilists"). Those monied interests took the form of banks, insurance agencies, vast mercantile concerns, and even colonial ventures. Often, the lines between those different sets of corporate interests blurred, and the specific details of a corporation's rights and privileges depended on the context in which the monarch granted the charter. In any case, the new species of incorporations emerged from the corpus of medieval kingship. Monarchs generally benefited from the exchange, now focusing entirely on forging nation-states and imperial militaries. Corporate efforts at exploration, trade, colonization, and raw materials production could offset the costs and travails of governing global empires and ease many of the traditional problems of governing Europeans. Such great transitions marked the shift from feudalism to capitalism, the Medieval to the Early Modern periods, the Dark Ages to the Renaissance and the Enlightenment—however one would like to cast the change, it was one of the most important historical situations humans had encountered to that point. The fusion of corporation and state power tended to encourage the very worst elements of both, producing a flood of enslavement, slave trading, the almost complete extermination of Native Americans from the planet, the construction of the largest and most powerful empires that ever existed, and world wars that consumed massive portions of the global population.

As we see below, even in a rebelliously liberated country such as the Netherlands, turning innocuous trading firms into militarized arms of statecraft took only a few decades. The first charter selected is a general proclamation that any agencies that demonstrated a sustained ability to carry out colonial trade stood to receive permanent and exclusive (monopoly) charters in the future. By the end of the year, the States-General granted a long list of capital-rich individuals the exclusive rights to trade "in America between New France and Virginia . . . called New Netherland." The company directly governed the colony and its extremely small population; only a decade later, the States-General turned its gaze to the far richer southern reaches of the Atlantic. The Dutch West India Company's charter is barely recognizable as a business enterprise and reads much more like a diplomatic arrangement between an empire and its client state. The company is granted wide latitude to govern colonies, deal with natives, and exploit its monopoly on trade in the entire Atlantic zone from the Caribbean to the Straits of Magellan. The company's duties to the government are enumerated in excruciating detail, giving the reader a perhaps too generous taste of modernity's origins.

General Charter for Those who Discover Any New Passages, Havens, Countries, or Places; March 27, 1614

Be it known, whereas we understand it would be honorable, serviceable, and profitable to this country and for the promotion of its prosperity, as well as for the maintenance of seafaring people, that the good inhabitants should be excited and encouraged to employ and occupy themselves in seeking out and discovering passages, havens, countries, and places that have not before now been discovered nor frequented; and being informed by some traders that they intend, with God's merciful help, by diligence, labor, danger, and expense, to employ themselves thereat, as they expect to derive a handsome profit therefrom if it pleased us to privilege, charter, and favor them that they alone might resort and sail to and frequent the passages, havens, countries, and places to be by them newly found and discovered for six voyages as a compensation for their outlays, trouble and risk, with interdiction to all, directly or indirectly to resort or sail to or frequent the said passages, havens, countries, or places before and until the first discoverers and finders thereof shall have completed the aforesaid six voyages. Therefore, we, having duly weighed the aforesaid matter and finding, as hereinbefore stated, the said undertaking to be laudable, honorable, and serviceable for the prosperity of the united provinces and wishing that the experiment be free and open to all and every of the inhabitants of this country, have invited and do hereby invite all and every of the inhabitants of the United Netherlands to the aforesaid search, and, therefore, have granted and consented, grant and consent hereby that whosoever any new passages, havens, countries, or places shall from now henceforward discover, shall alone resort to the same or cause them to be frequented for four voyages, without any other person directly or indirectly sailing, frequenting or resorting from the United Netherlands to the said newly discovered and found passages, havens, countries, or places until the first discoverer and finder shall have made or cause to be made the said four voyages, on pain of confiscation of the goods and ships wherewith the contrary attempt shall be made, and a fine of fifty thousand Netherlands ducats to the profit of the aforesaid finder or discoverer.

Grant of Exclusive Trade to New Netherland by the States-General of the United Netherlands; October 11, 1614

Whereas [a list of merchant-proprietors], all now associated in one company, have respectfully represented to us that they, the petitioners, after great expenses and damages by loss of ships and other dangers, had, during the present year, discovered and found with the above named five ships certain new lands situate in America between New France and Virginia, the sea coast whereof lie between forty and forty-five degrees of latitude, and now called New Netherland. And whereas we did, in the month of March last, for the promotion and increase of commerce, cause to be published a certain general consent and charter setting forth that whosoever should thereafter discover new havens, lands, places, or passages might frequent or cause to be frequented, for four voyages, such newly discovered and found places, passages, havens, or lands to the exclusion of all others from visiting or frequenting the same from the United Netherlands until the said first discoverers and finders shall themselves have completed the said four voyages or cause the same to be done within the time prescribed for that purpose, under the penalties expressed in the said octroy [grant of privilege, concession], etc.; they request that we would accord to them due act of the aforesaid octroy in the usual form.

Which, being considered, we, therefore, in our Assembly, having heard the pertinent report of the petitioners relative to the discoveries and finding of the said new countries between the above named limits and degrees and also of their adventures, have consented and granted, and by these presents do consent and grant, to the said petitioners now united into one company that they shall be privileged exclusively to frequent or cause to be visited the above newly discovered lands . . . now named New Netherland . . . and that for four voyages within the term of three years . . . without it being permitted to any other person from the United Netherlands, to sail to, navigate, or frequent the said newly discovered lands, havens, or places, either directly or indirectly within the said three years, on pain of confiscation of the vessel and cargo wherewith infraction hereof shall be attempted, and a fine of fifty thousand Netherland ducats for the benefit of said discoverers or finders; provided, nevertheless, that by these presents we do not intend to prejudice or diminish any of our former grants or charters. And it is also our intention that if any disputes or differences arise from these our concessions, they shall be decided by ourselves.

Charter of Privileges and Exemptions of the Dutch West India Company; June 7, 1629

Be it known, that we knowing the prosperity of these countries, and the welfare of their inhabitants depends principally on navigation and trade, which in all former times by the said Countries were carried on happily, and with a great blessing to all countries and kingdoms; and desiring that the aforesaid inhabitants should not only be preserved in their former navigation, traffic, and trade, but also that their trade may be encreased as much as possible in special conformity to the treaties, alliances, leagues and covenants for traffic and navigation formerly made with other princes, republics and people, which we give them to understand must be in all parts punctually kept and adhered to: And we find by experience, that without the common help, assistance, and interposition of a General Company, the people designed from hence for those parts cannot be profitably protected and maintained in their great risque from pirates, extortion and otherwise, which will happen in so very long a voyage. We have, therefore, and for several other important reasons and considerations as thereunto moving, with mature deliberation of counsel, and for highly necessary causes, found it good, that the navigation, trade, and commerce, in the parts of the West-Indies, and Africa, and other places hereafter described, should not henceforth be carried on any otherwise than by the common united strength of the merchants and inhabitants of these countries; and for that end there shall be erected one General Company, which we out of special regard to their common well-being, and to keep and preserve the inhabitants of those places in good trade and welfare, will maintain and strengthen with our Help, Favour and assistance as far as the present state and condition of this Country will admit: and moreover furnish them with a proper Charter, and with the following Priveleges and Exemptions, to wit, That for the Term of four and twenty Years, none of the Natives or Inhabitants of these countries shall be permitted to sail to or from the said lands, or to traffic on the coast and countries of Africa from the Tropic of Cancer to the Cape of Good Hope, nor in the countries of America, or the West-Indies, beginning at the fourth end of Terra Nova, by the streights of Magellan, La Maire, or any other streights and passages situated thereabouts to the straights of Anian, as well on the north sea as the south sea, nor on any islands situated on the one side or the other, or between both; nor in the western or southern countries reaching, lying, and between both the meridians, from the Cape of Good Hope, in the East, to the east end of New Guinea, in the West, inclusive, but in the Name of this United Company of these United Netherlands. And whoever shall presume without the consent of this Company, to sail or to traffic in any of the Places within the aforesaid Limits granted to this Company, he shall forfeit the ships and the goods which shall be found for sale upon the aforesaid coasts and lands; the which being actually seized by the aforesaid Company, shall be by them kept for their own Benefit and Behoof. . . .

II. That, moreover, the aforesaid Company may, in our name and authority, within the limits herein before prescribed, make contracts, engagements and alliances with the princes and natives of the countries comprehended therein, and also build any forts and fortifications there, to appoint and discharge Governors, people for war, and officers of justice, and other public officers, for the preservation of the places, keeping good order, police and justice, and in like manner for the promoting of trade; and again, others in their place to put, as they from the situation of their affairs shall see fit: Moreover, they must advance the peopling of those fruitful and unsettled parts, and do all that the service of those countries, and the profit and increase of trade shall require: and the Company shall successively communicate and transmit to us such contracts and alliances as they shall have made with the aforesaid princes and nations; and likewise the situation of the fortresses, fortifications, and settlements by them taken.

III. Saving, that they having chosen a governor in chief, and prepared instructions for him, they shall be approved, and a commission given by us, And that further, such governor in chief, as well as other deputy governors, commanders, and officers, shall be held to take an oath of allegiance to us and also to the Company.

IV. And if the aforesaid Company in and of the aforesaid places shall be cheated under the appearance of friendship, or badly treated, or shall suffer loss in trusting their money or Goods, without having restitution, or receiving payment for them, they may use the best methods in their power, according to the situation of their affairs, to obtain satisfaction.

V. And if it should be necessary for the establishment, security and defence of this trade, to take any troops with them, we will, according to the constitution of this country, and the situation of affairs furnish the said Company with such troops, provided they be paid and supported by the Company.

VI. Which troops, besides the oath already taken to us and to his excellency, shall swear to obey the commands of the said Company, and to endeavour to promote their interest to the utmost of their ability.

VII. That the provosts of the Company on shore may apprehend any of the military, that have inlisted in the service of the aforesaid company, and may confine them on board the ships in whatever city, place, or jurisdiction they may be found; provided, the provosts first inform the officers and magistrates of the cities and places where this happens.

VIII. That we will not take any ships, ordnance, or ammunition belonging to the company, for the use of this country, without the consent of the said company.

IX. We have moreover incorporated this company, and favoured them with privileges, and we give them a charter besides this, that they may pass freely with all their ships and goods without paying any toll to the United Provinces; and that they themselves may use their liberty in the same manner as the free inhabitants of the cities of this country enjoy their freedom, notwithstanding any person who is not free may be a member of this company. . . .

XI. And that this company may be strengthened by a good government, to the greatest profit and satisfaction of all concerned, we have ordained, that the said government shall be vested in five chambers of managers. . . . And the Provinces in which there are no chambers shall be accommodated with so many managers, divided among the respective chambers, as their hundred thousand guilders in this company shall entitle them to. . . .

XIII. And the States of the respective United Provinces are authorized, to lay before their High Mightinesses' ordinary deputies, or before the magistrates of the cities of these Provinces, any order for registering the members, together with the election of managers, if they find they can do it according to the constitution of their Provinces. . . .

XIV. That the first managers shall serve for the term of six years, and then one-third part of the number of managers shall be changed by lot; and two years after a like third part, and the two next following years, the last third part; and so on successively the oldest in the service shall be dismissed. . . .

XVI. That every six years they shall make a general account of all outfits and returns, together with all the gains and losses of the company; to wit, one of their business, and one of the war, each separate; which accounts shall be made public by an advertisement, to the end that every one who is interested may, upon hearing of it, attend; and if by the expiration of the seventh year, the accounts are not made out in manner aforesaid, the managers shall forfeit their commissions, which shall be appropriated to the use of the poor. . . .

XVII. No one shall, during the continuance of this charter, withdraw his capital, or sum advanced, from this company; nor shall any new members be admitted. If at the expiration of four and twenty years it shall be found good to continue this company, or to erect a new one, a final account and estimate shall be made by the nineteen, with our knowledge, of all that belongs to the company, and also of all their expences, and any one, after the aforesaid settlement and estimate, may withdraw his money, or continue it in the new company, in whole or in part, in the same proportion as in this; And the new company shall in such case take the remainder, and pay the members which do not think fit to continue in the company their share, at such times as the nineteen, with our knowledge and approbation, shall think proper.

XVIII. That so often as it shall be necessary to have a general meeting of the aforesaid chambers, it shall be by nineteen persons. . . .

XIX. By which general meeting of the aforesaid chambers, all the business of this Company which shall come before them shall be managed and finally settled, provided, that in case of resolving upon a war, our approbation shall be asked.

XX. The aforesaid general meeting being summoned, it shall meet to resolve when they shall fit out, and how many vessels they will send to each place, the company in general observing that no particular chamber shall undertake any thing in opposition to the foregoing resolution, but shall be held to carry the same effectually into execution. And if any chamber shall be found not following the common resolution, or contravening it, we have authorized, and by these presents do authorize, the said meeting, immediately to cause reparation to be made of every defect or contravention, wherein we, being desired, will assist them. . . .

XXIII. And if it should happen that in the aforesaid general meeting, any weighty matter should come before them wherein they cannot agree, or in case the vote are equally divided, the same shall be left to our decision; and whatever shall be determined upon shall be carried into execution. . . .

XXVIII. The managers shall have for commissions one per cent, on the outfits and returns, besides the Prince's; and an half per cent, on gold and silver: which commission shall be divided. . . .

XXXI. The manager shall not deliver or sell to the Company, in whole or in part, any of their own ships, merchandise or goods; nor buy or cause to be bought, of the said Company, directly or indirectly, any goods or merchandize nor have any portion or part therein on forfeiture of one year's commissions for the use of the poor, and the loss of Office. . . .

XXXVII. So when any ship shall return from a voyage, the generals or commanders of the fleets, shall be obliged to come and report to us the success of the voyage of such ship or ships, within ten days after their arrival, and shall deliver and leave with us a report in writing, if the case requires it.

XXXVIII. And if it happens (which we by no means expect) that any person will, in any manner, hurt or hinder the navigation, business, trade, or traffic of this Company, contrary to the common right, and the contents of the aforesaid treaties, leagues, and covenants, they shall defend it against them, and regulate it by the instructions we have given concerning it.

XXXIX. We have moreover promised and do promise, that we will defend this Company against every person in free navigation and traffic, and assist them with a million of guilders, to be paid in five years, whereof the first two hundred thousand guilders shall be paid them when the first payment shall be made by the members; Provided that we, with half the aforesaid million of guilders, shall receive and bear profit and risque in the same manner as the other members of this Company shall.

XL. And if by a violent and continued interruption of the aforesaid navigation and traffic, the business within the limits of their Company shall be brought to an open war, we will, if the situation of this country will in any wise admit of it, give them for their assistance sixteen ships of war, the least one hundred and fifty lasts burthen; with four good well sailing yachts, the least, forty lasts burthen, which shall be properly mounted and provided in all respects, both with brass and other cannon, and a proper quantity of ammunition, together with double suits of running and standing rigging, sails, cables, anchors, and other things thereto belonging, such as are proper to be provided and used in all great expeditions; upon condition, that they shall be manned, victualled, and supported at the expense of the Company, and that the Company shall be obliged to add thereto sixteen like ships of war, and four yachts, mounted and provided as above, to be used in like manner for the defence of trade and all exploits of war: Provided that all the ships of war and merchant-men (that shall be with those provided and manned as aforesaid) shall be under an admiral appointed by us according to the previous advise of the aforesaid General Company, and shall obey our commands, together with the resolutions of the Company, if it shall be necessary, in the same manner as in time of war; so notwithstanding that the merchantmen shall not unnecessarily hazard their lading.

XLI. And if it should happen that this country should be remarkably eased of its burthens, and that this Company should be laid under the grievous burthen of a war, we have further promised, and do promise, to encrease the aforesaid subsidy in such a manner as the situation of these countries will admit, and the affairs of the Company shall require.

XLII. We have moreover ordained, that in case of a war, all the prizes which shall be taken from enemies and pirates within the aforesaid limits, by the Company or their assistants; also the goods which shall be seized by virtue of our proclamation, after deducting all expenses and the damage which the Company shall suffer in taking each prize, together with the just part of his excellency the admiral . . . and the tenth part for the officers, sailors and soldiers, who have taken the prize, shall await the disposal of the managers of the aforesaid Company. . . .

XLIV. The managers of this Company shall solemnly promise and swear, that they will act well and faithfully in their administration, and make good and just accounts of their trade: That they in all things will consult the greatest profit of the Company, and as much as possible prevent their meeting with losses. . . .

XLV. All which privileges, freedoms and exemptions, together with the assistance herein before mentioned, in all their particulars and articles, we have, with full knowledge of the business, given, granted, promised and agreed to the aforesaid Company; giving, granting, agreeing and promising moreover that they shall enjoy them peaceably and freely; ordaining that the same shall be observed and kept by all the magistrates, officers and subjects of the United Netherlands, without doing anything contrary thereto directly or indirectly, either within or out of these Netherlands, on penalty of being punished both in life and goods as obstacles to the common welfare of this country, and transgressors of our ordinance. . . . And that none may pretend ignorance hereof, we command that the contents of this charter shall be notified by publication, or an advertisement, where, and in such manner, as is proper; for we have found it necessary for the service of this country.

Given under our Great Seal, and the Signature and Seal of our Recorder, at the Hague, on the third day of the month of June, in the year sixteen hundred and twenty one.

3

Thomas Morton's New English Canaan

For Thomas Morton, the New World truly was a new English Canaan. As one of the very earliest English settlers on the Massachusetts coast, Morton experienced the New World as a singular and direct contrast to life in late feudal or Early Modern Europe. Born in Devon, England, in 1579, Thomas was educated as a lawyer and wrote extensive personal notes and observations about social reform, inspired primarily by his time among Native Americans. His birthplace stamped Morton with the mark of High Church Anglicanism, considered by the rising tide of Puritans to be far too close to Catholicism. Morton spent the early part of his life traveling Elizabethan England, representing the "Old England" popular interest against the growing power of Crown and court. When not reveling in Renaissance England's libertinism—including, naturally enough, plays by Shakespeare and Ben Jonson—Morton sought to alleviate the sufferings of those displaced during the long centuries of land enclosure and structural unemployment. Ever fearful of peasant rebellion, espe-cially in London itself, Crown forces orchestrated a series of cam-paigns to stock the New World with indentured servants and free settlers. Men such as Sir Ferdinando Gorges led the coloniza-tion efforts, investing in land and labor. Gorges was personally granted a patent for what became Maine, the land between the Merrimack and Kennebec rivers, and in 1618 Thomas Morton agreed to help Gorges oversee his American holdings.

Morton visited the New World for several months in 1622 and again from 1624 to 1630. He drew on those experiences later in life, marketing his knowledge to eager London readers. The first book of Morton's *New English Canaan* is dedicated to the natural and social history of the Americas before the arrival of Europeans. Morton proceeded first under the assumption that virtually no place on Earth was better suited for colonization than New England. The practically perfect location and relative lack of concentrated population prepared an almost endless frontier for the British surplus population. Although Morton incorrectly esti-mated that Native Americans spoke a sort of transmuted Greek or Latin, he was quite correct in his belief that a "great mortality" had destroyed most of the native population. To Westerners, that fact generally spoke once again to the divinely chosen nature of the land and its preparation as a home to white-skinned, Christian peoples. Nevertheless, Morton does not fall into the Puritan mode of stand-ing in moral judgment over those with different lifestyles or histor-ical situations. He remarks with great reverence and respect on the generosity and friendliness of the natives; he notes their extensive trading practices, including the use of money; and, perhaps most importantly, Morton determines that the Indians live happily and in relative abundance. It was true, he held, that the Indians lacked the knowledge of important arts and sciences (notably navigation), but they enjoyed full stomachs all around and contented, leisurely lives—things most of London's poor had never known.

When Thomas Morton wrote of the "New English Canaan," he alluded back to the mists of time before Christ. The ancient Canaanites, according to chroniclers and theologians, were brethren of the famed Phoenicians and the infamous Carthaginians. As a seafaring, trade-seeking, settler-colonizing people, the Phoenicians founded what became Hannibal's great Carthaginian Empire and innumerable cities dotting the Mediterranean coasts over the course of two millennia. Ancient Canaan looked little different from modern Israel on the map, and it is precisely that territory that God marks for Abraham's descendants. Canaan was God's gift to his chosen people—a paradisiacal land of plenty reserved as Israel. To 17th century Englishmen, North America was the New Canaan. The Native Americans and their white Indian allies from places such as Morton's Merrymount, moreover, were the New Canaanites. The Puritans fancied themselves God's instruments to cleanse and purify the New World, preparing the New Israel for millennial battles against Satan. That convoluted, highly problematic theological pairing of defeated, dispossessed, and displaced Canaanites with victorious, prosperous, and powerful Israelite colonists established the tone of historical conflict through early New English history.

Yet in 1627, Thomas Morton and the residents, friends, and allies of Merrymount gathered together for a celebration of life and leisure. The settlement was a bustling little burgh, pleasantly situated on the fringes of Puritan Massachusetts Bay. Having previously felled one of New England's many mighty pines, the revelers marked their New World holy day by building a grand Maypole. In a very conscious imitation of the ancient, pagan world, the crowd decked their construction in garlands and intertwined ribbons, topping the whole with a formidable set of antlers. Morton constructed what historian Peter Linebaugh claims were "the first lyric verses penned in America," and he nailed the infamous "Bacchanalian song" to the Maypole itself, in proud defiance of the Puritan norms prevailing elsewhere in Massachusetts. In Merrymount, Native Americans and English lived alongside one another peacefully: they traded, they enjoyed mutual and consensual romantic and sexual relationships, and they mutually mixed philosophies and perspectives in convivial atmospheres such as the May Day festival.[8]

The Puritans viewed all of those practices with nothing short of horror and contempt. Whereas the Merrymounters saw Natives as brothers and sisters, the Puritans saw them as Satan's minions inhabiting the darkest corners of their New Israel. They called the Maypole "an Idoll" and the free settlement "Mount Dagon." As Linebaugh notes, in its short life, Merrymount had become "a refuge for Indians, the discontented, gay people, runaway servants, and what [Governor Bradford] called 'all the scume of the countrie.'" Convinced that the free settlers and May Day revelers were devils in human skins, Miles Standish and a Puritan contingent destroyed the settlement with fire, and the Maypole got the axe. In Linebaugh's estimation, Merrymount was but one short-lived—though powerful—example of the modern era's evolving "rainbow coalition" of radicals and those who dared to live free among the great empires.

In his short, fictionalized story on the subject, Nathaniel Hawthorne believed this episode determined "the future complexion of New England." Hawthorne explained that "Two hundred years ago, and more, the old world and its inhabitants became mutually weary of each other. Men voyaged by thousands to the West: some to barter glass beads, and such like jewels, for the furs of the Indian hunter." The white traders and their Indian customers mixed together socially, culturally, and biologically across the North American frontier zone, establishing a new era in history—the Early Modern—and a new geographic region—the Atlantic. Along with traders came "some to conquer virgin empires; and one stern band to pray. But none of these motives had much weight with the colonists of Merry Mount." "Should the grizzly saints establish their jurisdiction over the gay sinners," Hawthorne wrote, "then would their spirits darken all the clime, and make it a land of clouded visages, of hard toil, of sermon and psalm forever." Should the free settlers prevail, "sunshine would break upon the hills, and flowers would beautify the forest, and late posterity do homage to the Maypole." Puritan victory inflicted irreparable damages to liberty in the New World. With the Maypole and Merrymount left in heaps of ashes, Hawthorne concludes, "As the moral gloom of the world overpowers all systematic gayety, even so was their home of wild mirth made desolate amid the sad forest. They returned to it no more."[9]

Morton continues his story from May Day, 1627. The settlement is in cinders and the revelers in custody or scattered to
the countryside. Historian Peter Linebaugh's rainbow coalition
of "masterless men and women," Native Americans, and social
deviants of all sorts seemed to be destroyed along with their
Maypole. The currents of popular culture, however, revived dozens of images from ancient history and myth to tell a very different story. Morton's poem "Baccanall Triumphe," perhaps written
with assistance from popular playwright Ben Jonson, made its way
from mouth to ear through the streets of London. The lines burst
with subversive imagery and a very modern, humanistic critique
of fanaticism: the Puritans' commitments to demonology threatened the existence of a very real and very wonderful New Canaan.
Morton (and possibly Jonson) cried out to his English audiences
that they, too, could enjoy free, prosperous, and leisurely lives in
the New World but for the militant, charter-mongering "Separatists," who saw monsters around every corner and devils behind
every face. To the Puritans, all individuals not Elect—from homo-
sexuals to Native Americans, Africans, and poor people—were
tools of Satan, the many heads of the same hydra. Massachusetts
Bay hacked off the Merrymount head, but many others remained
to snap and bite another day.

In the last item of the present series, moderate royalist and
Anglican Thomas Morton loosed arrow after arrow in the
Puritans' general direction, chastising them before the English
public for their reckless destruction of his settlement. Morton's
attack was made all the more significant given the shift in context
from his days in Merrymount to the publication of *New English*

Canaan. Morton left New England in the late 1620s and published his memoir a decade later. By the time he did so, Puritan Massachusetts Bay battled for its very survival. Detailing "the Practice of their Church," Morton primarily focuses his criticism on the outward orientation of Separatism. He begins by noting that virtually anyone can become a Puritan preacher so long as he publicly professes a faith experience demonstrating Elect status before his peers. Once deemed Elect, "These are all public preachers," who enjoy the monopoly privileges of office holding and voting. Yet the trappings and emoluments of both spiritual and temporal office failed to cleanse the Puritan's moral slate. After all, "what is bred in the bone will not out of the flesh, nor the stepping into the pulpit can make the person fit for the employment." Morton admits that although he has not known many Puritan preachers personally, "If a man observe these people in the exercise of their gifts, he may thereby discern the tincture of their proper calling, the asses' ears will peep through the lion's hide." Most of all, the Puritan proudly puffed himself full of self-love and bluster, convinced of his own divine agency in the New World frontier zone, surrounded by Satan and his demons. Morton concludes of it all, "I am sorry they cannot discern their own infirmities." The current selection finishes Morton's critique of the Puritans and their pretensions to moral superiority, with special reference to his capture by Miles Standish, who then marooned Morton in the Isles of Shoals off the Maine coast. Bitter, fuming with anger, and stranded by religious zealots, Morton longed for the day when New English pride finally aroused sufficient divine vengeance. Little did he know that *new* New Canaanites such as

Anne Hutchinson, Roger Williams, and hundreds like them back in England were busily, diligently turning the world upside down.

Anne Hutchinson, the brilliant wife of a well-to-do English merchant, arrived with her family in Boston in 1634. The colony was never quite the same. Anne and her cohort of new Puritan immigrants to America's New Israel carried with them a dangerous combination of hyper-individualistic theology and revolutionary political philosophy. The Hutchinsonians suggested that the Puritans—so called because they wanted to "purify" the Anglican church of its remaining Catholic elements—were far from pure. In fact, Hutchinson argued in her (*gasp!*) mixed-sex Bible studies groups that the Puritan church followed Catholicism in preaching a covenant of works. Whereas Catholics believe that God's covenant with man requires the performance of specified "good works," including the sacraments, Hutchinson's "antinomians" carried the Protestant "covenant of grace" to its logical extreme. Rather than performing a series of worldly actions commanded by the worldly powers of church and state, Hutchinson believed that faith alone admitted individuals to God's family. Antinomians threatened the Massachusetts Bay Elect because they questioned the legitimacy of all worldly authorities and their commands. To make matters worse for the Elect, their colony was then in the middle of the Pequot War (ca. 1634–1638), and the prospect of soldiers disobeying temporal authorities, laying down arms, and perhaps even joining the Indians spelled New Israel's utter destruction. If Hutchinson were not stopped in her tracks, the Merrymount hydra would surely recover, gathering Satan's forces once again beneath a heathen Maypole.

New English Canaan; or New Canaan: Containing an Abstract of New England

The First Book. Containing the original of the Natives, their manners & Customs, with their tractable nature and love towards the English.[10]

> Chap. I: Proving New England the principal part of all America, and most commodious and fit for habitation.

The wise Creator of the universall Globe hath placed a golden mean betwixt two extremes; I mean the temperate Zones, betwixt the hot and cold; and every Creature, that participates of Heavens blessings with in the Compass of that golden mean, is made most apt and fit for man to use, who likewise by that wisdom is ordained to be the Lord of all. This globe may be his glass, to teach him how to use moderation and discretion, both in his actions and intentions. The wise man says, give me neither riches nor poverty; why? Riches might make him proud like Nebuchadnezar, and poverty despair like Jobs wife; but a mean between both . . .

Therefore the Creatures that participate of heat and cold in a mean, are best and holsomest: and so it is in the choice of love, the middle Zone between the two extremes is best . . .

Behold the secret wisdom of almighty God, and love unto our Salomon, to raise a man of a large heart, full of worthy abilities, to be the Index or Loadstar, that doth point out unto the English Nation with ease and comfort how to find it out. And this the noble minded Gentleman, Sir Ferdinando Gorges, Knight, zealous for the glory of God, the honor of his Majesty and the benefit of the wale publicke, hath done a great work for the good of his Country.

And herein this, the wondrous wisdom and love of God, is shown by sending to the place his Minister, to sweep away by heaps the Salvages; and also giving him length of days to see the same performed after his enterprise was begun, for the propagation of the Church of Christ.

This judicious Gentleman hath found this golden mean to be situated about the middle of those two extremes and for directions . . . and then keep us on that same side, and see what Land is to be found there, and we shall easily discern that New England is on the South side of that Center.

For that country doth begin her boundes at 40 Degrees . . . and ends at 45 Degrees . . . and doth participate of heat and cold indifferently, but is oppressed with neither: and therefore may be truly said to be within the compass of that golden mean most apt and fit for habitation and generation, being placed by Almighty God, the great Creator, under that Zone called Zona temperata; and is therefore most fit for the generation and habitation of our English nation, of all other. . . This Country of new England is by all judicious men accounted the principal part of all America for habitation and the commodiousness of the Sea, Ships, there not being subject to worms as in Virginia and other places, and not to be paralleled in all Christendom. The Massachusetts, being the middle part thereof, is a very beautiful Land, not mountainy nor inclining to mountainy . . . and hath as yet the greatest number of inhabitants; and hath a very large bay to it divided by islands into 4 great bays, where shipping may safely ride, all winds and weathers. . . The riches of which Country I have set forth in this abstract as in a Landskipp, for the better information of Travellers; which he may peruse and plainly perceive by the demonstration of it, that it is nothing inferior to Canaan of Israel, but a king of parallel to it in all points.

Chap. II: Of the Original of the Natives.

In the year since the incarnation of Christ, 1622, it was my chance to be landed in the parts of New England, where I found two sorts of people, the one Christians, the other Infidels; these I found most full of humanity, and more friendly then the other: as shall hereafter be made apparent in due course by their several actions from time to time, whilest I lived among them. After my arrival in those parts, I endeavored by all the ways and means that I could to find out from what people, or nation, the Natives of New England might be conjectured originally to proceed; and by continuance and conversation amongst them, I attained to so much of their language, as by all probable conjecture may make the same manifest: for it hath been found by divers, and those of good judgement, that the Natives of this Country do use very many words, both of Greek and Latin, to the same signification that the Latins and Greeks have done . . . so that it may be thought that these people heretofore have had the name of Pan in great reverence and estimation, and it may be have worshipped Pan the great God of the Heathens: Howsoever they do use no manner of worship at all now: and it is most likely that the Natives of this Country are descended from people bred upon that part of the world which is toward the Tropick of Cancer . . . the Natives of New-England may proceed from the race of the

Tartars, and come from Tartaria into those parts, over the frozen Sea, I see no probability for any such Conjecture . . . But it may perhaps be granted that the Natives of this Country might originally come from the scattered Trojans: For after that Brutus, who was the forth from Aneas, left Latium upon the conflict had with the Latins . . . this people were dispersed: there is no question but the people that lived with him, by reason of their conversation with the Grecians and Latins, had a mixed language that participated of both, whatsoever was that which was proper to their own nation at first I know not: for this is commonly seen where two nations traffick together, the one endeavoring to understand the others meaning makes them both many times speak a mixed language, as is approved by the Natives of New England, through the covetous desire they have to commerce with our nation and we with them . . .

Chap. III: Of a great mortality that happened amongst the Natives of New England, near about the time that the English came there to plant.

If fortuned some few years before the English came to inhabit at new Plymouth, in New England, that upon some distaste given in the Massachusetts bay by Frenchmen, then trading there with the Natives for beaver, they set upon the men at such advantage that they killed many of them, burned their ship, then riding at Anchor by an Island there . . . distributing them unto 5 Sachems, which were Lords of the several territories adjoining: they did keep them so long as they lived, only to sport themselves at them, and made these five Frenchmen fetch them wood and water, which is the general work that they require of a servant. One of these five men, out living the rest, had learned so much of their language as to rebuke them for their bloody deed, saying that God would be angry with them for it, and that he would in his displeasure destroy them; but the Savages (it seems boasting of their strength,) replied and said, that they were so many that God could not kill them.

But contrary wise, in short time after the hand of God fell heavily upon them, with such a mortal stroke that they died on heaps as they lay in their houses; and the living, that were able to shift for themselves, would run away and let them die, and let there Carcasses lie above the ground without burial. For in a place where many inhabited, there hath been but one left alive to tell what became of the rest; the living being (as it seems) not able to bury the dead, they were left for Crows, Kites and vermin to pray [prey] upon. And the bones and skulls upon the several places of their habitations made such a spectacle after my coming into those parts, that, as I travelled in that Forest near the Massachusetts, it seemed to me a new found Golgatha.

But otherwise, it is the custom of those Indian people to bury their dead ceremoniously and carefully, and then to abandon that place, because they have no desire the place should put them in mind of mortality: and this mortality was not ended when the Brownists of new Plymouth were settled at Patuxet in New England: and by all likelihood the sickness that these Indians died of was the Plague, as by conference with them since my arrival and habitation in those parts, I have learned. And by this means there is as yet but a small number of Savages in New England, to that which hath been in former time, and the place is made so much the more fit for the English Nation to inhabit in, and erect in it Temples to the glory of God.

Chap. IV: Of their Houses and Habitations.

. . . In the night they take their rest; in the day time, either the kettle is on with fish or flesh, by no allowance, or else the fire is employed in roasting of fishes, which they delight in. The air doth beget good stomachs, and they feed continually, and are no niggards of their vittels; for they are willing that any one shall eat with them. Nay, if any one that shall come into their houses and there fall asleep, when they see him disposed to lie down, they will spread a mat for him of their own accord, and lay a roll of skins for a boulster, and let him lie. If he sleep until their meat be dished up, they will set a wooden bowl of meat by him that sleepeth, and wake him saying, *Cattup keene Meckin*: That is, If you be hungry, there is meat for you, where if you will eat you may. Such is their Humanity.

Likewise, when they are minded to remove, they carry away the mats with them; other materials the place adjoining will yield. They use not to winter and summer in one place, for that would be a reason to make fuel scarce; but, after the manner of the gentry of Civilized natives, remove for their pleasures; some times to their hunting places, where they remain keeping good hospitality for that season; and sometimes to their fishing places, where they abide for that season likewise: and at the spring, when fish comes in plentifully, they have meetings from several places, where they exercise themselves in gaming and playing in juggling tricks and all manner of Revels, which they are delighted in; so that it is admirable to behold what pastime they use of several kinds, every one striving to surpass each other. After this manner they spend their time . . .

Chap. XII: Of their traffick and trade one with another.

Although these people have not the use of navigation, whereby they may traffick as other nations, that are civilized, use to do, yet do they barter for such commodities as they have, and have a kind of beads, instead of money, to buy withal such things as they want, which they call Wampampeak: and it is of two sorts, the one is white, the other is of a violet color. These are made of the shells of fish. The white with them is a silver with us; the other as our gold: and for these beads they buy and sell, not only amongst themselves, but even with us.

We have used to sell them any of our commodities for this Wampampeak, because we know we can have beaver again of them for it: and these beads are current in all the parts of New England, from one end of the Coast to the other.

And although some have endeavored by example to have the like made of the same kind of shells, yet none hath ever, as yet, attained to any perfection in the composure of them, but that the Savages have found a great difference to be in the one and the other; and have known the counterfeit beads from those of their own making; and have, and do slight them.

The skins of beasts are sold and bartered, to such people as have none of the same kind in the parts where they live . . .

So likewise (at the season of the year) the Savages that live by the Sea side for trade with the inlanders for fresh water . . . chestnuts, and such like useful things as one place affordeth, are sold to the inhabitants of another, where they are a novelty accounted amongst the natives of the land. And there is no such thing to barter withal, as is their Wampampeak . . .

Chap. XX. That the Savages live a contented life.

A Gentleman and a traveler, that had been in the parts of New England for a time, when he returned again, in his discourse of the Country, wondered, (as he said,) that the natives of the land lived so poorly in so rich a Country, like to our Beggars in England. Surely that Gentleman had not time or leisure while he was there truly to inform himself of the state of that Country, and the happy life the Savages would lead were they once brought to Christianity.

I must confess they want the use and benefit of Navigation, (which is the very finnus of a flourishing Commonwealth,) yet are they supplied with all manner of needful things for the maintenance of life and livelihood. Food and raiment are the chief of all that we make true use of; and of these they find no want, but have, and may have, them in a most plentiful manner.

If our beggars of England should, with so much ease as they, furnish themselves with food at all seasons, there would not be so many starved in the streets, neither would so many jails be stuffed, or gallows furnished with poor wretches, as I have seen them.

But they of this sort of our own nation, that are fit to go to this Canaan, are not able to transport themselves; and most of them unwilling to go from the good ale tap, which is the very loadstone of the land by which our English beggars steer their Course; it is the Northpole to which the flower-du-luce of their compass points. The more is the pity that the Commonalty of our Land are of such leaden capacities as to neglect to brave a Country, that doth so plentifully seed many lusty and a brave, able men, women and children, that have no[t] the means that a Civilized Nation hath to purchase food and raiment; which that Country with a little industry will yield a man in a very comfortable measure, without overmuch carking.

I cannot deny but a civilized Nation hath the preeminence of an uncivilized, by means of those instruments that are found to be common amongst civil people, and the uncivil want the use of, to make themselves masters of those ornaments that make such a glorious show, that will give a man occasion to cry, *sic transit Gloria Mundi* ["thus passes Earthly Glory"].

Now since it is but food and raiment that men that live needeth, (though not all alike,) why should not the Natives of New England be said to live richly, having no want of either? Cloths are the badge of sin; and the more variety of fashions is but the greater abuse of the Creature: the beasts of the forest there do serve to furnish them at any time when they please: fish and flesh they have in great abundance, which they both roast and boil.

They are indeed not served in dishes of plate with variety of Sauces to procure appetite; that needs not there. The rarity of the air, begot by the medicinable quality of the sweet herbs of the Country, always procures good stomachs to the inhabitants.

I must needs commend them in this particular, that, though they buy many commodities of our Nation, yet they keep but few, and those of special use.

They love not to be cumbered with many utensils, and although every proprietor knows his own, yet all things, (so long as they will last), are used in common amongst them: A Biscuit cake given to one, that one breaks it equally into so many parts as there be persons in his company, and distributes it. Plato's Commonwealth is so much practiced by these people.

According to human reason, guided only by the light of nature, these people leads the more happy and freer life, being void of care, which torments the minds of so many Christians: They are not delighted in baubles, but in useful things.

Their natural drink is of the Cristal fountaine, and this they take up in their hands, by joining them close together. They take up a great quantity at a time, and drink at the wrists. It was the sight of such a feat which made Diogenes hurl away his dish, and, like one that would have this principal confirmed, *Natura paucis contentat* [nature is satisfied by meager things], used a dish no more.

I have observed that they will not be troubled with superfluous commodities. Such things as they find they are taught by necessity to make use of, they will make choice of, and seek to purchase with industry. So that, in respect that their life is so void of care, and they are so loving also that they make use of those things they enjoy, (the wife only excepted,) as common goods, and are therein so compassionate that, rather than one should starve through want, they would starve all. Thus do they pass away the time merrily, not regarding our pomp, (which they see daily before their faces,) but are better content with their own, which some men esteem so meanly of.

They may be rather accounted to live richly, wanting nothing that is needful; and to be commended for leading a contented life, the younger being ruled by the Elder, and the Elder ruled by the Powahs, and the Powahs are ruled by the Devil; and then you may imagine what good rule is like to be amongst them . . .

Book III

Chap. XIV. Of the Revels of New Canaan.

The inhabitants of Pasonagessit, (having translated the name of their habitation from that ancient Savage name to Merrymount, and being resolved to have the new name confirmed for a memorial to after ages,) did devise amongst themselves to have it performed in a solemn manner, with Revels and merriment after the old English custom; [they] prepared to set up a Maypole upon the festival day of Philip and Jacob, and therefore brewed a barrel of excellent beer and provided a case of bottles, to be spent, with other good cheer, for all comers of that day. And because they would have it in a complete form, they had prepared a song fitting to the time and present occasion. And upon Mayday they brought the Maypole to the place appointed, with drums, guns, pistols and other fitting instruments for that purpose; and there erected it with the help of Savages, that came thether of purpose to see the manner of our Revels. A goodly pine tree of 80 foot long was reared up, with a pair of buckshorns nailed on somewhat near unto the top of it: where it stood, as a fair sea mark for directions how to find out the way to mine Host of Merrymount.

And because it should more fully appear to what end it was placed there, they had a poem in readiness made, which was fixed to the Maypole, to show the new name confirmed upon that plantation; which, although it were made according to the occurrents

of the time, it, being Enigmatically composed, puzzled the Separatists most pitifully to expound it, which, (for the better information of the reader,) I have here inserted.

THE POEM.

Rise Oedipus, and, if thou canst, unfold
What means Caribdis underneath the mold,
When Scilla solitary on the ground
(Sitting in form of Niobe,) was found,
Till Amphitrites Darling did acquaint
Grim Neptune with the Tenor of her plaint,
And caused him send forth Triton with the sound
Of Trumpet loud, at which the Seas were found
So full of Protean forms that the bold shore
Presented Scilla a new paramour
So strong as Sampson and so patient
As Job himself, directed thus, by fate,
To comfort Scilla so unfortunate.
I do profess, by Cupids beauteous mother,
Heres Scogans choise for Scilla and none other;
Though Scilla's sick with grief, because no sign
Can there be found of virtue masculine.
Esculapius come; I know right well
His labor's lost when you may ring her Knell.
The fatal sisters doom none can withstand,
Nor Cithareas power, who points to land
With proclamation that the first of May
At Merrymount shall be kept holy day.

The setting up of this Maypole was a lamentable spectacle to the precise separatists, that lived at New Plymouth. They termed it an Idol; yea, they called it the Calf of Horeb, and stood at defiance with the place, naming it Mount Dagon; threatening to make it a woeful mount and not a merry mount.

The Riddle, for want of Oedipus, they could not expound; only they made some explication of part of it, and said it was meant by Sampson Job, the carpenter of the ship that brought over a woman to her husband, that had been there long before and thrived so well that he sent for her and her children to come to him; where shortly after he died: having no reason, but because of the sound of those two words; when as, (the truth is,) the man they applied it to was altogether unknown to the Author.

There was likewise a merry song made, which, (to make their Revels more fashionable,) was sung with a Chorus, every man bearing his part; which they performed in a dance, hand in hand about the Maypole, whilest one of the Company sung and filled out the good liquor, like Ganymede and Jupiter.

THE SONG.

Cor.

Drink and be merry, merry, merry boys;
Let all your delight be in the Hymens joys;
So to Hymen, now the day is come,
About the merry Maypole take a Room.
Make green garlands, bring bottles out
And fill sweet Nectar freely about.

Uncover thy head and fear no harm,
For heres good liquor to keep it warm.
Then drink and be merry, etc.
So to Hymen, etc.
Nectar is a thing assigned
By the Deities own mind
To cure the heart oppressed with grief,
And of good liquors is the chief.
Then drink, etc.
So to Hymen, etc.
Give to the Melancholy man
A cup or two of it now and then;
This physic will soon revive his blood,
And make him be of a merrier mood.
Then drink, etc.
So to Hymen, etc.
Give to the Nymph that's free from scorn
No Irish stuff nor Scotch over worn.
Lasses in beaver coats come away,
Yee shall be welcome to us night and day.
To drink and be merry etc.
So to Hymen, etc.

This harmless mirth made by young men, (that lived in hope to have wives brought over to them, that would save them a labor to make a voyage to fetch any over,) was much distasted of the precise Separatists, that keep much ado about the tyth of [Mint] and Cumin, troubling their brains more than reason would require about things that are indifferent: and from that time sought occasion against my honest Host of Merrymount, to overthrow his undertakings and to destroy his plantation quite and clean. But because they presumed with their imaginary gifts, (which they have out of Phaos box,) they could expound hidden mysteries, to convince them of blindness, as well in this as in other matters of more consequence, I will illustrate the poem, according to the true intent of the authors of these Revels, so much distasted by those Moles.

Oedipus is generally received for the absolute reader of riddles, who is invoked: Silla and Caribdis are two dangerous places for seamen to encounter, near unto Venice; and have been by poets formerly resembled to man and wife. The like licence the author challenged for a pair of his nomination, the one lamenting for the loss of the other as Niobe for her children. Amphitrite is an arm of the Sea, by which the news was carried up and down of a rich widow, now to be tane [taken] up or laid down. By Triton is the same spread that caused the Suitors to muster, (as it had been to Penelope of Greece;) and, the Coast lying circular, all our passage to and fro is made more convenient by Sea than Land. Many aimed at this mark; but he that played Proteus best and could comply with her humor must be the man that would carry her; and he had need have Sampsons strength to deal with a Dallila, and as much patience as Job that should come there, for a thing that I did observe in the life-time of the former.

But marriage and hanging, (they say,) comes by destiny and Scogans choice tis better [than] none at all. He that played Proteus, (with the help of Priapus,) put their noses out of joint, as the Proverb is.

And this the whole company of the Revelers at Merrymount knew to be the true sense and exposition of the riddle that was fixed to the Maypole, which the Separatists were at defiance with. Some of them affirmed that the first institution thereof was in memory of a whore; not knowing that it was a Trophe erected at first in honor of Maja, the Lady of learning which they despise, vilifying the two universities with uncivil terms, accounting what is there obtained by study is but unnecessary learning; not considering that learning does enable mens minds to converse with elements of a higher nature than is to be found within the habitation of the Mole.

Chap. XV. Of a great Monster supposed to be at Merrymount; and the Preparation made to Destroy it.

The Separatists, envying the prosperity and hope of the Plantation at Merrymount, (which they perceived began to come forward, and to be in a good way for gain in the Beaver trade,) conspired together against mine Host especially, (who was the owner of that Plantation,) and made up a party against him; and mustered up what aid they could, accounting of him as of a great Monster.

Many threatening speeches were given out both against his person and his Habitation, which they divulged should be consumed with fire: And taking advantage of the time when his company, (which seemed little to regard their threats,) were gone up into the Inlands to trade with the Savages for Beaver, they set upon my honest host at a place called Wessaguscus, where, by accident, they found him. The inhabitants there were in good hope of the subversion of the plantation at Merrymount, (which they principally aimed at;) and the rather because mine host was a man that endeavored to advance the dignity of the Church of England; which they, (on the contrary part,) would labor to vilify with uncivil terms: envying against the sacred book of common prayer, and mine host that used it in a laudable manner amongst his family, as a practice of piety.

There he would be a means to bring sacks to their mill, (such is the thirst after Beaver,) and helped the conspirators to surprise mine host, (who was there all alone;) and they charged him, (because they would seem to have some reasonable cause against him to set a gloss upon their malice,) with criminal things; which indeed had been done by such a person, but was of their conspiracy; mine host demanded of the conspirators who it was that was author of that information, that seemed to be their ground for what they now intended. And because they answered they would not tell him, he as peremptorily replied, that he would not say whether he had, or he had not done as they had been informed.

The answer made no matter, (as it seemed,) whether it had been negatively or affirmatively made; for they had resolved what he should suffer, because, (as they boasted,) they were now become the greater number: they had shaked of their shackles of servitude, and were become Masters, and masterless people.

It appears they were like bears whelps in former time, when mine hosts plantation was of as much strength as theirs, but now, (their being stronger,) they, (like overgrown bears,) seemed monsterous. In brief, mine host must indure to be their prisoner until they could contrive it so that they might send him for England, (as they said,) there to suffer according to the merit of the fact which they intended to father upon him; supposing, (belike,) it would prove a heinous crime.

Much rejoicing was made that they had gotten their capital enemy, (as they concluded him;) whom they purposed to hamper in such sort that he should not be able to uphold his plantation at Merrymount.

The conspirators sported themselves at my honest host, that meant them no hurt, and were so jocund that they feasted their bodies and fell to tippling as if they had obtained a great prize; like the Trojans when they had the custody of Hippeus pinetree horse.

Mine host feined grief, and could not be persuaded either to eat or drink; because he knew emptiness would be a means to make him as watchful as the Geese kept in the Roman Capital; whereon, the contrary part, the conspirators would be so drowsy that he might have an opportunity to give them a slip, instead of a tester. Six persons of the conspiracy were set to watch him at Wessaguscus: But he kept waking; and in the dead of night, (one lying on the bed for further surety,) up gets mine Host and got to the second door that he was to pass, which, notwithstanding the lock, he got open, and shut it after him with such violence that it affrighted some of the conspirators.

The word, which was given with an alarme, was, 'Oh he's gon, he's gon, what shall we do, he's gon!' The rest, (half asleep,) start up in a maze, and, like rams, ran their heads one at another full butt in the dark.

Their grand leader, Captain Shrimp [Miles Standish], took on most furiously and tore his clothes for anger; to see the empty nest, and their bird gone.

The rest were eager to have torn their hair from their heads; but it was so short that it would give them no hold. Now Captain Shrimp thought in the loss of this prize, (which he accounted his Masterpiece,) all his honor would be lost forever.

In the mean time mine Host was got home to Ma-re Mount [Merrymount] through the woods, eight miles round about the head of the river Monatoquit that parted the two Plantations, finding his way by the help of the lightening, (for it thundered as he went terribly;) and there he prepared powder, with bullets of several sizes, three hundred or thereabouts, to be used if the conspirators should pursue him thether: and these two persons promised their aides in the quarrel, and confirmed that promise with health in good *rosa solis*.

Now Captain Shrimp, the first Captain in the Land, (as he supposed,) must do some new act to repair this loss, and, to vindicate his reputation, who had sustained blemish by this oversight, begins now to study, how to repair or survive his honor: in this manner, calling of Council, they conclude.

He takes eight persons more to him, and, (like the nine Worthies of New Canaan,) they imbarque with preparation against Ma-re-Mount, where this Monster of a man, as their prase was, had his den; the whole number, had the rest not been from home, being but seven, would have given Captain Shrimp, (a quondam Drummer,) such a welcome as would have made him wish for a Drum as big as Diogenes' tub, that he might have crept into it out of sight.

Now the nine Worthies are approached, and mine Host prepared: having intelligence by a Savage, that hastened in love from Wessaguscus to give him notice of their intent.

One of mine Hosts' men proved a craven: the other had proved his wits to purchase a little valour, before mine Host had observed his posture.

The nine worthies coming before the Den of this supposed Monster, (this seven headed hydra, as they termed him,) and began, like Don Quixote against the Windmill, to beat a parly, and to offer quarter, if mine Host would yield; for they resolved to send him for England; and bade him lay by his arms.

But he, (who was the Son of a Soldier,) having taken up arms in his just defence, replied that he would not lay by those arms, because they were so needful at Sea, if he should be sent over. Yet, to save the effusion of so much worthy bounty, as would have issued out of the vaynes of these nine worthies of New Canaan, if mine Host should have played upon them out at his port holes, (for they came within danger like a flock of wild geese, as if they had been tied one to another, as colts to be sold at a fair,) mine Host was content to yield upon quarter; and did capitulate with them in what manner it should be for more certainty, because he knew what Captain Shrimp was.

He expressed that no violence should be offered to his person, none to his goods, nor any of his Household: but that he should have his arms, and what else was requisite for the voyage: which their Herald returns, it was agreed upon, and should be performed.

But mine Host no sooner had set upon the door, and issued out, but instantly Captain Shrimp and the rest of the worthies stepped to him, laid hold of his arms, and had him down: and so eagerly was every man bent against him, (not regarding any agreement made with such a carnal man,) that they fell upon him as if they would have eaten him: some of them were so violent that they would have a slice with scabbert, and all for haste; until an old Soldier, (of the Queens', as the Proverb is,) that was there by accident, clapt his gunner under the weapons, and sharply rebuked these worthies for their unworthy practices. So the matter was taken into more deliberate consideration.

Captain Shrimp, and the rest of the nine worthies, made themselves, (by this outrageous riot,) Masters of mine Host of Mar-re Mount, and disposed of what he had at his plantation.

This they knew, (in the eye of the Savages,) would add to their glory, and diminish the reputation of mine honest Host; whom they practiced to be rid of upon any terms, as willingly as if he had been the very Hydra of the time.

Chap. XVII. Of the Baccanall Triumph of the nine worthies of New Canaan.

The Separatists were not so contended, (when mine Host of Ma-re-Mount was gone,) but they were as much discontended when he was returned again: and the rather because their passages about him, and the business, were so much derided and in songs exemplified: which, (for better satisfaction of such as are in that kind affected,) I have set forth, as it was then in use by the name of the Baccanall Triumphe, as followeth:

THE POEM

Sing th' adventures of nine worthy wights,
And pity 't is I cannot call them Knights,
Since they had brawn and brain, and were right able

To be installed of Prince Arthur's table;
Yet all of them were Squires of low degree,
As did appear by rules of heraldry.
The Magi told of a prodigious birth
That shortly should be found upon the earth,
By Archimedes art, which they misconster
Unto their Land would prove a hideous monster;
Seven heads it had, and twice so many feet,
Arguing the body to be wondrous great,
Besides a forked tail heav'd up on high
As if it threaten'd battle to the sky.
The Rumor of this fearful prodigy
Did cause th' effeminate multitude to cry
For want of great Alcides aid, and stood
Like People that have seen Medusa's head.
Great was the grief of heart, great was the moan,
And great the fear conceived by every one
Of Hydra's hideous form and dreadful power,
Doubting in time this Monster would devour
All their best flocks, whose dainty wool comforts
It self with Scarlet in all Princes Courts.
Not Jason nor the adventurous youths of Greece
Did bring from Colcos any richer Fleece.
In Emulation of the Gretian force
These Worthies nine prepar'd a wooden horse,
And, prick'd with pride of like success, divise
How they may purchase glory by this prize;
And, if they give to Hydra's head the fall,

It will remain a platform unto all
Their brave achievements, and in time to come,
Per fas aut nefas, they'l erect a throne.
Clubs are turn'd trumps: so now the lot is cast:
With fire and sword to Hydra's den they haste,
Mars in th' ascendant, Sol in Cancer now,
And Lerna Lake to Pluto's court must bow.
What though they [be] rebuk'd by thund'ring Jove,
Tis neither Gods nor men that can remove
Their minds from making this a dismal day.
These nine will now be actors in this play,
And Summon Hydra to appear anon
Before their witless Combination:
But his undaunted Spirit, nursed with meat
Such as the Cyclops gave their babes to eat,
Scorn'd their base actions; for with Cyclops charm
He knew he could defend himself from harm
Of Minos, Eacus, and Radamand,
Princes of Limbo; who must out of hand
Consult bout Hydra, what must now be done:
Who, having sat in Council, one by one
Return this answer to the Siggean [Stygian] fiends;
And first grim Minos spake: most loving friends,
Hydra prognosticks ruin to our state
And that our Kingdom will grow desolate;
But if one head from thence be taken away
The Body and the members will decay.
To take in hand, quoth Eacus, this task,

Is such as hairbrained Phaeton did ask
Of Phebus, to begird the world about;
Which granted put the Netherlands to rout;
Presumptuous fools learn wit at too much cost,
For life and labor both at once he lost.
Stern Radamantus, being last to speak,
Made a great hum and thus did silence break:
What if, with rattling chains or Iron bands,
Hydra be bound either by feet or hands,
And after, being lashed with smarting rods,
He be conveyed by Styx unto the gods
To be accused on the upper ground
Of Lesae Majestatis, this crime found
T'will be unpossible from thence, I trowe,
Hydra shall come to trouble us below.
This sentence pleased the friends exceedingly,
That up they tossed their bonnets, and did cry,
Long live our Court in great prosperity.
The Sessions ended, some did straight devise
Court Revels, antiques and a world of joys,
Brave Christmas gambols: there was open hall
Kept to the full, and sport, the Devil and all:
Labour's despised, the looms are laid away,
And this proclaim'd the Stigean Holiday.
In came grim Mino, with his motley beard,
And brought a distillation well prepar'd;
And Eacus, who is as sure as text,
Came in with his preparatives the next;

Then Radamantus, last and principal,
Feasted the Worthies in his sumptuous hall.
There Charon Cerberus and the rout of fiends
Had lap enough: and so their pastimes ends.

THE ILLUSTRATIONS.

Now to illustrate this Poem, and make the sense more plain, it is to be considered that the Persons at Ma-re-Mount were seven, and they had seven heads and 14 feet; these were accounted Hydra with the seven heads: and the Maypole, with the Horns nailed near the top, was the forked tail of this supposed Monster, which they (for want of skill) imposed: yet feared in time, (if they hindered not mine Host), he would hinder the benefit of their Beaver trade, as he had done, (by means of this help,) in Kennebec river finely, ere they were awares; who, coming too late, were much dismayed to find that mine Host his boat had gleaned away all before they came; which Beaver is a fit companion for Scarlet: and I believe that Jason's golden Fleece was either the same, or some other Fleece not of so much value.

This action bred a kind of heart burning in the Plymouth Planters, who after sought occasion against mine Host to overthrow his undertakings and to destroy his Plantation; whom they accounted a main enemy to their Church and State.

Now when they had begun with him, they thought best to proceed: forasmuch as they thought themselves far enough from any control of Justice, and therefore resolved to be their own carvers: (and the rather because they presumed upon some incouragement they had from the favorites of their Sect in England:) and with fire and sword, nine in number, pursued mine Host, who had escaped their hands, in scorn of what they intended, and betook him to his habitation in a night of great thunder and lightening, when they durst not follow him, as hardy as these nine worthies seemed to be.

It was in the Month of June that these Marshallists had appointed to go about this mischievous project, and deal so crabbidly with mine Host.

After a parly, he capitulated with them about the quarter they proferred him, if he would consent to go for England, there to answer, (as they pretended,) some thing they could object against him principal to the general: But what it would be he cared not, neither was it any thing material.

Yet when quarter was agreed upon, they, contrary wise, abused him, and carried him to their town of Plymouth, where, (if they had thought he durst have gone to England,) rather then they would have been any more affronted by him they would have dispatched him, as Captain Shrimp [Miles Standish] in a rage professed that he would do with his Pistol, as mine Host should set his foot into the boat. Howsoever, the chief Elders voice in that place was more powerful than any of the rest, who concluded to send mine Host without any other thing to be done to him. And this being the final agreement, (contrary to Shrimp and others,) the nine Worthies had a great Feast made, and the furmity pot was provided for the boats gang by no allowance: and all manner of pastime.

Captain Shrimp was so overjoyed in the performance of this exploit, that they had, at that time, extraordinary merriment, (a thing not usual amongst those precisians); and when the wind served they took mine Host into their Shallop, hoisted Sail, and carried him to the Northern parts; where they left him upon a Island.

Chap. XXVII. Of the Practice of their Church.

The Church of the Separatists is governed by Pastors, Elders and Deacons, and there is not any of these, though he be but a Cow keeper, but is allowed to exercise his gifts in the public assembly on the Lord's day, so as he do not make use of any notes for the help of his memory: for such things, they say, smell of Lamp oil, and there must be no such unsavory perfume admitted to come into the congregation.

These are all public preachers. There is amongst these people a deconesse, made of the sisters, that uses her gifts at home in an assembly of her sex, by way of repetition or exhortation: such is their practice.

The Pastor, (before he is allowed of,) must disclaim his former calling to the Ministry as heretical; and take a new calling after their fantastical inventions: and then he is admitted to be their Pastor.

The manner of disclaiming is, to renounce his calling with bitter execrations, for the time that he hath heretofore lived in it: and after his new election, there is great joy conceived at his commission.

And their Pastors have this preeminence above the Civil Magistrate: He must first consider of the complaint made against a member: and if he be disposed to give the party complained of an admonition, there is no more to be said: if not; He delivers him over to the Magistrate to deal with him in a course of Justice, according to their practice in cases of that nature.

Of these pastors I have not known many: some I have observed together with their carriage in New Canaan, and can inform you what opinion hath been conceived of their conditions in the particular. There is one who, (as they give it out there that think they speak it to advance his worth,) has been expected to exercise his gifts in an assembly that stayed his coming, in the middest of his Journey falls into a fit, (which they term a zealous meditation,) and was 4 miles past the place appointed before he came to himself, or did remember where abouts he went. And how much these things are different from the actions of mazed men, I leave to any indifferent man to judge; and if I should say they are all much alike, they that have seen and heard what I have done, will not condemn me altogether.

Now, for as much as by the practice of their Church every Elder or Deacon may preach, it is not amiss to discover their practice in that particular, before I part with them.

It has been an old saying, and a true, what is bred in the bone will not out of the flesh, nor the stepping into the pulpit that can make the person fit for the employment. The unfitness of the person undertaking to be the Messenger has brought a blemish upon the message, as in the time of Louis XI, King of France, who, (having advanced his Barber to place of Honor, and graced him with eminent titles), made him so presumptuous to undertake an Embassage to treat with foreign princes of Civil affairs.

But what was the issue? He behaved himself so unworthily, (yet as well as his breeding would give him leave,) that both the Messenger and the message were despised; and had not he, (being discovered,) conveyed himself out of their territories, they had made him pay for his barbarous presumption.

Socrates says, *loquere ut te videam* ["speak, that I might see you"]. If a man observe these people in the exercise of their gifts, he may thereby discern the tincture of their proper calling, the asses' ears will peep through the lion's hide. I am sorry they cannot discern their own infirmities. I will deal fairly with them, for I will draw their pictures *cap a pe*, that you may discern them plainly from head to foot in their postures, that so much bewitch, (as I may speak with modesty,) these illiterate people to be so fantastical, to take Jona's task upon them without sufficient warrant.

One steps up like the Minister of Justice with the balance only, not the sword for fear of affrighting his auditory. He points at a text, and handles it as evenly as he can; and teaches the auditory, that the thing he has to deliver must be well weighed, for it is a very precious thing, yes, much more precious than gold or pearl: and he will teach them the means how to weigh things of that excellent worth; that a man would suppose he and his auditory were to part stakes by the scale; and the like distribution they have used about a bag pudding.

Another, (of a more cutting disposition,) steps in his steed [stead]; and he takes a text, which he divides into many parts: (to speak truly) as many as he list. The fag end of it he pares away, as a superfluous remnant.

He puts his auditory in comfort, that he will make a garment for them, and teach them how they shall put it on; and incourages them to be in love with it, for it is of such a fashion as doth best become a Christian man.

He will assure them that it shall be armor of proffer against all assaults of Satan. This garment, (says he,) is not composed as the garments made by a carnal man, that are sowed with a hot needle and a burning thread; but it is a garment that shall outlast all the garments: and, if they will make use of it as he shall direct them, they shall be able, (like saint George,) to terrify the great Dragon, error; and defend truth, which error with her wide chaps would devour: whose mouth shall be filled with the shreds and parings, which he continually gapes for under the cutting board.

A third, he supplies the room: and in the exercise of his gifts begins with a text that is drawn out of a fountain that has in it no dregs of popery. This shall prove unto you, (says he,) the Cup of repentence: it is not like unto the Cup of the Whore of Babylon, who will make men drunk with the dregs thereof: It is filled to the brim with comfortable joys, and will prove a comfortable cordial to a sick soul, says he. And so he handles the matter as if he dealt by the pint and the quart, with Nic and Froth.

Another, (a very learned man indeed,) goes another way to work with his auditory; and exhorts them to walk upright, in the way of their calling, and not, (like carnal men,) tread awry. And if they should fail in the performance of that duty, yet they should seek for amendment whiles it was time; and tells them it would be too late to seek for help when the shop windows were shut up: and pricks them forward with a friendly admonition not to place their delight in worldly pleasures, which will not last, but in time will come to an end; but so to handle the matter that they may be found to wax better and better, and then they shall be doubly rewarded for their work: and so closes up the matter in a comfortable manner.

But stay: Here is one stept up in haste, and, (being not minded to hold his auditory in expectation of any long discourse,) he takes a text; and, (for brevity's sake,) divides it into one part: and then runs so fast afore with the matter, that his auditory cannot follow him. Doubtless his Father was some Irish footman; by his speed it seems so. And it may be at the hour of death, the son, being present, did participate of his Father's nature, (according to Pythagoras,) and so the virtue of his Fathers nimble feet being infused into his brains, might make his tongue outrun his wit.

Well, if you mark it, these are special gifts indeed: which the vulgar people are so taken with, that there is no persuading them that it is so ridiculous . . .

Chap. XXVIII. Of their Policy in public Justice.

Now that I have anatomized the two extreme parts of this Politique Commonwealth, the head and the inferior members, I will show you the heart, and read a short lecture over that too; which is Justice.

I have a petition to exhibit to the high and mighty Mr. Temperwell; and I have my choice whether I shall make my plaint in a case of conscience, or bring it with in the Compass of a point in law. And because I will go the surest way to work, at first, I will see how others are answered in the like kind, whether it be with hab or nab, as the Judge did the Countryman.

Here comes Mr. Hopewell: his petition is in a case of conscience, (as he says.) But, see, great Joshua allows conscience to be of his aide: yet cuts him off with this answer; Law is flat against him. Well let me see another. I marry: Here comes one Master Doubtnot: his matter depends, (I am sure,) upon a point in Law: alas, what will it not do, look ye it is affirmed that Law is on his side: but Conscience, like a blanket, over spreads it. This passage is like to the Procustes of Rome, me thinks; and therefore I may very well say of them,

Even so, by racking out the joints & chopping off the head,
Procustes fitted all his guests unto his Iron bed.

And, if these speed no better, with whom they are friends, that neither find Law nor Conscience to help them, I do not wonder to see mine Host of Ma-re-Mount speed so ill, that has been proclaimed an enemy so many years in New Canaan to their Church and State.

Chap. XXIX. How Mine Host was put into a whale's belly.

The Separatists, (after they had burned Ma-re-Mount they could not get any ship to undertake the carriage of mine Host from thence, either by fair means or foul,) they were inforced, (contrary to their expectation,) to be troubled with his company: and by that means had time to consider more of the man, then they had done of the matter: wherein at length it was discovered that they, (by means of their credulity of the intelligence given them in England of the matter, and the false Character of the man,) had run themselves headlong into an error, and had done that on a sodaine [sudden] which they repented at leisure, but could not tell which way to help it as it stood now. They could debate upon it and especially upon two difficult points, whereof one must be concluded upon: if they suffer him to stay, and put him in *status quo prius* ["the status quo before"], all the vulgar people will conclude they have been too rash in burning a house that was useful, and count them men unadvised.

So that it seems, (by their discourse about the matter,) they stood betwixt Hawk and Bussard: and could not tell which hand to incline unto. They had founded him secretly: he was content with it, go which way it would. Nay Shackles himself, (who was employed in the burning of the house, and therefore feared to be caught in England,) and others were so forward in putting mine Host in *status quo prius*, after they had found their error, (which was so apparent that Luceus eies would have served to have found it out in less time,) that they would contribute 40 shillings a piece towards it; and affirmed, that every man according to his ability that had a hand in this black design should be taxed to a Contribution in like nature: it would be done exactly.

Now, (whiles this was in agitation, and was well urged by some of those parties to have been the upshot,) unexpected, (in the depth of winter, when all ships were gone out of the land,) in comes Mr. Wethercock, a proper Mariner; and, they said, he could observe the wind: blow it high, blow it low, he was resolved to lie at Hull rather than encounter such a storm as mine Host had met with: and this was a man for their turne.

He would do any office for the brethren, if they (who he knew had a strong purse, and his conscience waited on the strings of it, if all the zeal he had) would bear him out in it: which they professed they would. He undertakes to rid them of mine Host by one means or another. They gave him the best means they could, according to the present condition of the work, and letters of credence to the favors of that Sect in England; with which, (his business there being done, and his ship cleared,) he hoist the Sails and put to Sea: since which time mine Host has not troubled the brethren, but only at the Counsel table: where now *Sub iudice lis est* ["the case is before the judge"].

Chap. XXX. Of Sir Christopher Gardiner Knight, and how he sped amongst the Separatists.

Sir Christopher Gardiner, (a Knight, that had been a traveler both by Sea and Land; a good judicious gentleman in the Mathematick and other Sciences useful for Plantations, Chemistry, &c. and also being a practical Engineer,) came into those parts, intending discovery.

But the Separatists love not those good parts, when they proceed from a carnal man, (as they call every good Protestant); in short time [they] had found the means to pick a quarrel with him. The means is that they pursue to obtain what they aim at: the word is there, the means.

So that, when they find any man like to prove an enemy to their Church and state, then straight the means must be used for defense. The first precept in their Politics is to defame the man at whom they aim, and then he is a holy Israelite in their opinions who can spread that fame broadest, like butter upon a loaf: not matter how thin, it will serve for a veil: and then this man, (who they have thus depraved,) is a spotted unclean leaper [leper]: he must out, lest he pollute the Land, and them that are clean.

If this be one of their gifts, then Machiavelli had as good gifts as they. Let them raise a scandal on any, though never so innocent, yet they know it is never wiped clean out: the stained marks remains; which hath been well observed by one in these words of his,

> *Stick Candles gainst a Virgin walls white back;*
> *If they'l not burn yet, at the least, they'l black.*

And thus they dealt with Sir Christopher: and plotted by all the ways and means they could, to overthrow his undertakings in those parts.

And therefore I cannot choose but conclude that these Separatists have special gifts: for they are given to envy and malice extremely.

The knowledge of their defamation could not please the gentleman well, when it came to his ear; which would cause him to make some reply, as they supposed, to take exceptions at, as they did against Fair cloth: and this would be a means, they thought, to blow the coal, and so to kindle a brand that might fire him out of the Country too, and send him after mine Host of Ma-re-Mount.

They take occasion, (some of them,) to come to his house when he was gone up into the Country, and (finding he was from home,) so went to work that they left him neither house nor habitation nor fervent, nor any thing to help him, if he should return: but of that they had no hope, (as they gave it out,) for he was gone, (as they affirmed,) to lead a Savage life, and for that cause took no company with him: and they having considered of the matter, thought it not fit that any such man should live in so remote a place, within the Compass of their patent. So they fired the place, and carried away the persons and goods.

Sir Christopher was gone with a guide, (a Savage,) into the inland parts for discovery: but, before he was returned, he met with a Savage that told the guide, Sir Christopher would be killed: Master Temperwell, (who had now found out matter against him,) would have him dead or alive. This he related; and would have the gentleman not to go to the place appointed, because of the danger that was supposed.

But Sir Christopher was nothing dismayed; he would on, whatsoever came of it; and so met with the Savages: and between them was a terrible skirmish: But they had the worst of it, and he escaped well enough.

The guide was glad of it, and learned of his fellows that they were promised a great reward for what they should do in this employment.

Which thing, (when Sir Christopher understood,) he gave thanks to God; and after, (upon this occasion to solace himself,) in his table book he composed this sonnet, which I have here inserted for a memorial.

THE SONNET.

Wolves in Sheep's clothing, why will ye
Think to deceive God that doth see
Your simulated sanctity?
For my part, I do wish you could
Your own infirmities behold,

For then you would not be so bold.

Like Sophists, why will you dispute

With wisdom so? You do confute

None but yourselves. For shame, be mute,

Least [Lest] great Jehovah, with his power,

Do come upon you in a hour

When you least think, and you devour.

This Sonnet the Gentleman composed as a testimony of his love towards them, that were so ill-affected towards him; from whom they might have received much good, if they had been so wise to have embraced him in a loving fashion.

But they despise the help that shall come from a carnal man, (as they termed him,) who, after his return from those designs, finding how they had used him with such disrespect, took shipping, and disposed to himself for England; and discovered their practices in those parts towards his Majesty's true hearted Subjects, which they made wary of their abode in those parts.

Chap. XXXI. Of mine Host of Ma-re-Mount how he played Jonah after he had been in the Whale's belly for a time.

Mine Host of Ma-re-Mount, being put to Sea, had delivered him, for his release by the way, (because the ship was unvittled, and the Seamen put to straight allowance, which could hold out but to the Canaries,) a part of his own provision, being two months proportion; in all but 3 small pieces of pork, which made him expect to be famished before the voyage should be ended, by all likelihood. Yet he thought he would make one good meal, before he died: like the Colony servant in Virginia, that, before he should go to the gallows, called to his wife to set on the loblolly pot, and let him have one good meal before he went; who had committed a petty crime, that in those days was made a capital offense.

And now, mine Host being merrily disposed, on went the pieces of pork, wherewith he feasted his body, and cherished the poor Sailors; and got out of them what Mr. Wethercock, their Master, purposed to do with him that he had no more provision: and along they sailed from place to place, from Island to Island, in a pitiful weather-beaten ship, where mine Host was in more danger, (without all question,) than Jonah, when he was in the Whale's belly; and it was the great mercy of God that they had not all perished. Vittled they were but for a month, when they wayed [weighed] Anchor and left the first port.

They were a prey for the enemy for want of power, if they had met them: besides the vessel was a very slug, and so unserviceable that the Master called a council of all the company in general, to have their opinions which way to go and how to bear the helm, who all under their hand affirmed the ship to be unserviceable: so that, in fine, the Master and men and all were at their wits end about it: yet they employed the Carpenters to search and caulk her sides, and do their best whiles they were in her. Nine months they made a shift to use her, and shifted for supply of vittles at all the Islands they touched at: though it were so poorly, that all those helps, and the short allowance of a biscuit a day, and a few Lemons taken in at the Canaries, served but to bring the vessel in view of the lands end.

They were in such a desperate case, that, (if God in his great mercy had not favoured them, and disposed the winds fair until the vessel was in Plymouth road,) they had without question perished; for when they let drop an Anchor, near the Island of S. Michaels, not one bit of food left, for all that starving allowance of this wretched Weathercock, that, if he would have launched out his beaver, might have bought more vittles in New England than he, and the whole ship with the Cargazoun, was worth, (as the passengers he carried who vittled themselves affirmed). But he played the miserable wretch, and had possessed his men with the contrary; who repented them of waying anchor before they knew so much.

Mine Host of Ma-re-Mount, (after he had been in the Whale's belly,) was set ashore, to see if he would now play Jonah, so metamorphosed with a long voyage that he looked like Lazarus in the painted cloth.

But mine Host, (after due consideration of the premises,) thought it fitter for him to play Jonah in this kind, then [than] for the Separatists to play Jonah in that kind as they do. He therefore bid Weathercock tell the Separatists, that they would be made in due time to repent those malicious practices, and so would he too; for he was a Separatist amongst the Separatists, as far as his wit would give him leave; though when he came in Company of basket makers, he would do his endeavor to make them pin the basket, if he could, as I have seen him. And now mine Host, being merrily disposed, having past many perilous adventures in that desperate Whale's belly, began in a posture like Jonah, and cried, "Repent you cruel Separatists, repent; there are as yet but 40 days, if Jove vouchsafe to thunder, Charter and the Kingdom of the Separatists will fall asunder: Repent you cruel

Schismatics, repent." And in that posture he greeted them by letters returned into New Canaan; and ever, (as opportunity was fitted for the purpose,) he was both heard and seen in the posture of Jonah against them, crying, "repent you cruel Separatists, repent; there are as yet but 40 days; if Jove vouchsafe to thunder, the Charter and the Kingdom of the Separatists will fall asunder: Repent, you cruel Schismatics, repent. If you will hear any more of this proclamation meet him at the next markettown, for *Cynthius aurem vellet*." [The Latin is a quote from Vergil's sixth *Eclogue*—literally "Apollo twitched my ear," translated by John Dryden as "Apollo checked my pride."]

The Saga of Pirate Captain John Gow

John Gow was born in Thurso, in the far north of Scotland, in about 1689 and moved to the Orkneys as a young man. Gow was in many ways the typical pirate of his era, the "Golden Age of Piracy." Of humble origins, with inordinate knowledge of sailing and a quenchless thirst for vengeance against the innumerable wrongs done to him throughout his life at the bottom of European society, Gow long harbored the desire to "turn pirate," and he simply awaited the opportune moment. Gow rallied fellow crewmembers to his cause while sailing under the command of one Captain Ferneau, employed in goods transport for Amsterdam merchants. Protesting Ferneau's management of the ship, his crew steadily rejected their captain's authority and seized control of the ship for themselves. Gow and his crewmates murdered their captain and several other officers, determined to "go on Account," making war upon constituted authority and living only for themselves. Having declared war on the existing sociopolitical order, pirates in the "Golden Age" remade society at sea, each vessel a novel social organization spontaneously and (mostly) democratically ordered.

The crew, declaring themselves the enemies of all nations, terrorized the coast of Portugal and the Portuguese Madeira Islands in the Atlantic. During their endless search for wine (which includes scaring a colonial governor so much that he soiled himself), Gow resolved to convince his crew that easy yet rich pickings awaited them in the Orkney Islands. Although the Orkneys were a far cry from the standard pirate stomping grounds in the Caribbean and West Africa, Gow assured his crew that his extensive knowledge of the coasts and the wealthy, landed population guaranteed success against any meager, locally raised resistance. With the ship anchored so near many sailors' homes, though, the bulk of Gow's crew deserted him as soon as they had the opportunity and betrayed their captain to mainland authorities. In a desperate attempt to gather what spoils he could and possibly to avenge himself against his homeland, Gow ordered his men to attack one Mr. Fea, a wealthy member of the Orkney gentry. Triumphing over the pirates, Fea captured those who remained, including Gow, and denied his final wish of being shot sword-in-hand. Fea delivered Gow to the local sheriff, who then transported him to London for execution. Gow, however, had declared war not only on the enemies of his youth, not only on the empires and other constituted authorities of his day, but he also had declared war on all earthly forces, including Death itself. When hanged on the gallows in 1726, Gow managed to break his noose through sheer brute force. The assembled crowd cheered Gow's final grand act of piracy, jeering at and ridiculing the British officials who led the condemned to his second hanging. The second time took.

An Account of the Conduct and Proceedings of the late John Gow alias Smith, Captain of the late Pirates, Executed for Murder and Piracy by Daniel Defoe.[11]

Tho' this Work seems principally to enter into the History of one Man . . . it may indeed be call'd the History of all the late Pirates so far as they acted together in these wicked Adventures . . . for 'tis eminently known, that among such Fellows as these, when once they have abandon'd themselves to such a dreadful hight of Wickedness, there is so little Government or Subordination among them, that they are, on Occasion, all Captains, all Leaders. And tho' they generally put in this or that Man to act as Commander for this or that Voyage, or Enterprise, they frequently remove them again upon the smallest Occasion, nay, even without any Occasion at all, but as Humours and Passions govern at those Times: And this is done so often, that I once knew a Buccaneering Pirate Vessel, whose Crew were upwards of 70 Men, who, in one Voyage, had so often changed, set up, and pull'd down their Captains and other Officers, that above seven and Forty of the Ships Company had, at several Times, been in Office of one kind or other; and among the rest they had, in particular had, 13 Captains. . .

At Amsterdam . . . Gow ship'd himself afore the Mast, (as the Seamen call it) that is to say, as a Common Sailor, on Board an English Ship of 200 Tons Burden, call'd the George Galley . . . Appearing to be an active skillful Sailor he obtain'd the Favour of being made Second Mate . . .

Captain Ferneau being a Man of Reputation among the Merchants at Amsterdam, got a Voyage for his Ship from thence to Santa Cruz, on the Coast of Barbary, to Load Bees Wax, and to carry it to Genoa . . . but not being able to Man themselves wholly with English or Scots, they were oblig'd to take some Swedes, and other Seamen to make up his Compliment, which was 23 in all; among the latter Sort . . . both of them Swedes by Nation, but as wicked too as Gow and his other Fellows were . . .

'Tis evident, that this Gow, in particular, whatever the rest might have done, had entertain'd this bloody Resolution in General, (I mean of turning Pirate) long before this Voyage; he had endeavour'd to put it in Practice, at least once before . . . and had only fail'd for want of being able to bring over a sufficient Gang of Rogues to his Party . . . but it seems he had not been able to bring it to pass till now, when finding some little Discontent among the Men, on account of their Provisions, he was made the Devil's Instrument to run up those Discontents to such a dreadful hight of Fury and Rage, as we shall find they did . . .

. . . We must content ourselves with beginning where he began, that is to say, when they seiz'd the Captain, murdered him and his Men, and run away with the Ship, on the Coast of Barbary, in the Mediterranean Sea . . .

[At a meeting with a group of merchants,] Three of the Men, (viz.) Winter and Peterson, two Swedes, and Maccauly a Scotchman, came rudely upon the Quarter-Deck, and as if they took that Opportunity because the Merchants were present, believing the Captain would not use any Violence with them, in the presence of the Merchants, they made a long Complaint of their ill Usage, and particularly of their Provisions and Allowance (as they said) being not sufficient, nor such as was ordinarily made in other Merchant Ships . . .

In their making this Complaint, they seemed to direct their Speech to the Merchants, as well as to the Captain . . .

The Captain was highly provok'd at this Rudeness, as indeed he had reason . . . however, he restrain'd his Passion, and gave them not the least angry Word, only, that if they were aggreiv'd they had no more to do, but to have let him known it, that if they were ill used it was not by his Order, that he would enquire into it, and that if any thing was amiss it should be rectify'd . . .

Peterson . . . answered in a surly Tone, and with a kind of Disdain, So as we Eat so shall we Work: This he spoke aloud so as that he might be sure the Captain should hear him, and the rest of the Men also; and 'twas evident, that as he spoke in the plural Number *We*, so he spoke their Minds as well as his Own, and Words which they had all agreed to before . . .

Soon after this the Calm went off, and the Land-Breeze sprung up, as if usual on that Coast, and they immediately weigh'd and stood off to Sea; but the Captain having had those two Ruffles with his Men, just at their putting to Sea, was very uneasy in his Mind . . . The Captain told [the First Mate] he thought it was absolutely necessary to have a Quantity of finall Arms brought immediately into the great Cabbin, not only to defend themselves if there should be occasion, but also that he might be in a Posture to correct those Fellows for their Insolence . . .

But two Mistakes in this Part was the ruin of them all. (1). That the Captain spoke it without due Cation, so that Winter and

Peterson, the two principal Malecontents, and who were expressly mentioned by the Captain to be corrected, overheard it, and knew by that Means what they had to expect, if they did not immediately bestir themselves to prevent it. (2.) . . . The Captain unhappily bad [the Mate] go immediately to Gow, the second Mate and Gunner, and give him Orders to get the Arms cleared and loaded for him, and so to bring them up to the great Cabbin; which was, in short, to tell the Conspirators that the Captain was preparing to be too strong for them if they did not fall to work with him immediately . . .

They fell downright to the Point, which Gow had so long form'd in his own Mind, (viz.) to seize upon the Captain and Mate, and all those that they could not bring to joyn with them; in short, to throw them into the Sea, and to go upon the Account.

All those who are acquainted with the Sea Language, know the Meaning of that Expression and that it is in few Words, to run away with the Ship and turn Pirates . . .

They came to this short but hellish Resolution, (viz.) That they would immediately, that very Night, murder the Captain, and such others as they nam'd, and afterwards proceed with the Ship as they should see Cause . . .

The Persons they had immediately design'd for Destruction, were four, (viz.) the Captain, the Mate, the Super Cargo, and the Surgeon, whereof all, but the Captain, were gone to Sleep; the Captain himself being upon the Quarter-deck.

Between Nine and Ten at Night, all being quiet and secure, and the poor Gentlemen, that were to be Murdered, fast asleep, the Villains, that were below, gave the Watch-Word, which was, *who Fires next?* At which they all got out of their Hammocks, with as little Noise as they could, and going, in the Dark, to the Hammocks of the Chief Mate, Super Cargo, and Surgeon, they cut all their Throats . . . The Mate, whose Throat was cut, but not his Windpipe, had struggled Vigorously with the Villain, that attempted him . . . and the Super Cargo, in the same Condition, got forwards between Decks, under some Deals, and both of them begg'd, with the most moving Cries and Intreaties, for their Lives; and when nothing could prevail, they beg'd, with the same Earnestness, but for a few Moments to Pray to God, and Recommdn their Souls to his Mercy; but alike, in Vain, for the wretched Murderers, heated with Blood, were pass'd all Pitty; and not being able to come at them with their Knives, with which they had begun the Execution, they shot them with their Pistols, Firing several times upon each of them, till they found they were quite dead. . . .

The Captain . . . call'd out, and ask'd, what was the Matter? . . . when Winter, Rowlinson and Melvin, coming that Moment behind him, lay'd Hands on him, and lifting him up, at once attempted to throw him Overboard into the Sea; but he being a nimble, strong Man, got hold of the Shrouds, and struggled so hard with them, that they could not break his Hold; but turning his Head, to look behind him, to see who he had to deal with, one of them cut his Throat with a broad Dutch Knife . . . He constantly cry'd out to God for Mercy, for he found there was no Mercy to be expected from them: During this Struggle, another of the Murderers stab'd him with a Knife in the Back, and that with such Force, that the Villain could not draw the

Knife out again to repeat his Blow, which he would otherwise have done.

At this Moment Gow came up from the Butchery he had been at between Decks, and seeing the Captain still alive, he went close up to him, and shot him (as he confess'd) with a Brace of Bullets . . .

The first thing they did afterward, was to call up all Eight upon the Quarter-Deck, where they congratulated one another, and shook Hands together engaging to proceed, by unanimous Consent, in their resolved Design, that is to say, of turning Pirates . . .

They had drawn in four more of the Men to approve of what they had done, and promise to Joyn with them, so that now they were twelve in Number, and being but 24 at first, whereof four were Murdered, they had but either Men to be Apprehensive of, and those they could easily look after . . . They were told by Gow, what his Resolution was, viz. to go a Crusing, or to go upon the Account, (as above) that if they were willing to Joyn with them, and go into their Measures, they should be well used, and there should be no Distinction among them, but they should all fare alike, that they had been forced by the barbarous Usage of Ferneau to do what they had done, but that now there was no looking back; and therefore as they had not been concern'd in what was past, they had nothing to do but to act in Concert, do their Duty as Sailors, and obey Orders for the good of the Ship, and no Harm should be done to any of them . . . Tho' such of them as sometimes afterward shewed any Reluctance to act as Principals, were never Trusted, always Suspected, and often severely Beaten, and some of them were many ways inhumanly

Treated, and that particularly by Williams, the Lieutenant, who was, in his Nature, a merciless, cruel, and inexorable Wretch . . .

They were now in a new Circumstance of Life, and acting upon a different Stage of Business, tho' upon the same Stage as to the Element, the Water . . . But they were now a Crew of Pirates, or . . . Corsaires, Bound no where, but to look out for Purchase and Spoil wherever they could find it.

In pursuit of this wicked Trade, they first chang'd the Name of the Ship, which was before call'd the George Galley, and which they call now the Revenge, a Name indeed suitable to the bloody Steps they had taken . . .

Instead of pursing [pursuing] their Voyage to Genoa with the Ships Cargo, they took a clear contrary Course, and resolv'd to Station themselves upon the Coasts of Spain and Portugal, and to Cruise upon all Nations; but what they chiefly aim'd at, was a Ship with Wine, if possible, for that they wanted Extreamly.

The first Prize they took was an English Sloop . . . This was a Prize of no Value to them, for they knew not what to do with the Fish; so they took out the Master . . . and his Men . . . and what else they found worth taking out, and sunk the Vessel . . .

The next Prize they took was a Scotch Vessel . . . with Herring and Salmon . . . This Vessel was likewise of little Value to them, except that they took out, as they had done from the other, their Arms, Ammunition, Cloths, Provisions, Sails, Anchors, Cables, &c. and every Thing of Value, and therefore they sunk her too, as they had done the Sloop . . . They were very unwilling to leave the Coast of Portugal, till they had got a Ship with Wine, which they very much wanted.

They Cruised eight or ten Days after this, without seeing so much as one Vessel upon the Seas . . . when they descried a Sail . . . being a Ship about as big as their own . . . hoisting up French Colours, and standing away . . . The Frenchman chang'd his Course in the Night, and so got clear of them . . .

They resolved to stand away for the Maderas, which they knew was not far off, so they accordingly made the Island in two Days more . . . expecting to meet with some Portuguese Vessel going in or coming out; but 'twas in Vain . . .

They stood away for Porto Santa, about ten Leagues to the Windward of Maderas, and belonging also to the Portuguese; here putting up British Colours, they sent their Boat ashore with Captain Somervills Bill of Health, and a present to the Governour of three Barrels of Salmon, and six Barrels of Herrings, and a very civil Message, desiring leave to Water, and to buy some Refreshments . . .

The Governour very courteously granted their Desire . . . went off himself, with about Nine or ten of his principal People, to pay the English Captain a Visit . . .

However, Gow, handsomely dress'd, receiv'd them with some Ceremony . . . for a while . . . and when the Governour and his Company rose up to take their leave, they were, to their great Surprize, suddenly surrounded with a gang of Fellows with Musquets and an Officer at the Head of them, who told them in so many Words, they were the Captains Prisoners, and must not think of going on Shore any more, till the Water and Provisions, which were promised, should come on Board . . .

The poor Governour was so much more than half Dead with the Fright, that he really Befoul'd himself in a piteous Manner;

and the rest were in no much better Condition; they trembled, cry'd, begg'd, cross'd themselves, and said their Prayers as Men going to Execution. . . They were however well enough Treated, except the Restraint of their Persons, and were often ask'd to Refresh themselves, but they would neither Eat or Drink any more all the while they stay'd on Board . . .

Having no better Success in this out of the way run, to the Maderas, they resolved to make the best of their way back again to the Coast of Spain or Portugal . . .

They met with a New England Ship . . . laden with Staves, and bound for Lis[b]on, and being to Load there with Wine for London; this was a Prize also of no Value to them, and they began to be very much discouraged with their bad Fortune. However they . . . gave the Ship to Captain Wise . . . who they took at first in a Sloop . . . and made them Satisfaction . . . He gave to Captain Wise and his Mate 24 Cerons of Bees Wax, and to each of his Men . . . two Cerons of Wax each; thus he pretended Honesty, and to make Reperation of Damages by giving them the Goods which he had robb'd the Dutch Merchants of, whose Super-Cargo he had Murdered . . .

They met with a French Ship from Cadiz, laden with Wine, Oyl, and Fruit; this was, in some respect, the very Thing they wanted; so they Mann'd her with their own Men, and stood off to Sea, that they might divide the Spoil of her with more Safety, for they were then too near the Land . . .

They gave that Ship to Captain Somerville, the Glascow Captain, whose Ship they had sunk, and to Captain Cross, the New England Captain, who they had taken but just before; and to do Justice, as they call'd it, here also, they gave half the Ship and Cargo to Somerville, one quarter to his Mate, and the other quarter to Captain Cross, and 16 Cerons of Wax to the Men to be shar'd among them. . . Cross's Men where all detain'd, whether by Force, or by their own Consent . . .

Two days after this they took a Bristol Ship bound from Newfoundland to Oporto with Fish; they let her Cargo alone, for they had no occasion for Fish, but they took out also almost all their Provisions, all the Ammunition, Arms, &c. all her good Sails, also her best Cables, and forced two of her Men to go away with them, and then put 10 of the French Men on Board her, and let her go . . .

This was the last Prize they took, not only on the Coast of Portugal, but any where else . . .

Some [were] for going to the Coast of Guinea . . . others were for going to the West Indies, and to Cruize among the Islands, and take up their Station at Tobago; others . . . propos'd the standing in the Bay of Mexico, and to joyn in with some of a new sort of Pirates at St. Fago de la Cuba, who are all Spaniards, and call themselves . . . Guardships for the Coast; but under that pretence make Prize of Ships of all Nations, and sometimes even of their own Countrymen too, but especially of the English; but when this was propos'd it was answered, they durst not trust the Spaniards.

Another sort was for going to the North of America, and after having taken a Sloop or two on the Coast of New England, or New-York, laden with Provisions for the West-Indies, which would not have been very hard to do . . . then to have gone away to the South Seas; but Gow objected, that they were not Mann'd sufficiently for such an Undertaking; and likewise, that they had not sufficient Stores of Ammunition, especially of Powder, and of Small Arms for any considerable Action with the Spaniards.

Then it was offered . . . to go away to the Honduras, and to the Bay of Campeachy among the Buccaniers and Logwood Cutters, and there they should in the first Place be sure to pick up forty or fifty stout Fellows, good Sailors, and bold, enterprising Men, who understand the Spaniards, and the Spanish Coast on both sides of America as well as any Men in the World . . .

Others said they should go first to the Islands of New-Providence, or go to the Mouth of the Gulph of Florida, and then crusing on the Coast of North-America . . . upon the Coast of Carolina, and as high as the Capes of Virginia. But nothing could be resolv'd on; till at last Gow let them into the Secret of a Project, which . . . he had long had in his Thoughts . . . to go away to the North of Scotland, near the Coast of which, as he said, he was Born and Bred; and where he said, if they met with no Purchase upon the Sea, he could tell them how they should Enrich themselves by going on Shore . . .

About the middle of last January, they arriv'd . . . in the Isles of Orkney, and came to an Anchor in a Place, which Gow told them, was safe Riding under the Lee of a finall Island at some Distance from the Port . . .

But now their Misfortunes began to come on, and Things look'd but with an indifferent Aspect upon them; for several of their Men, especially such of them as had been forc'd or decoy'd into their Service, began to think of making their Escape from them; and to cast about for Means to bring it to pass. The first was a young Man, who was originally one of the Ships Company, but was Forced by fear of being Murdered . . . to give a silent Assent to go with them, he took an Opportunity to get away . . . escaped to Kirkwall, a Market-Town, and the Chief of the Orkneys, about 12 Miles from the Place where the Ship lay . . .

But the next Disaster that attended them, was, (for Misfortunes seldom come alone) more fatal than this, for 10 of Gow's Men, most of them likewise Men forced into their Service, went away with the long Boat, making the best of their Way for the main Land of Scotland . . . These Men . . . were taken in the Firth of Edenburg, and made Prisoners there . . .

But harden'd for his own Destruction, and Justice evidently pursuing him, he grew the Bolder for the Disaster; and notwithstanding that the Country was alarm'd, and that he was fully discover'd, instead of making a timely Escape, he resolved to Land upon them, and to put his intended Projects, (viz.) of Plundering the Gentlemens Houses, in Execution, whatever it cost him.

In order to this, he sent the Boatswain and 10 Men on Shore . . . directing them to go to the House of Mr. Honnyman of Grahamsey, Sheriff of the County, and who was himself at that Time, to his great good Fortune, from Home . . .

Mrs. Honnyman and her Daughter were extreamly Frighted at the sight of so many Armed Men coming into the House, and ran screaming about, like People Distracted, while the Pirates, not regarding them, were looking about for Chests and Trunks, where they might expect to find some Plunder . . . She recovered some Courage, and ran back into the House immediately; and knowing, to be sure, where her Money lay, which was very

Considerable, and all in Gold, she put the Bags in her Lap and boldly . . . carried it all off, and so made her Escape with the Treasure. The Boatswain being inform'd that the Money was carried off, resolved to revenge himself by burning the Writings and Papers, which they call there, the Charters of their Estates, and are always of great Value in Gentlemens Houses of Estates; but the young Lady . . . tying the most considerable of them up in a Napkin, threw them out of the Window, jumpt after them herself, and Escaped without the Damage . . .

And now Gow resolved to make the best of his Way for the Island of Eda, to Plunder the House of Mr. Fea, a Gentleman of a considerable Estate, and who Gow had some Acquaintance with, having been at School together when they were Youths . . .

[Fea and his men-at-arms manage to capture Gow's Boatswain and his company of pirates.]

They were all five now in his Power, and he sent them away under a good Guard to a Village in the middle of the Island, where they were kept separate from one another, and sufficiently secur'd. Then Mr. Fea dispatch'd Expresses to the Gentlemen in the neighbouring Islands, to acquaint them with what he had done, and to desire their speedy Assistance; also desiring earnestly that they would take care that no Boat should go within reach of the Pirate's Guns; and at Night he, Mr. Fea, caus'd Fires to be made upon the Hills round him, to alarm the Country . . .

Next day . . . it blew very hard all Day; and in the Evening . . . the Ship run directly on Shore on the Calf Island; nor could all their Skill prevent it: Then Gow, with an Air of Desperation, told them they were all dead Men . . . for having lost the only Boat they had, and five of their best Hands, they were able to do little or nothing towards getting their Ship off . . .

On the 17th, in the Morning, contrary to Expectation, Gow himself came on Shore, upon the Calf-Island, unarm'd, except his Sword, and alone, except one Man at a distance, carrying a white Flag, making Signals for a Parlee . . .

Mr. Fea made no Hesitation, but told him in short he was his Prisoner; at which Gow starting, said, it ought not to be so, since there was a Hostage delivered for him. Mr. Fea said he gave no Order for it . . . but advis'd Gow, as he expected good Usage himself, that he would send the Fellow, who carried his white Flag, back to the Ship, with Orders for them to return [the hostage] and to desire Winter and Peterson to come with him.

Gow declin'd giving any such Orders; but the Fellow said he would readily go and fetch them, and did so, and they came along with him. When Gow saw them, he reproached them for being so easily imposed, and order'd them to go back to the Ship immediately . . . They demanded Gow to deliver his Sword, but he said he would rather dye with it in his Hand, and begg'd them to shoot him: But that was deny'd . . .

Being thus brought up to London . . . and the Government being fully inform'd what black uncommon Offenders they were, it was thought proper to bring them to speedy Justice . . .

But as they Acted together, Justice requir'd they should Suffer and accordingly Gow and Williams, Belvin, Melvin, Winter, Peterson, Rollson, Mackawley, receiv'd the Reward of their Cruelty and Blood at the Gallows, being all Executed together the 11th, of June.

N. B. Gow as if Providence had directed that he should be twice Hang'd, his Crimes being of a Two-fold Nature, and both Capital; soon after he was turn'd off, fell down from the Gibbet, the Rope breaking by the Weight of some that pull'd his Legs to put him out of Pain; he was still alive and sensible, tho' he had Hung four Minutes, and able to go up the Ladder the second Time, which he did with very little Concern'd, and was Hang'd again; and since that a third Time (viz.) in Chains over-against Greenwich, as Williams is over-against Blackwall.

Slavery & Empire: The Destruction of Whydah by Dahomey

British slave trader William Snelgrave recorded accounts of his various voyages and details of the daily lives of Europeans and Africans in the trans-Atlantic atmosphere of the West African coast. Among the more notable and historically important anecdotes he relates is the rising Empire of Dahomey and its utter destruction of neighboring polities.

A New Account of Some Parts of Guinea, and the Slave-Trade[12]

By William Snelgrave

Book I: Containing an Account of the Destruction of the Kingdom of Whidaw, or Fida; the Author's Journey to the King of Dahome's Camp; with several other remarkable Particulars.

For the better understanding of the following Relation, it is necessary to prefix some Account of the late State of the Country of Whidaw, before the terrible Destruction and Desolation thereof, in the Month of March 1726–7.

The pre-Dahomey West African coastal states (ca. 1500–1720s) practiced extensive agriculture, herding, and internal trade so complex and highly developed that regular market fairs in Allada and Whydah often were larger than those in contemporary Amsterdam. Although kings theoretically possessed absolute power, important and influential noblemen and popular custom both tremendously limited royal rule. Rulers taxed production and trade while also demanding corvee labor in the royal fields. Kings exercised monopoly rights over the slave trade, either absolutely monopolizing it or claiming the right of first sale.

The Reader then is to observe, That the Sea-coast of this Kingdom lies in 6 Degrees 40 Minutes North Latitude. Sabee, the chief Town of the Country, is situate about seven Miles from the Sea side. In this Town the King allowed the Europeans convenient Houses for their Factories; and by him we were protected in our Persons and Goods, and, when our Business was finish'd, were permitted to go away in Safety. The Road where Ships anchored, was a free Port for all European Nations trading to those Part for Negroes. And this Trade was so very considerable, that it is computed, while it was in a flourishing State, there were above twenty thousand Negroes yearly exported from thence, and the neighbouring Places, by the English, French, Dutch, and Portuguese. As this was the principal Part of all the Guinea Coast for the Slave Trade, the frequent Intercourse that Nation had for many Years carried on with the white People (a) had rendered them so civilized, that it was a Pleasure to deal with them . . .

The Custom of the Country allows Polygamy to an excessive degree . . . whereby the Land was become so stock'd with People, that the whole Country appeared full of Towns and Villages: And being a very rich Soil, and well cultivated by the Inhabitants, it looked like an intire Garden. Trade having likewise flourished for a long time, had greatly enriched the People; which, with the Fertility of their Country, had unhappily made them so proud, effeminate, and luxurious, that tho' they could have brought at least one hundred thousand Men into the Field, yet so great were their Fears, that they were driven out of their principal City, by two hundred of their Enemies; and at last lost their whole Country, to a Nation they formerly had contemned. And tho' this may appear to the Reader very incredible, yet it will sufficiently be illustrated by the following Account . . .

The last King of Whydah ascended to his throne at the age of 14, with a penchant for violence in his temperament and "indolent and lascivious" living. Whydah's "Great Men," powerful landowners and advisers to the King, exploited the sovereign's weakness, carving out their own zones of "petty tyranny." Their attempts to control increasingly lucrative trade with European powers drew West African kings and warlords into conflict over time. By conquering enemy states in the interior, selling captives to

Europeans as slaves, and quickly incorporating Western weapons into his army, the King of Dahomey destroyed his coastal rivals and monopolized the slave trade. In the selection below, Snelgrave describes the origins of Dahomey as an interior slave-trading state engaged in what historian Robin Law has called the "slave-raiding mode of production."[13]

> *This common Enemy was the King of Dahome, a far inland Prince, who for some Years past had rendered himself famous, by many Victories gained over his Neighbours. He sent an Ambassador to the King of Whidaw, requesting to have an open Traffick to the Sea side, and offering to pay him his usual Customs on Negroes exported: which being refused, he from that time resolved to resent it, when Opportunity offered . . .*

> *[The King of Dahome] had such Success against his Neighbours, in a few Years, that he conquered towards the Sea Coast, as far as the Kingdom of Ardra, which is the next inland Country adjoining to Whidaw; and then resolved to remain quiet for some time, in order to settle his Conquests . . .*

> *The Conquest of Appragah gave the King an easy Entrance into the Heart of the Country; but he was obliged to halt there by a river . . . For the Pass of the River was of that Nature, it might have been defended against his whole Army, by five hundred resolute Men; but instead of guarding it, these cowardly luxurious People, thinking the fame of their numbers sufficient to deter the Dahomes from attempting it, kept no set Guard . . .*

The King of Whydah remained content to offer sacrifices to the gods, counting on the power of religion over arms.

There is a constant Tradition amongst them, that whenever any Calamity threatens their Country, by imploring the Snake's Assistance, they are always delivered from it. However this fell out formerly, it now stood them in no stead; neither were the Snakes themselves spared after the Conquest. For they being in great Numbers, and a kind of domestick Animals, the Conquerors found many of them in the Houses, which they treated in this manner: They held them up by the middle, and spoke to them in this manner: If you are Gods, speak and save your selves: Which the poor Snakes not being able to do, the Dahomes cut their Heads off, ripped them open, broiled them on the Coals, and eat them. It is very strange, the Conquerors should so far contemn the Gods of this Country, since they are so barbarous and savage themselves, as to offer human Sacrifices whenever they gain a Victory over their Enemies; and Eye-Witness to which I was, as hereafter shall be related . . .

Upon hearing Dahomey war drums, the King of Whydah immediately fled his capital with as many of his people as were able to follow. They escaped by canoe to an easily defensible river island,

But a great many that could not have the same Benefit, being hurried on by their Fears, were drowned in the Rivers, in attempting to swim to the Islands lying near Popoe; which was the next neighbouring Country to their own, on the Sea Coast to the Westward; and where they might have been

secure from their Enemies, had they escaped. Moreover, many thousands of these poor People that sheltered themselves up and down the Country among the Bushes, perished afterwards by Sword and Famine . . .

While Dahomey soldiers burned the capital city, both they and local Europeans stood in amazement at the ease of conquest. As both sets of imperialists, Dahomeian and European, commiserated over the ongoing destruction of Whydah, race decidedly did not divide them for long. In the exchanges between the Europeans and the Empire of Dahomey, we see the union of slavery and empire in the process of military conquest and the institutional relegation of conquered foes to the status of slaves—an institutional designation Europeans then transferred to their own colonies in the New World.

Mr. Duport, who was then the African Company's Governour, told me, that when the Dahome Soldiers, who had never seen white Men before, came to his House, they stood in amaze, and would not venture near him, till he beckon'd and held out his Hand to them. Whereupon they laid hold on him, and finding him a Man like themselves in all Respects, except Colour, soon laid aside their Reverance; and taking from him what he had valuable in his Pockets, made him Prisoner, with about forty other white Men, English, French, Dutch, and Portuguese, who were served in the same manner . . .

Those Europeans were soon released from bondage, however, at about the time Snelgrave arrived in West Africa and recorded their stories of the conquest. As the Dahomey state grew and centralized control over the flow of slaves, overall trade from the "Slave Coast" decreased, leading Snelgrave to lament the rise of such a ruthlessly destructive power. The example of Dahomey provided Europeans such as Snelgrave a convenient opportunity to charge Africans with full moral responsibility for plantation slavery in the Americas, but to modern historians it has provided an example of the "gun-slave cycle" in action.

As soon as the King of Dahome had conquered Ardra, the Lord of [Jaqueen, a tributary state of Ardra] sent his Submission, offering the usual Tribute he used to pay the conquered King; which was readily accepted. This shews the Policy of the King of Dahome; for tho' he had made a terrible Destruction of the Inhabitants of the inland Countries he had conquered from Time to Time; yet he knew his Interest too well, to destroy the People of this Country in the same manner; for having now obtained his Desires, in gaining a free Passage to the Sea-Side, he judged the Jaqueens would be very useful to him, because they understood Trade, and now by their means, he should never want a supply of Arms and Gunpowder, to carry on his designed Conquests. Moreover these People had ever been Rivals to the Whidaws in Trade, and had an inveterate Hatred against them, because they had drawn almost the whole trade from the Jaqueens, to their own Country. For, the Pleasantness thereof, with the good Government in former Times, had induced the Europeans to carry on the far greater part of the Trade, at their principal Town of Sabee . . .

Although some historians have denied anything more than a coincidental relationship between Dahomeian militarism and the slave trade, readers will likely be painfully aware of the careless regard for fellow human beings exercised by all parties involved.

[Snelgrave is invited by the King of Dahomey to visit court.]

The Country, as we travelled along, appeared beautiful and pleasant, and the Roads good; but desolated by the War, for we saw the remains of abundance of Towns and Villages, with a great quantity of the late Inhabitants bones strewed about the Fields . . .

We were plagued with a Vermin that greatly annoyed us; and that was such an infinite number of Flies, that tho' we had several Servants with Flappers, to keep them off our Victuals, yet it was hardly possible to put a bit of Meat into our Mouths, without some of those Vermin with it. These Flies, it seems, were bred by a great number of dead Mens Heads, which were piled on Stages, not far from our Tent, tho' we did not know so much at that time.

After we had dined, a Messenger came to us, about three o'clock in the afternoon, from the Great Captain, desiring us to go to the King's Gate; accordingly we went, and in our way saw two large Stages, on which were heaped a great number of dead Men's Heads, that afforded no pleasing sight or smell. Our Interpreter told us, they were the Heads of four thousand of the Whidaws, who had been sacrificed by the Dahomes to their God, about three week before, as an Acknowledgement of the great Conquest they had obtain'd . . .

His Majesty was in a large Court palisaded round, fitting (contrary to the Custom of the Country) on a fine gilt Chair, which he had taken from the King of Whidaw . . .

The King had a Gown on, flowered with Gold, which reached as low as his Ancles; an European embroidered Hat on his Head; with Sandals on his Feet . . .

As part of the ceremonies attending new conquests, the King ordered many prisoners executed as religious sacrifices, and the rest were made slaves "for his own use; or to be sold to the Europeans." Merchants traded cowrie shell money (imported by Europeans from India) to purchase slaves, most of whom were immediately sent to the coast and from thence to the Americas. The King then paid the soldiers for their kills, adding their heads to the growing collection.

We saw many other Persons sacrificed in this lamentable manner, and observed, That the Men went to the side of the Stages, bold and unconcerned; but the Cries of the poor Women and Children were very moving, and much affected the Dutch Captain and My self, tho' in a different manner: For he expressed his Fears to me, That the Priests might take it into their Heads, to serve us in the same manner, if they should fancy white People would be more acceptable to their God, than persons of their own colour. This notion raised some fear in me . . . Soon after, a principal Man of the Court came and stood by us, and bid the Interpreter ask us, "How we liked the Sight?" To which we replied, "Not at all: For our God had expressly forbid us using Mankind in so cruel a manner: That our Curiosity had drawn us to come and see it; which if we had not done, we could never have believed it . . . I observed to him, that the grand Law both of Whites and Blacks, with all their Fellow Creatures was: To do to others no otherwise, than as they desired to be done unto: And that our God had enjoined this to us on pain of very severe Punishments." To which he answered, This was the Custom of his Country; and so he left us . . .

Snelgrave asks the linguist if those sacrificed might be better used as slaves or sold to Europeans.

He answered, "It was best to put [the old men] to death; for being grown wise by their Age and long Experience, if they were preserved, they would be ever plotting against their Masters, and to disturb the Country; for they never would be easy under Slavery, having been the chief Men in their own Land. Moreover, if they should be spared, no European would buy them, on account of their Age . . ."

Snelgraves then returned to the coast.

The King of Dahome being desirous of the Portuguese Gold, which they bring to purchase Negroes with, his Majesty sent a great many Slaves down to Whidaw, which made Trade dull with us at Jaqueen. For tho' formerly great Numbers came to this place, from other Nations now destroyed by the Dahomes, there remains at present only one Country called Lucamee, lying towards the North-East, for the Jaqueens to trade to . . .

The King of Whydah and his people, entrenched on their barren river island, continued to sell themselves one-by-one into slavery to the residents of Popoe to obtain provisions. The effort remained fruitless, and Whydah never revived.

> *It seems the King of Dahome is grown exceedingly cruel towards his People, being always suspicious, that Plots and Conspiracies are carrying on against him: So that he frequently cuts off some of his great Men on bare Surmises. This . . . has so soured his Temper, that he is likewise greatly altered towards the Europeans . . .*
>
> *From this and the foregoing Account the Reader may observe, that now all the Countries near the Sea side, which the King of Dahome could possibly get at, are not only conquered, but also turned into Desolation, with the Inland Parts, in so terrible a manner, that there is no Prospect of Trade's reviving there again for many Years, or at least so long as the Conqueror lives. What little there is, is carried on chiefly at Appah, a place secured from him by a Morass and a River.*

Although some historians have argued that the Dahomey militarism and the slave trade were merely coincidental, the foregoing account strongly suggests otherwise. From both imperial perspectives offered in his account of the destruction of Whydah—Snelgrave's British Empire and the King of Dahomey's new West African empire—the slave trade and imperialism were inextricably linked in daily action and systematic thinking. Perhaps it is a mistake for historians to conceptually disentangle them whatsoever; Snelgrave never did.

6

Slavery's Defenders versus the First Abolitionists

William Snelgrave was a British slave trader and occasional sufferer of pirate attacks and captivity. Snelgrave regularly traded and even lived a significant portion of his life in West Africa, one of the many hundreds and thousands of powerful linchpins in the developing world of trans-Atlantic slavery, capitalism, and empires. Snelgrave's accounts of slavery, the slave trade, and piracy remain some of the most complete and detailed that have ever been written, and they are positively riddled with biases toward merchants' interests; white, European, and Christian supremacy; and writing that often engages with the imagination of his readership more so than presenting an honest portrayal of his subject. In the following extracts from Snelgrave's *A New Account of Some Parts of Guinea, and the Slave-Trade*, the author endeavors to defend his peculiar trade as entirely lawful and indeed beneficial to all parties involved.

A New Account of Some Parts of Guinea, and the Slave-Trade[14]

By William Snelgrave

BOOK II. The manner how the Negroes become Slaves. The Numbers of them yearly exported from Guinea to America. The Lawfulness of that Trade. Mutinies among them on board the Ships where the Author has been, &c.

As for the Manner how those People become Slaves; it may be reduced under these several Heads.

1. It has been the Custom among the Negroes, time out of Mind, and is so to this day, for them to make Slaves of all the Captives they take in War. Now, before they had an Opportunity of selling them to the white People, they were often obliged to kill great Multitudes, when they had taken more than they could well employ in their own Plantations, for fear they should rebel, and endanger their Masters safety.

2dly. Most Crimes amongst them are punished by Mulcts and Fines; and if the Offender has not wherewithal to pay his Fine, he is sold for a Slave: This is the Practice of the inland People, as well as of those on the Sea side.

3dly. Debtors who refuse to pay their Debts, or are insolvent, are likewise liable to be made Slaves; but their Friends may redeem them: And if they are not able or willing to do it, then they are generally sold for the Benefit of their Creditors. But few of these come into the hands of the Europeans, being kept by their Countrymen for their own use.

4thly. I have been told, That it is common for some inland People, to sell their Children for Slaves, tho' they are under no Necessity for so doing; which I am inclined to believe. But I never observed, that the People near the Sea Coast practice this, unless compelled thereto by extreme Want and Famine, as the People of Whidaw have lately been.

Now, by these means it is that so many of the Negroes become Slaves, and more especially by being taken Captives in War. Of these the Number is so great, that I may safely affirm, without any Exaggeration, that the Europeans of all Nations, that trade to the Coast of Guinea, have, in some Years, exported at least seventy thousand. And tho' this may no doubt be thought at first hearing a prodigious Number; yet when 'tis considered how great the Extent of this Coast is, namely from Cape Verd to Angola, which is about four thousand Miles in length; and that Polygamy is allowed in general amonst them, by which means the Countries are full of People, I hope it will not be thought improbable that so many are yearly exported from thence.

Snelgrave thus produces the standard defense of slavery from his day, developed in part by thinkers such as John Locke, which justified slavery as an extension of the state of war. In fact, because most slaves became such as a result of defeat and capture in battle, Snelgrave argued that he and his slave ships rescued those captives from execution by adding trade value to their lives and labor. Despite the slaves' and European moralizers' ignorance, Snelgrave and his fellow human-dealers fancied themselves the

African's benefactor. What strikes the modern reader as almost assuredly his real reason for defending slavery, however, is the fabulous wealth and power African slave labor channeled to the English Nation-State:

> *Several Objections have often been raised against the Lawfulness of this Trade, which I shall not here undertake to refute. I shall only observe in general, That tho' to traffick in human Creatures, may at first sight appear barbarous, in-human, and unnatural; yet the Traders herein have as much to plead in their own Excuse, as can be said for some other Branches of Trade, namely, the Advantage of it: And that not only in regard of the Merchants, but also of the Slaves themselves, as will plainly appear from these following Reasons.*

> *First, It is evident, that abundance of Captives, taken in War, would be inhumanly destroyed, was there not an Opportunity of disposing of them to the Europeans. So that at least many Lives are saved, and great Numbers of useful Persons kept in being.*

> *Secondly, When they are carried to the Plantations, they generally live much better there, than they ever did in their own Country; for as the Planters pay a great price for them, 'tis their interest to take care of them.*

> *Thirdly, By this means the English Plantations have been so much improved, that 'tis almost incredible, what great Advantages have accrued to the Nation thereby; especially to the Sugar Islands, which lying in a Climate near as hot as the*

Coast of Guinea, the Negroes are fitter to cultivate the Lands there, than white People.

Then as to the Criminals amongst the Negroes, they are by this means effectually transported, never to return again; a Benefit which we very much want here.

In a word, from this Trade proceed Benefits, far outweighing all, either real or pretended Mischiefs and Inconveniencies. And, let the worst that can, be said of it, it will be found, like all other earthly Advantages, tempered with a mixture of Good and Evil . . .

As Snelgrave's narratives of slave ship mutinies demonstrate, the slaves were quite far from appreciating their new status. His narrative reminds us that the first abolitionists were not stuffy Puritans or radical Quakers without regard to social order and realism; rather, the first abolitionists were the slaves themselves. Slaves fought the crystallization of their status as property at every opportunity, many of them resorting to suicidal attempts at rebellion and, failing that, casting themselves overboard, starving and strangling themselves to death, and even conspiring to and actually committing mass suicide both at sea and on plantations.

I have been several Voyages, when there has been no Attempt made by our Negroes to mutiny; which, I believe, was owing chiefly, to their being kindly used, and to my Officers Care in keeping a good Watch. But sometimes we meet with stout stubborn People amongst them, who are never to be made easy;

and these are generally some of the Cormantines, a Nation of the Gold Coast. I went in the year 1721, in the Henry of London, a Voyage to that part of the Coast, and bought a good many of these People. We were obliged to secure them very well in Irons, and watch them narrowly: Yet they nevertheless mutinied, tho' they had little prospect of succeeding . . .

This Mutiny began at Midnight (the Moon then shining very bright) in this manner. Two Men that stood Centry at the Fore-hatch way, where the Men Slaves came up to go to the house of Office, permitted four to go to that place; but neglected to lay the Gratings again, as they should have done: Where-upon four more Negroes came on Deck, who had got their Irons off, and the four in the house of Office having done the same, all the eight fell on the two Centries, who immediately called out for help. The Negroes endeavoured to get their Cutlaces from them, but the Lineyards (that is the Lines by which the handles of the Cutlaces were fastened to the Men Wrists) were so twisted in the Scuffle, that they could not get them off before we came to their Assistance. The Negroes perceiving several white Men coming towards them, with Arms in their hands, quitted the Centries, and jumped over the Ship's side into the Sea.

I being by this time come forward on the Deck, my first care was to secure the Gratings, to prevent any more Negroes from coming up; and then I ordered People to get into the Boat, and save those that jumped over-board, which they luckily did; For they found them all clinging to the Cables the Ship was moored by.

After we had secured these People, I called the Linguists, and ordered them to bid the Men-Negroes between Decks be quiet; (for there was a great noise amongst them.) On their being silent, I asked, "What had induced them to mutiny?" They answered, I was a great Rogue to buy them away from their own Country; and that they were resolved to regain their Liberty if possible. I replied, "That they had forfeited their Freedom before I bought them, either by Crimes or by being taken in War, according to the Custom of their Country; and they being now my Property, I was resolved to let them feel my Resentment, if they abused my Kindness: Asking at the same time, Whether they had been ill used by the white Men, or had wanted for any thing the Ship afforded?" To this they replied, "They had nothing to complain of." Then I observed to them, "That if they should gain their Point and escape to the Shore, it would be no Advantage to them, because their Countrymen would catch them, and sell them to other Ships." This served my purpose, and they seemed to be convinced of their Fault, begging, "I would forgive them, and promising for the future to be obedient, and never mutiny again, if I would not punish them this time." This I readily granted, and so they went to sleep. When Day-light came we called the Men Negroes up on Deck, and examining their Irons, found them all secure. So this Affair happily ended, which I was very glad of; for these People are the stoutest and most sensible Negroes on the Coast: Neither are they so weak as to imagine as others do, that we buy them to eat them; being satisfied we carry them to work in our Plantations, as they do in their own Country.

However, a few days after this, we discovered they were plotting again, and preparing to mutiny. For some of the Ringleaders proposed to one of our Linguists, If he could procure them an Ax, they would cut the Cables the Ship rid by in the night; and so on her driving (as they imagined) ashore, they should get out of our hands, and then would become his Servants as long as they lived.

For the better understanding of this I must observe here, that these Linguists are Natives and Freemen of the Country, whom we hire on account of their speaking good English, during the time we remain trading on the Coast; and they are likewise Brokers between us and the black Merchants.

This Linguist was so honest as to acquaint me with what had been proposed to him; and advised me to keep a strict Watch over the Slaves: For tho' he had represented to them the same as I had done on their mutinying before, That they would be all catch'd again, and sold to other Ships, in case they could carry their Point, and get on Shore; yet it had no effect upon them.

This gave me a good deal on Uneasiness. For I knew several Voyages had proved unsuccessful by Mutinies; as they occasioned either the total loss of the Ship and the white Mens Lives; or at least by rendring it absolutely necessary to kill or wound a great number of the Slaves, in order to prevent a total Destruction. Moreover, I knew many of these Cormantine Negroes despised Punishment, and even Death it self: It having often happened at Barbadoes and other Islands, that on their being any ways hardly dealt with, to break them of their Stubbornness in refusing to work, twenty or more have hang'd themselves at a time in a Plantation.

We also see in this document early notions of race as a sociopolitical construction, a category linking one's legal status and one's skin color. In this case, the final paragraphs of the document starkly show skin color as the dividing line of those within the protection of the law and those literally without it. A month later, another mutinous slave killed a white man aboard Snelgrave's ship. The crew captured the slave.

Accordingly we acquainted the Negroe, that he was to die in an hour's time for murdering the white Man. He answered, "He must confess it was a rash Action in him to kill him; but he desired me to consider, that if I put him to death, I should lose all the Money I had paid for him." To this I bid the Interpreter reply, "That tho' I knew it was customary in his Country to commute for Murder by a Sum of Money, yet it was not so with us; and he should find that I had no regard to my Profit in this respect: For as soon as an Hour-Glass, just then turned, was run out, he should be put to death;" At which I observed he shewed no Concern.

Hereupon the other Commanders went on board their respective Ships, in order to have all their Negroes upon Deck at the time of Execution, and to inform them of the occasion of it. The Hour-Glass being run out, the Murderer was carried on the Ship's Forecastle, where he had a Rope fastened under his Arms, in order to be hoisted up to the Fore-yard Arm, to be shot to death. This some of his Countrymen observing, told him, (as the Linguist informed me afterwards) "That they would not have him be frightened; for it was plain I did not design to put him to death, otherwise the Rope would have been put about his neck, to hang him." For it seems they had no thought of his being shot . . . But they immediately saw the contrary; for as soon as he was hoisted up, ten white Men who were placed behind the Barricado on the Quarter-deck, fired their Musquets, and instantly killed him. This struck a sudden Damp upon our Negroe-Men, who thought, that, on account of my Profit, I would not have executed him.

The Body being let down upon the Deck, the Head was cut off, and thrown overboard. This last part was done, to let our Negroes see, that all who offended thus, should be served in the same manner. For many of the Blacks believe, that if they are put to death and not dismembered, they shall return again to their own Country, after they are thrown overboard. But neither the Person that was executed, nor his Countrymen of Cormantee (as I understood afterwards,) were so weak as to believe any such thing; tho' many I had on board from other Countries had that Opinion.

When the Execution was over, I ordered the Linguist to acquaint the Men-Negroes, "That now they might judge, no one that killed a white Man should be spared . . ."

"Their Voyage to Hell": Piracy, Thick and Thin

Book III of William Snelgrave's account of slave-trading life on the coast of West Africa is undoubtedly the most enjoyable section of his book to read, for it is the section in which the slave-trader narrator is captured and abused by pirates. Although they spared his life, it was only upon the word of his former sailors, who attested to his having treated them well.

A New Account of Some Parts of Guinea, and the Slave-Trade (1734)

By William Snelgrave

BOOK III. Containing an Account of the Author's being taken by Pirates, on the North part of the Coast of Guinea, in the Bird Galley of London, belonging to the late Humphrey Morrice Esq; who was sole Owner of the said Ship. Interspersed with several Instances of the Author's many Deliverances, and narrow Escapes from Death, during the time he was detain'd Prisoner by the Pirates.

[Off the West African Coast.]

As it was dark, I could not yet see the Boat, but heard the noise of the rowing very plain: Whereupon I ordered the second Mate to hail the Boat, to which the People in it answered, "They belonged to the Two Friends, Captain Eliot of Barbadoes." At this, one of the Officers who stood by me, said, "He knew the Captain very well, and that he commanded a Vessel of that name." I replied, "It might be so; but I would not trust any Boat in such a place;" and ordered him to hasten the first Mate, with the People and Arms upon Deck, as I had just before ordered. By this time our Lanthorns and Candles were brought up, and I ordered the Boat to be hailed again: To which the People in it answered, "They were from America." And at the same time fired a volley of small Shot at the Ship, tho' they were then above Pistol shot from us; which showed the Boldness of these Villains: For there was in the Boat only twelve of them, as I understood afterwards, who knew nothing of the Strength of our Ship; which was indeed considerable, we having 16 Guns, and 45 Men on board. But as they told me after we were taken, "They judged we were a small Vessel of little force. Moreover, they depended on the same good fortune as in the other Ships they had taken; having met with no resistance: For the People were generally glad of an opportunity of entering with them:" Which last was but too true.

When they first began to fire, I called aloud to the first Mate, to fire at the Boat out of the Steerage Port-holes; which not being done, and the people I had ordered upon Deck with small Arms not appearing, I was extremely surprised; and the more, when an Officer came and told me, "The People would not take Arms." I went thereupon down into the Steerage, where I saw a great many of them looking at one another. Little thinking that my first Mate had prevented them from taking Arms, I asked them with some Roughness, "Why they had not obeyed my Orders?" Calling upon some brisk Fellows by name, that had gone a former Voyage with me, to defend the Ship; saying, "It would be the greatest Reproach in the World to us all, if we should be taken by a Boat." Some of them replied, "They would have taken Arms, but the Chest they were kept in could not be found." The reason of which will be related hereafter.

By this time the Boat was along the Ship's Side, and there being no body to oppose them, the Pirates immediately boarded us; and coming on the Quarter-deck, fired their Pieces several times down into the Steerage, and shot a Sailor in the Reins, of which Wound he died afterwards. They likewise threw several Granado-shells, which burst amongst us, so that 'tis a great wonder several of us were not killed by them, or by their Shot.

At last some of our People bethought themselves to call out for Quarter; which the Pirates granting, the Quarter-master came down into the Steerage, enquiring, "Where the Captain was?" I told him, "I had been so till now." Upon that he asked me, "How I durst order my People to fire at their Boat out of the Steerage? Saying, that they had heard me repeat it several times." I answered "I thought it my Duty to defend the Ship, if my People would have fought." Upon that he presented a Pistol to my Breast, which I had but just time to parry before it went off; so that the Bullet past between my Side and Arm. The Rogue finding he had not shot me, gave me such a Blow on the Head as stunned me; so that I fell upon my Knees; but immediately recovering my self, I forthwith jumped out of the Steerage upon the Quarter-deck, where the Pirate Boatswain was.

He was a bloody Villain, having a few days before killed a poor Sailor, because he did not do something so soon as he had ordered him. This cruel Monster was asking some of my People, "Where their Captain was." So at my coming upon Deck, one of them, pointing to me, said, "There he is . . ." Whereupon lifting up his broad Sword, he swore, "No Quarter should be given to any Captain that offered to defend his Ship," aiming at the same time a full stroke at my Head. To avoid it I stooped so low, that the Quarter-deck Rail received the Blow; and was cut in at least an inch deep: Which happily saved my Head from being cleft asunder: And the Sword breaking at the same time, with the force of the Blow on the Rail, it prevented his cutting me to pieces.

By good Fortune his Pistols, that hung at his Girdle, were all discharged; otherwise he would doubtless have shot me. But he took one of them, and with the But-end endeavoured to beat out my Brains, which some of my People that were then on the Quarter-deck observing, cried out aloud, "For God's sake don't *kill our Captain, for we never were with a better Man." This turned the Rage of him and two other Pirates on my People, and saved my Life: But they cruelly used my poor Men, cutting and beating them unmercifully. One of them had his Chin almost cut off; and another received such a Wound on his Head, that he fell on the Deck as dead; but afterwards, by the care of our Surgeon he recovered . . .*

Then the Quarter-master took me by the hand, and told me, "My Life was safe provided none of my People complained against me." I replied, "I was sure none of them could . . ."

Then I was ordered to go on the Quarter-deck to their Commander, who saluted me in this manner. "I am sorry you have met with bad usage after Quarter given, but 'tis the Fortune of War sometimes. I expect you will answer truly to all such Questions as I shall ask you: otherwise you shall be cut to pieces; but if you tell the Truth, and your Men make no Complaints against you, you shall be kindly used; and this shall be the best Voyage you ever made in your Life, as you shall find by what shall be given you." I thanked him for his good Intentions, telling him, "I was content to stand on the footing he had proposed to me . . ."

The most significant component of Snelgrave's narrative for modern historians and libertarians is the ideology of piracy he describes. Snelgrave wrote of events during what historian Marcus Rediker calls the "Golden Age of Piracy" (1710s–1720s), in which pirates generally considered themselves revolutionaries warring against constituted authority the world over. Rediker has described piracy in the Golden Age as part of a "dialectic of terror," in which mercantile and imperial powers exploited and brutalized sailors in their service and sailors responded by "turning pirate," exploiting and murdering the exploiters and murderers. Pirates in the Golden Age rejected their sociopolitical status in the order of nation-states, empires, and massively growing mercantile interests. They revolted against the social order, remade their sociopolitical world at sea, and declared permanent war against their oppressors. The empires responded by prosecuting their own ruthless wars against pirate fleets, exterminating the last significant crews in the Atlantic around the same time William Snelgrave published his *New Account*.

> *As, in this whole Affair, I greatly experienced the Providence of Almighty God, in his Goodness delivering me from the hands of these Villains, and from many Dangers; so the same good Providence gave me such a presence of Mind, that when I believe I was upon the point of being killed, such Terrors did not arise, as I had formerly experienced, when in danger of Shipwrack; and tho' I fare very hard, and endured great Fatigues during the time I was there Prisoner; yet praised be God, I enjoyed my Health: Submitting with that Resignation to the Will of the Almighty, as a Man ought to do in such severe Misfortunes . . .*
>
> *I come now to relate, How Mr. Simon Jones, my first Mate, and ten of my Men entred with the Pirates. The Morning after we were taken, he came to me, and said, "His Circumstances*

were bad at home: Moreover, he had a Wife whom he could not love; and for these Reasons he had entred with the Pirates, and signed their Articles." I was greatly surprised at this Declaration, and told him, "I was very sorry to hear it, for I believ'd he would repent when too late; and as he had taken this Resolution rashly, without communicating it to me, all I could say now would be to no Purpose; neither would it be proper for me, for the future, to have any Discourse with him in private." I saw this poor Man afterwards despised by his Brethren in Iniquity; and have since been informed, he died a few Months after they left the River Sieraleon. However, I must do him the Justice to own, He never shewed any Disrespect to me; and the ten People he persuaded to enter with him, remained very civil to me, and of their own accord, always manned the side for me, whenever I went on board the Ship they belonged to.

Several of these unhappy People soon after repented, and desired me to intercede for them, that they might be cleared again; for they durst not themselves mention it to the Quartermaster, it being death by their Articles: But it was too nice a matter for me to deal in; and therefore I refused them.

Some days after this, one of these poor Men . . . discovered things to me, of which I only had a suspicion before. After cursing Mr. Jones for persuading him to enter with the Pirates, he said to me, "That several times in the Night-watch, before we came to Sieraleon, he had heard him say, That he hoped we should meet with Pirates when we came to that River . . . "

Then I asked them the Reason why the Chest of Arms was put out of the place where it usually stood at the Steerage; and where it was hid in the time we were taken? They answered . . . That when I called to the People in the Steerage to fire on the Pirate-boat, supposing Mr. Jones had delivered them Arms according to my Order, many of the Men would have broken the Chest open, but he prevented them, by declaring, This was an opportunity he had wished for; and that if they fired a Musquet, they would be all cut to pieces. And they further assured me, that to induce them to enter with the Pirates, he had declared to them, That I had promised him to enter my self. Putting all this together, with what several of the Pirates told me afterwards, namely, That he had been the chief occasion of their keeping my Ship, it was a wonder that I escaped so well, having such a base Wretch for my principal Officer . . .

[The pirate captain invites Snelgrave to accompany him on a tour of the conquered ship.]

Soon after we were on board, we all went into the great Cabin, where we found nothing but Destruction . . . Two large Chests that had Books in them were empty; and I was afterwards informed, they had been all thrown overboard; for one of the Pirates, upon opening them, swore, "There was Jaw-work enough (as he called it) to serve a Nation, and proposed they might be cast into the Sea; for he feared, there might be some Books amongst them, that might breed Mischief enough; and prevent some of their Comrades from going on in their Voyage to Hell, whither they were all bound." Upon which the Books were all flung out of the Cabin-windows into the River . . .

They . . . made such Waste and Destruction, that I am sure a numerous set of such Villains would in a short time, have ruined a great City. They hoisted upon Deck a great many half Hogsheads of Claret, and French Brandy; knock'd their Heads out, and dipp'd Canns and Bowls into them to drink out of: And in their Wantonness threw full Buckets of each sort upon one another. . . As to bottled Liquor of many sorts, they made such havock of it, that in a few days they had not one Bottle left . . .

As to Eatables, such as Cheese, Butter, Sugar, and many other things, they were as soon gone. For the Pirates being all in a drunken Fit, which held as long as the Liquor lasted, no care was taken by any one to prevent this Destruction: Which they repented of when too late . . .

[A pirate attempts to steal Snelgrave's spare clothes, to which he objects.]

I had hardly done speaking, when he lifted up his broad Sword, and gave me a Blow on the Shoulder with the flat side of it; whispering at the same time these Words in my Ear, "I give you this Caution, never to dispute the Will of a Pirate: For, suppose I had cleft your Scull asunder for your Impudence . . . assure your self my Friends would have brought me off on such an Occasion." I gave him thanks for his Admonition, and soon after he put on the Clothes, which in less than half an hour after, I saw him take off and throw overboard. For some of the Pirates seeing him dress'd in that manner, had thrown several Buckets of Claret upon him . . .

The next day, which was the third since my being taken, Le Bouse's Crew were permitted to come on board the Prize: Where they finished what was left of Liquors and Necessaries; acting in the same destructive manner as their vile Brethren in Iniquity had done before . . .

The Quarter-master [a few days later fell] into a Delirium, [and] died before morning in terrible Agonies; cursing his Maker in so shocking a manner, that it made a great Impression on several new entered Men: and they afterwards came privately to me, begging, "that I would advise them how to get off from so vile a Course of Life, which led them into Destruction both of Body and Soul . . . I declined it; Exhorting them in general, Not to be guilty of Murder, or any other Cruelty to those they should take. For if ever they should, by a general consent, resolve to embrace the King's Pardon [which rewarded those who assisted in capturing or killing pirates], it would be a great Advantage to them, to have the unfortunate People they had taken give them a good Character in that respect . . ."

From thence I took occasion to observe to them, "That if they thought fit to embrace his Majesty's most gracious Pardon, there was not only time enough for them to return to the West Indies, (there being still three Months to come of the time limited in the Proclamation) but now that War was declared

*against Spain, they would have an opportunity of inriching
themselves in a legal way, by going a privateering, which
many of them had privately done." This seemed to be relished
by many: but several old Buccaneers, who had been guilty of
Murder and other barbarous Crimes, being no ways inclined
to it, they used the King's Proclamation with great contempt,
and tore it in pieces . . .*

*[One day during his period of capture, pirates stole Snelgrave's
embroidered coat.]*

*They were going on Shore amongst the Negroe-Ladies . . .
[and as the pirate's new] Coat was Scarlet embroidered with
Silver, they believed he would have the preference of them,
(whose Coats were not so showy) in the opinion of their
Mistresses. This making him easy, they all went on Shore
together.*

*It is a Rule amongst the Pirates, not to allow Women to be on
board their Ships, when in the Harbour. And if they should
take a Prize at Sea, that has any Women on board, no one
dares, on pain of death, to force them against their Inclina-
tions. This being a good political Rule to prevent distur-
bances amongst them, it is strictly observed. So now being in a
Harbour, they went on Shore to the Negroe-women, who were
very fond of their Company, for the sake of the great Presents
they gave them. Nay, some white Men that lived there, did
not scruple to lend their black Wives to the Pirates, purely on
account of the great Rewards they gave . . .*

Snelgrave's captors were clearly divided. First were the new recruits—young men either recently terrified into joining the crew or sadly disappointed with the results of their voluntarily joining. Second were the grizzled, veteran pirates—older men literally cast out of all polite society, denied all protections from "lawful" authorities. The two distinct factions of pirates show distinct piratical ideologies; the first based in the "thin" concerns of daily life for poor young men, the second based in "thick" declarations of war on God himself.[15] Whereas the young pirates do not yet fully recognize the implications of life as outlaws in a world of powerful nation-states and empires, the veterans embraced their villainy and steered a course for Hell. One evening, a fire broke out in one portion of one of the pirate ships.

> *Whilst I stood musing with my self on the Quarter-deck, I heard a loud shout upon the Main-deck, with a Huzza, "For a brave blast to go to Hell with," which was repeated several times. This not only much surprised me, but also many of the new entered Pirates; who were struck with a Pannick Fright, believing the Ship was just blowing up . . . I heard these poor wretches say, in a lamentable Voice, one to another; "Oh! That we could be so foolish as to enter into this vile course of Life! The Ship will be immediately blown up, and we shall suffer for our Villainies in Hell Fire." So that when the old harden'd Rogues on the Main-deck, wish'd for a blast to go to Hell with, the other poor wretches were at the same time under the greatest Consternation at the thoughts of it . . .*

Two days after this, a small Vessel came into the River, and was taken by them: It was called the Dispatch Captain Wilson, belonging to the Royal African Company. Mr. Simon Jones, formerly my first Mate, who had entered with the Pirates . . . told them, on this occasion, "That he had once commanded a Ship, which was hired and freighted by the African Company; and that he had been very unjustly used by them; so he desired the Dispatch might be burned, that he might be revenged of them." This being immediately consented to, and forthwith ordered to be executed, one John Stubbs, a witty brisk fellow, stood up, and desired to be heart first; saying, "Pray, Gentlemen, hold a little, and I will prove to you, if this Ship is burnt, you will thereby greatly serve the Company's Interest." This drawing every one's attention, they bid him go on: Then he said, "The Vessel has been out these two years on her Voyage, being old and crazy, and almost eaten to pieces by the Worms; besides, her Stores are worth little; and as to her Cargoe, it consists only of a little Redwood and Melegette-pepper; so if she should be burned, the Company will lose little; but the poor People that now belong to her, and have been so long a Voyage, will lose all their Wages, which, I am sure, is three times the Value of the Vessel, and of her trifling Cargoe; so that the Company will be highly obliged to you for destroying her." The rest of the Crew being convinced by these Reasons, the Vessel was spared, and delivered again to Captain Wilson and his People, who afterwards came safe to England in it . . .

Part Two:

The Revolutionary Nineteenth Century

8

Walker's Appeal

In 1828, small businessman and free African American David Walker presided as the de facto leader of Boston's black community and abolitionist movement. Through his powerful speeches and writing, Walker galvanized audiences' attention and consciences, wresting them from all sorts of slumber, rousing them to excited action against the slavery menace. Where no formal abolition movement existed, Walker's rhetoric and publications provided the ideological and spiritual elements. In 1829, he published a series of articles rocketing him to infamy nationwide. Walker spread his *Appeal* throughout the vast, informative social networks linking free black communities (often through sailors and couriers) with their yet-enslaved brethren. As Walker's inflammatory text worked its way down the coasts and penetrated the southern countryside—threatening to stir shackled minds to resistance wherever it went—southern governments responded with vigor and fury to match. Slave states banned the movement of black sailors and the dissemination of any information deemed hazardous to "public safety."

In the preface and first two articles, Walker channels deep spiritual faith and innumerable material sufferings into an impassioned abolitionist plea to his fellows, though his prose often addresses white Americans as well. He compares the positions of African Americans in the United States to the slaves of civilizations past and their brothers-in-chains throughout the Atlantic world. He seeks to expose the root sources of African miseries in the Americas. The first article explains those miseries with reference to the long history of trans-Atlantic African slavery, a system novel in its brutality, its level of control over the individual slave, and its perpetual expulsion of former slaves from citizenship. In previous eras, freed slaves could rise to the very heights of society, whereas flurries of state laws and even the American Constitution itself positively condemned African Americans to exist outside and fundamentally apart from white American culture, politics, and law. Walker concludes the first half of his series by denouncing ignorance and encouraging education, self-empowerment, and, ultimately, violent resistance when and where necessary.

He begins the third article with a history of African slavery in the New World, from its origins in the decrees of the Spanish king and Holy Roman Emperor and the first permissions to land 4,000 slaves in the Caribbean. Within a century, the hapless and half-starved settlers of Virginia eagerly imported African slaves to offset their constant monetary losses and shortage of capable labor. Over the centuries, economic need and base greed warped into "principled" and "religious" justifications for what was, according to Christian doctrine, an obvious evil. Finally, Walker identifies the primary political factor driving his *Appeal*: the veritable "scheme" called "colonization," through which American slaveholders from John Randolph of Roanoke to Henry Clay wished to separate freed and independent African Americans from their enslaved and ignorant brethren. Through colonization, planters could open a trans-Atlantic safety valve, offload their more troublesome black chattels (who could die in Africa, for all the planters cared), and rest comfortably in bed, assured of their safety. The *Appeal* concludes that Americans may indeed enjoy their peace, but they cannot—they will not be allowed to—have peace at the expense of justice.

Walker died a short year after publishing his *Appeal* (leading sympathetic newspapers to allege that he was poisoned). The *Appeal* appeared in the South circa 1830, followed soon after by Nat Turner's (apparently) unconnected rebellion in Virginia. The Turner slave revolt shocked and horrified Americans everywhere but especially in the slavery-heavy Deep South and Tidewater regions. Planters responded to Turner by spending the next three decades constructing a police state to enforce slave codes and suppress the ever-present threat of rebellion. Southern elites determined to do everything necessary to preserve their wealth and power, flatly denying the essentially Jeffersonian principles expressed in Walker's powerful and revolutionary text.

David Walker, Walker's Appeal, in Four Articles, Together with a Preamble to the Colored Citizens of the World, but in Particular and Very Expressly to Those of the United States of America (Excerpts). Boston. 1829.[16]

My dearly beloved Brethren and Fellow Citizens—

Having travelled over a considerable portion of these United States, and having in the course of my travels taken the most accurate observation of things as they exist—the result of my observation has warranted the full and unshaken conviction, that we (coloured people of these United States) are, the most degraded, wretched and abject set of beings, that ever lived since the world began, and I pray God, that none like us ever may live until time shall be no more. They tell us of the Israelites in Egypt, the Helots in Sparta, and of the Roman Slaves, which last, were made up from almost every nation under heaven, whose sufferings under those ancient and heathen nations, were, in comparison with ours, under this enlightened and Christian nation, no more than a cypher . . . little more . . . than the name and form of slavery; while wretchedness and endless miseries were reserved, apparently in a phial, to be poured out upon our fathers, ourselves, and our children by Christian Americans. . .

I am fully aware, in making this appeal to my much afflicted and suffering brethren, that I shall not only be assailed by those whose greatest earthly desires are, to keep us in abject ignorance and wretchedness, and who are of the firm conviction that heaven has designed us and our children, to be slaves and beasts of burden to them and their children.—I say I do not only expect to be held up to the public as an ignorant, impudent and restless disturber of the public peace, by such avaricious creatures, as well as a mover of insubordination—and perhaps put into prison or to death, for giving a superficial exposition of our miseries, and exposing tyrants . . . I will only ask one question here—Can our condition be any worse? Can it be more mean and abject? If there are any changes, will they not be for the better, though they may appear for the worst at first? Can they get us any lower? Where can they get us? They cannot treat us worse; for they well know the day they do it they are gone. But against all accusations, which may or can be preferred against me, I appeal to heaven for my motive in writing—who knows that my object is, if possible to awaken in the breasts of my afflicted, degraded and slumbering brethren, a spirit of enquiry and investigation respecting our miseries and wretchedness in this Republican land of Liberty!!!!!! . . .

And as the inhuman system of slavery, is the source from which most of our miseries proceed, I shall begin with that curse to nations; which has spread terror and devastation through so many nations of antiquity . . . The fact is, the labor of slaves comes so cheap to the avaricious usurpers, and is of such great utility to the country where it exists, that those who are actuated only by sordid avarice, overlook the evils . . . And being a just and holy Being, [God] will at one day appear fully in behalf of the oppressed, and arrest the progress of the avaricious oppressors . . . The Lord our God will bring other destructions upon them—for not unfrequently will he cause them to rise up one against another, to be split and divided, and to oppress each other, and sometimes to open hostilities with sword in hand. Some may ask what is the matter with this united and happy people? Some say it is caused by political usurpers, tyrants, oppressors, &c. But has not the Lord an oppressed and suffering people among them? Does the Lord condescend to hear their cries, and see their tears in consequence of oppression? Will he let the oppressors rest comfortably and happy always? Will he not cause the very children of the oppressors to rise up against them, and oftimes put them to death? God works in many ways his wonders to perform. . .

Has he not the hearts of all men in his hand? Will he suffer one part of his creatures to go on oppressing and treating another like brutes, always, with impunity? . . . I ask every man who has a heart and is blessed with the privilege of believing—Is not God, a God of justice to all his creatures? . . . I say, if God gives you peace and tranquility and suffers you thus to go on, afflicting us and our children . . . would he be to us a God of justice? . . .

Article 1. Our Wretchedness in Consequence of Slavery.

My beloved brethren:—The Indians of North and of South America—the Greeks—the Irish, subjected under the king of Great Britain—the Jews, that ancient people of the Lord—the inhabitants of the Islands of the Sea—in fine, all the inhabitants of the Earth, (except, however the sons of Africa) are called men, and of course are, and ought to be free.—But we, (colored people) and our children are brutes, and of course are, and ought to be slaves to the American people and their children, forever—to dig their mines and work their farms; and thus go on enriching them, from one generation to another with our blood and our tears!!!!!! . . .

Now, I appeal to Heaven and to Earth, and particularly to the American People themselves, who cease not to declare that our condition is not hard . . . Show me a coloured President, a Governor, a Legislator, a Senator, a Mayor, or an Attorney at the Bar . . . Show me a man of colour, who holds the low office of a constable, or one who sits in a Juror Box, even on a case of one of his wretched brethren, throughout this great Republic!! . . .

Do they not institute laws to prohibit us from marrying among the whites? I would wish, candidly, however, before the Lord, to be understood, that I would not give a pinch of snuff to be married to any white person I ever saw in all the days of my life. And I do say it, that the black man, or man of colour, who will leave his own colour (provided he can get one, who is good for any thing) and marry a white woman, to be a double slave to her, just because she is white, ought to be treated by her, as he surely will be, viz: as a Neger!!!! It is not, indeed, what I care about inter-marriages with the whites, which induced me to pass this subject in review; for the Lord knows, that there is a day coming when they will be glad to get into the company of the blacks, notwithstanding we are, in this generation, levelled by them, almost on a level with the brute creation: and some of us they treat even worse than they do the brutes that perish. . .

I ask those people who treat us so well, Oh! I ask them, where is the most barren spot of land which they have given unto us? . . . Can a man of color buy a piece of land and keep it peaceably? Will not some white man try to get it from him, even if it is a mud hole? I need not comment any farther on a subject which all, both black and white will readily admit. But I must, really, observe that in this very city, when a man of colour dies, if he owned any real estate it most generally falls into the hands of some white person—the wife and children of the deceased may weep and lament if they please, but the estate will be kept snug enough by its white possessor. . .

The Spartans chained, and hand-cuffed the Helots, and dragged them from their wives and children, children from their parents, mothers from their suckling babes, wives from their husbands, driving them from one end of the country to the other? Notice the

Spartans were heathens, who lived long before our Divine Master made his appearance in the flesh. Can Christian Americans deny these barbarous cruelties? Have you not Americans, having us subjected under you, added to these miseries, by insulting us in telling us to our face, because we are helpless, that we are not of the human family? . . .

But the slaves among the Romans. Every body who has read history, knows, that as soon as a slave among the Romans obtained his freedom, he could rise to the greatest eminence in the State, and there was no law instituted to hinder a slave from buying his freedom. Have not the Americans instituted laws to hinder us from obtaining our freedom? Do any deny this charge? Read the laws of Virginia, North Carolina, &c. Further, have not the Americans instituted laws to prohibit a man of colour from obtaining and holding any office, whatever, under the government of the U. States of America? Now, Mr. Jefferson tell us, that our condition is not so hard, as the slaves were under the Romans!!!!!! . . .

At the close of the first Revolution in this country, with Great Britain, there were but thirteen States in the Union, now there are twenty four, most of which are, slave-holding States, and the whites are dragging us around in chains and in hand-cuffs to their new States and Territories to work their mines and farms, to enrich them and their children—and millions of them believing firmly that we being a little darker than they, were made by our creator to be an inheritance to them and their children forever— the same as a parcel of brutes!!!!!

Are we men?—I ask you, O! my brethren, are we men? Did our creator make us to be slaves to dust and ashes like ourselves? Are they not dying worms as well as we? Have they not to make their appearance before the tribunal of heaven, to answer for the deeds done in the body, as well as we?—Have we any other master but Jesus Christ, alone? Is he not their master as well as ours? What right then, have we to obey and call any other master but himself? . . .

Article 2. Our Wretchedness in Consequence of Ignorance.

Ignorance, my brethren, is a mist, low down into the very dark, and almost impenetrable abyss of which, our fathers for many centuries have been plunged. The Christians . . . instead of trying to enlighten them, by teaching them, that religion, and light with which God had blessed them, they have plunged them into wretchedness ten thousand times more intolerable, than if they had left them entirely to the Lord, and to add to their miseries, deep down into which they have plunged them, tell them, that they are an inferior and distinct race of beings. . .

When we take a retrospective view of the Arts and Sciences—the wise legislators, the Pyramids, and other magnificent buildings, the turning of the channel of the river Nile, by the sons of Africa or of Ham, among whom learning originated, and was carried thence into Greece, where it was improved upon and refined . . . I say, when I view retrospectively, the renown of that once mighty people, the children of our great progenitor I am indeed cheered. Yea, further, when I view that mighty son of Africa, Hannibal, one of the greatest generals of antiquity, who defeated and cut off so many thousands of white Romans or murderers, and who, carried his victorious arms, to the very gates of Rome, and I give it as my candid opinion, that, had Carthage been well united and had given him good support, he would have carried that cruel and barbarous city by storm. But they were disunited, as the coloured people are now in the United States of America, the reason our natural enemies are enabled to keep their feet on our throats.

Beloved brethren—here let me tell you and believe it, that the Lord our God . . . will give you a Hannibal, And when the Lord shall have raised him up, and given him to you for your possession. Oh! My suffering brethren, remember the divisions and consequent sufferings of Carthage and of Hayti. Read the History particularly of Hayti, and see how they were butchered by the whites, and do you take warning. The person whom God shall give you, give him your support, and let him go his length, and behold in him, the salvation of your God. God will indeed, deliver you through him, from your deplorable and wretched condition, under the Christians of America. I charge you this day before my God to lay no obstacle in his way, but let him go. . .

Article 3. Our Wretchedness in Consequence of the Preachers of the Religion of Jesus Christ.

It is well known to the Christian world, that Bartholomew Las Casas, that very notoriously avaricious Catholic priest or preacher, and adventurer with Columbus in his second voyage, proposed to his countrymen, the Spaniards in Hispaniola to import the Africans from the Portuguese settlement in Africa, to dig up gold and silver, and work their plantations for them . . . This man, ("Las Casas, the Preacher,") succeeded so well in his plans of oppression, that in 1503, the first blacks had been imported into the new world. Elated with this success, and stimulated by sordid avarice only, he importuned Charles V in 1511, to grant permission to a Flemish merchant, to import 4,000 blacks at one time. Thus we see, through the instrumentality of a pretended preacher of the Gospel of Jesus Christ our common master, our wretchedness first commenced in America, where it has been continued from 1503, to this day, 1829. A period of three hundred and twenty six years. But two hundred and nine, from 1620—when twenty of our fathers were brought into Jamestown, Virginia, by a Dutch man of war, and sold off like brutes to the highest bidders; and there is not a doubt in my mind, but that tyrants are in hopes to perpetuate our miseries under them and their children until the final consummation of all things.—But if they do not get dreadfully deceived, it will be because God has forgotten them. . .

The Pagans, Jews and Mahometans try to make proselytes to their religions, and whatever human beings adopt their religions they extend to them their protection. But Christian Americans, not only hinder their fellow creatures, the Africans, but thousands of them will absolutely beat a coloured person nearly to death, if they catch him on his knees, supplicating the throne of grace . . . Yes, I have known small collections of coloured people to have convened together, for no other purpose than to worship God Almighty, in spirit and in truth, to the best of their knowledge; when tyrants calling themselves patrols, would also convene and wait almost in breathless silence, for the poor coloured people to commence singing and praying to the Lord our God, and as soon as they had commenced the wretches would burst in upon them and drag them out and commence beating them as they would rattle-snakes—many of whom, they would beat so unmercifully that they would hardly be able to crawl for weeks and sometimes for months—Yet the American ministers send out missionaries to convert the heathen, while they keep us and our children sunk at their feet in the most abject ignorance and wretchedness that ever a people was afflicted with since the world began. . .

How can the preachers and people of America believe the Bible? Does it teach them any distinction on account of a man's colour? . . .

But the Americans having introduced slavery among them, their hearts have become almost seared as with an hot iron, and God has nearly given them up to believe a lie in preference to the truth!!!! And I am awfully afraid that pride, prejudice, avarice and blood will before long, prove the final ruin of this happy republic, or land of liberty!!!!! Can any thing be a greater mockery of religion than the way in which it is conducted by the Americans? It appears as though they are bent only on daring God Almighty to do his best. . .Will he not stop them, preachers and all? O! Americans! Americans!! I call God—I call angels—I call men, to witness, that your destruction is at hand, and will be speedily consummated, unless you repent.

Article 4. Our Wretchedness in Consequence of the Colonizing Plan.

My dearly beloved brethren:—This is a scheme . . .

That is to say, [it is] a plan to get those of the coloured people, who are said to be free, away from among those of our brethren, whom they unjustly hold in bondage so that they may be enabled to keep them the more secure in ignorance and wretchedness, to support them and their children, and consequently, they would have the more obedient slaves. For if the free are allowed to stay among the slaves, they will have intercourse together, and of course, the free will learn the slaves bad habits, by teaching them, that they are men, as well as other people, and certainly ought and must be free. . .

The Americans of North and of South America, including the West-India Islands—no trifling portion of whom, were, for stealing, murdering, &c. compelled to flee from Europe, to save their necks or banishment, have effected their escape to this continent, where God blessed them with all the comforts of life—He gave them a plenty of every thing calculated to do them good—not satisfied with this, however, they wanted slaves, and wanted us for their slaves, who belong to the Holy Ghost and no other, who we shall have to serve instead of tyrants.—I say, the Americans want us, the property of the Holy Ghost, to serve them. But there is a day fast approaching, when (unless there is a universal repentance on the part of the whites, which will scarcely be done, they have got to be so hardened in consequence of our blood, and so wise in their own conceit). To be plain and candid with you, Americans! I say that the day is fast approaching when there will be a greater time on the continent of America than ever was witnessed upon this earth . . . Some of you, have done us so much, that you will never be able to repent—Your cup must be filled—You want us for your slaves and shall have enough of us—God is just, who will give you your fill of us. . .

Do you believe that Mr. Henry Clay, late Secretary of State, and now in Kentucky, is a friend to the blacks further than his personal interest extends? Is it not his greatest object and glory upon earth, to sink us into miseries and wretchedness by making slaves of us, to work his plantation to enrich him and his family? Does he care a pinch of snuff about Africa—whether it remains a land of Pagans and of blood, or of Christians, so long as he gets enough of her sons and daughters to dig up gold and silver for him? . . . Would he work in the hot sun to earn his bread, if he could make an African work for nothing, particularly, if he could keep him in ignorance and make him believe that God made him for nothing else but to work for him? . . . I have been for some time taking notice of this man's speeches and public writings, but never to my knowledge have I seen any thing in his writings which insisted on the emancipation of slavery, which has almost ruined his country. Thus we see the depravity of men's hearts, when in pursuit only of gain. . .

Here is a demonstrative proof, of a plan got up, by a gang of slave-holders, to select the free people of colour from among the slaves, that our more miserable brethren may be the better secured in ignorance and wretchedness, to work their farms and dig their mines, and thus go on enriching the Christians with their blood and groans . . . This country is as much ours as it is the whites, whether they will admit it now or not, they will see and believe it by and by. They tell us about prejudice—what have we to do with it? Their prejudices will be obliged to fall like lightning to the ground, in succeeding generations; not, however, with the will and consent of all the whites, for some will be obliged to hold on to the old adage, viz: the blacks are not men, but were made to be an inheritance to us and our children, forever!!!!!! I hope the residue of the coloured people, will stand still and see the salvation of God, and the miracle which he will work for our delivery from wretchedness under the Christians!!!!!!!. . .

I say, from the beginning, I do not think that we were natural enemies to each other. But the whites having made us so wretched, by subjecting us to slavery and having murdered so many millions of us . . . Man, in all ages and all nations of the earth is the same. Man is a peculiar creature—he is the image of his God, though he may be subjected to the most wretched condition upon earth, yet that spirit and feeling which constitute the creature, man, can never be entirely erased from his breast, because the God who made him after his own image planted it in his heart, he cannot get rid of it. The whites knowing this, they do not know what to do, they know that they have done us so much injury they are afraid, that we, being men, and not brutes, will retaliate, and woe will be to them, therefore, that dreadful fear, together, with an avaricious spirit, and the natural love in them, to be called masters . . . bring them to the resolve, that they will keep us . . . as long as they possibly can, and make the best of their time while it lasts. Consequently they, themselves, (and not us,) render themselves, our natural enemies, by treating us so cruel. They keep us miserable now, and call us their property, but some of them will have enough of us by and by—their stomachs shall run over with us, they want us for their slaves, and shall have us to their fill. . .Let no man of us budge one step, and let slaveholders come to beat us from our country. America is more our country, than it is the whites—we have enriched it with our blood and tears. The greatest riches in all America have arisen from our blood and tears:—and will they drive us from our property and homes, which we have earned with our blood? They must look sharp or this very thing will bring swift destruction upon them. The Americans have got so far upon our blood and groans, that they have almost forgotten the God of armies. But let them go on. . .

I speak Americans for your good. We must and shall be free I say, in spite of you. . .And wo, wo, will be to you if we have to obtain our freedom by fighting. Throw away your fears and prejudices then, and enlighten us and treat us like men, and we will like you more than we do not hate you, and tell us no more about colonization, for—America is as much our country, as it is yours.—Treat us like men, and there is no danger but we all will live in peace and happiness together. For we are not like you, hard hearted, unmerciful, and unforgiving. What a happy country this will be, if the whites will listen. . . . Treat us then like men, and we will be your friends. And there is not a doubt in my mind, but that the whole of the past, will be sunk into oblivion, and we yet, under God, will become a united and happy people. The whites may say it is impossible, but remember, that nothing is impossible with God. . .

Should tyrants take it into their heads to emancipate any of you, remember that your freedom is your natural right. . .Whether you believe it or not, I tell you that God will dash tyrants, in combination with Devils, into atoms, and will bring you out from your wretchedness and miseries under these Christian People!!!!!! . . .

[Walker quotes the Declaration of Independence at length.]

Now, Americans! I ask you candidly, was your sufferings under Great Britain, one hundredth part as cruel and tyrannical as you have rendered ours under you? . . .

The Americans may be as vigilant as they please, but they cannot be vigilant enough for the Lord, neither can they hide themselves, where he will not find and bring them out.

The Equal Rights
or Locofoco Party
Declaration of Principles

On the evening of October 29, 1835, a great mass of radical liberal conspirators poured into Tammany Hall, fulfilling their carefully laid plans to overtake the local Democratic Party nominating conventions from the conservatives who controlled the Hall. The conservatives, clearly outnumbered, feared to lose their grasp on the nominating process and did everything possible to maintain it. Overpowered and shouted down by the steadily growing throng of rowdy and boisterous "Equal Rights" Democrats—as the radicals called themselves—the conservatives finally gave up, feebly declared the convention closed without nominations, and shut off the gas lights throughout Tammany Hall before abandoning their hijacked proceedings. The rump of radicals had come prepared to handle those sorts of dirty tricks, however, and they emptied their pockets. The conspirators lighted their newly invented friction matches, popularly called "locofocos," illuminating their second-class convention with candles. The radicals nominated their own slate of candidates representing what they considered the true principles of the Democratic Party.

The following morning, the hostile press condescendingly referred to the rump conventioneers as the "Locofoco Party," a name that the party adopted as a badge of honor in their quest to ideologically purify Jackson's democracy. On February 9, 1836, the Locofoco, or Equal Rights, Party met for its first county convention in New York City, where they drafted a Declaration of Principles. The document defined much of the movement—its ideology, intentions for American government, and political strategy. It became the litmus test for Equal Rights candidates during the two-year existence of the party. By late 1837, Locofocos had gained preeminence in the Van Buren administration, and Tammany Hall itself adopted the Declaration of Principles. For the next decade, Locofoco Democrats steered politics in many northern and western states. The Locofoco movement as such lasted until the 1870s, affecting American life in profound and understudied ways. The Declaration of Principles, therefore, stands as a clear articulation of radical liberal ideas and the first blast in a decades-long war on monopoly.

Declaration of Principles[17]

We, whose names are hereunto affixed, do associate ourselves, and unite, for the purpose of effecting Constitutional Reform in legislation, and to bring into practice the principles of which the governments of these United States were originally founded.

We utterly disclaim any intention or design of instituting any new party, but declare ourselves the original Democratic party, our whole object being political reformation by reviving the landmarks and principles of Democracy. We therefore hold with the revered Jefferson, that,

1st. "The true foundation of Republican Government is the equal rights of every citizen, in his person and property, and in their management."

2d. "The rightful power of all legislation is to declare and enforce only our natural rights and duties, and to take none of them from us. No man has a natural right to commit aggression on the equal rights of another; and this is ALL from which the law ought to restrain him. Every man is under the natural duty of contributing to the necessities of society; and this is all the law should enforce on him. When the laws have declared and enforced all this, they have fulfilled their functions."

3d. "The idea is quite unfounded that on entering into society, we give up any natural rights."

4th. Unqualified and uncompromising hostility to bank note and paper money as a circulating medium, because gold and silver is the only safe and constitutional currency.

5th. Hostility to any and all monopolies by legislation, because they are a violation of the equal rights of The People.

6th. Hostility to the dangerous and unconstitutional creation of vested rights by legislation, because they are a usurpation of the people's sovereign rights. And we hold that all laws or acts of incorporation passed by one Legislature can be rightfully altered or repealed by their successors.

Preamble & Resolutions of the Equal Rights Party Convention

Whereas—When, on the ever memorable 4th of July, 1776, the thirteen Colonies of North America renounced all political connection or subjection to the government of Great Britain, they founded their Declaration of Independence on the natural, equal, inalienable rights of man. And when subsequently, it became necessary to form Constitutions and governments for themselves, the democratic principle of the paramount sovereignty of the people, was constantly and emphatically set forth: hence, it was only as a matter of convenience, that the plan of legislating by representatives was adopted; but the worst prerogative of despotism, that of vesting privileges and divesting of rights, never could have been delegated to any government in the Union. Ours are governments of derived and specified powers, and not of original or independent authority; and, like the leaves of the forest, they are only of annual duration. Had the framers of our Constitutions considered it right in itself, consistent with the just rights of the people, or with our political system, for legislators to enact laws specifying any numbers of years, or a perpetuity of existence, would they have established annual elections and annual governments? If a legislature can enact any law to continue in force for as long a term of years as it chooses to designate, it can also as reasonably hold office and exercise power so long as it can pledge the public faith to its acts, and bind future generations.

It is well argued and demonstrated by Thomas Jefferson, that every generation of mankind has the sovereign right of changing the government and constructing a new Constitution. He averaged a generation at twenty years. Can a legislature, therefore, make laws more sacred than the Constitution, more binding on the people? Is the servant greater than his master? Is the legislature greater than the people, the paramount sovereign? Is a charter more irrevocable than the Constitution? And, in short, can they alter, repeal, or remake the one, and dare they not interfere with or repeal the other? If so, then is the paramount sovereignty in chartered companies, and not in the hands of the people.

Resolved—As the deliberate belief and solemn sentiment of this Convention, That it is usurpation of the worst and most dangerous character, for any legislature in the Union to grant charters of privileges or immunities, for any specified term of years, because legislatures cannot rightfully grant that to others which they never possessed themselves, and because they have no prospective authority as to futurity. They have no power, ability, competency, or means to add to or increase the rights of the great mass of the people, and therefore no authority to take from, limit, or diminish those rights. They have no right to tie up the hands of their successors on any subject of legislation that concerns or affects the community. The natural, the equal, inalienable, civil and social rights of the people, are always invaded where privileges are granted to individuals or companies. In fact, the people are not sovereign, nor freedom does not truly exist, when governments assume such prerogatives and exercise such injustice and despotism; our annual elections are an absurdity, the prohibition of privileged orders in the Constitution is a mere sounding brass and tinkling cymbal, so long as our legislative halls are charter manufactories.

Resolved, That our principles and measures are strictly democratic in accordance with the theory of our government and the happiness of our country. We require nothing exclusive for ourselves, no advantage but what we are desirous should be extended to each and every citizen of this republic. We "ask nothing but what is manifestly right, nor will we submit tamely to those abuses of legislation which are clearly wrong." We ask, "that the blessings of government, like the dews of Heaven, should descend equally on the high and the low, the rich and the poor."

We ask the repeal of all unequal, unjust, unconstitutional laws, granting powers or privileges to portions of the community, to the divesting of the rights and manifest injury of the majority.

We ask that the state legislatures will confine themselves to their proper sphere of action, as respects the currency, and that they will cease to usurp from the general government a power granted by the Constitution. We demand that the state governments will no longer authorize the issuing of bills of credit, commonly called bank notes, in open violation of the Constitution of the United States.

We ask that our legislators will legislate for the whole people and not for favored portions of our fellow-citizens, thereby creating distinct aristocratic little communities within the great community. It is by such partial and unjust legislation that the productive classes of society are compelled by necessity, to form unions for mutual preservation, and because they are not equally protected and respected as the other classes of mankind.

We ask to be reinstated in our equal and constitutional rights according to the fundamental truths in the Declaration of Independence, and as sanctioned by the Constitution of the United States, because it is "self-evident that all men are created equal; that they are endowed by their creator with certain inalienable rights; that among these are life, liberty and the pursuit of happiness; and that to secure those rights, governments are instituted among men."

In short, we ask nothing but what is consistent with Christian Democracy; for, in the declaration that "God is no respecter of persons, all are equal in his sight," we behold the universal equality of man:—In the denunciation of, "Woe unto you ye lawyers, for ye bind heavy burthens and grievous to be borne upon men's shoulders," we see the strongest form of command against unequal laws, or monopolies:—In the precept of "Do unto others as ye would that they should do unto you," is the divine doctrine of Equal Justice;—and in the injunction of "Be ye perfect, even as your father in heaven is perfect," we behold the great law of progress.

10

Theodore Sedgwick,
Monarchy vs. Democracy

In late 1835, the *New York Evening Post* faced an existential dilemma. The paper, once founded by Alexander Hamilton, had been owned for some time by the radical Locofoco Democrat William Cullen Bryant. As part of an effort to remake the *Post* from a staunch organ of federalism into a rejuvenated and luminously democratic paper, Bryant hired the young literary critic William Leggett and shortly put him to work writing political editorials. Leggett's writing, his career, and his reformist passions all caught fire in 1835 when New York abolitionists mailed sacks full of pamphlets to Charleston, South Carolina. When the local postmaster refused to deliver the mail and a mob publicly burned the sacks, the Jackson administration kept its peace. Leggett was incensed and turned the *Post*'s editorial pages against the administration, attacking those flagrant violations of the people's equal right to use the federal mails. Because of Leggett's radicalism, the Democratic

Party's national organ, the *Washington Globe*, read him out of the party, and Democratic leaders threatened to withdraw advertising and printing contracts with the *Post* if Leggett were not leashed. The fiery editor fell ill and was kept from his pen for most of the year 1836, however, and editorial duties fell to his genteel lawyer friend from Massachusetts, Theodore Sedgwick III.

Sedgwick hailed from a famous and modestly wealthy family of Federalists, and his radical ideas alienated him from much of New England life. He found an ideological homeland in New York, however, and heartily joined the *Post*'s ventures, as well as his friend Leggett's expeditions into abolitionism. In the following selections from Theodore Sedgwick's time at the *New York Evening Post*, our author explores the foundational principles of voluntary government and their relationship to private associations. Sedgwick believed that the United States was, properly conceived, a voluntary democracy, and all evidence of involuntary government resulted from corruptions in the people and their leaders. One such key font of corruption was the system of granting corporate charters and reserving for the legislature's pets the privilege of limiting shareholder liabilities. By controlling and limiting the people's ability to organize in corporate bodies, with their own contractual schemes for limiting shareholder liabilities, state legislatures in fact established a class of American aristocrats and moved the mode of governance closer to monarchy than to democracy. As a necessary corrective, Sedgwick demanded that the democratic principle be followed through by the people's representatives: "We ask of our legislators, therefore, the unrestricted power of managing our own private concerns."

"Monarchy vs. Democracy" By Theodore Sedgwick III[18]

We have before shown some reasons why incorporated Insurance Companies did not afford as complete security to the publick as schemes which human ingenuity would have devised if left unshackled. This is not all matter of theory. It has been in many instances reduced to successful practice. In London, in Philadelphia, in some of the New England States, and even in some parts of the State of New York, men have begun to understand that they can manage their own affairs, without depending upon a privileged order constituted and set apart by law to rule them in this branch of business. Voluntary associations are formed by which a number of individuals agree to apportion among the whole the loss sustained by each respectively. Such an association is truly republican. It is in perfect accordance with the fundamental principles of the social compact. A nation is nothing more than an assemblage of a great number of individuals, associated for the purpose of preventing or apportioning among all collectively the risks and burdens which would otherwise fall upon some of its members individually. Each pays a certain premium for the purpose of effecting an insurance upon his most important interests. Where the management of their common concerns is placed entirely under the control of a single individual, the organization is termed a Monarchy—when submitted to the regulation of a privileged class, it is denominated an Aristocracy; but where those interested undertake to manage their own affairs, it becomes a Democracy. We are all convinced of the superior efficacy of the last mode in the management of other matters—Can we be doubtful as to this?

We are not acquainted with the details of the organization of all the associations of this nature already formed. The general principle running through all is, that every one who is insured joins the association and becomes an insurer. A small premium is paid at first, the object of which is to defray the current expenses of managing the business of the company. Whenever a loss is sustained by any of the members, the amount is distributed among the whole, the portion paid by each as well as the amount of the original premium being as proportioned to the sum for which he is insured.

The mode adopted to prevent a failure in the payment of a loss is different in different cases. In some instances, a promissory note, with competent indorsers, or a mortgage upon unencumbered real estate, is required, at the same time the premium is paid. In others, a sum of money is deposited proportional to the amount insured. Which ever mode is adopted, the security given is restored at the expiration of the policy, subject to the claims thereon, arising in the mean time in consequence of the losses sustained. There are no dividends—the gains being realized in the diminished rates of insurance. The whole business loses the character of a gambling operation, in which great risks are encountered in hopes of great gains. Each one pays exactly as much as he should, and receives no more than he ought.

Similar to the associations already described is the Alliance Mutual Assurance formed in this city, and which we regard as a spontaneous tribute paid to the superiority of the free trade system. In great difficulties, men turn their eyes to what they sincerely believe the surest source of relief. In trivial complaints they may employ as a physician some family relative, some personal favourite, or some cheap-serving quack; but when life is at stake, economy, personal partiality, and family friendship are overlooked, and resort is had to the ablest and the best. On the recent occasion, when general ruin seemed to threaten large classes in this community, where did they look for succor? Did they call on the pretended Hercules to help them? No; they put their own shoulders to the wheel—they threw aside their slothfulness, their prejudices—they overlooked even the superior advantages Monopoly would still have conferred upon some of their number, and established a truly democratic association, wherein the people become their own defenders, and common dangers are encountered by common sacrifices.

We approve these institutions, and sincerely wish there were no obstacles to impede their general introduction. But our laws have interposed the most serious discouragements to the formation of such compacts, but which we trust will be speedily removed. We cannot believe that the policy of our government, or the interests of any considerable portion of our citizens, is opposed to the formation of these associations; but still our present laws, in effect, absolutely prohibit their establishment, except in an indirect manner. The principal obstacle thrown in the way is the disability to act in all cases in a corporate capacity. The laws grant no power by which associations of this kind can sue or be sued, without joining in the suit the names of every one of its members. It is true this inconvenience is thought to be obviated by the Alliance recently formed in this city; but great circuity was necessary to the attainment of that object, and after all some cases may be found to have been unprovided for. Now, this trouble is all unnecessary. There is good reason why a company doing business under a particular name should not be allowed to sustain actions at law in that name. A simple modification of the present law in this particular would remove one of the principal obstacles to the object we are seeking to accomplish. We shall resume this subject to-morrow.

5 January 1836

We stated yesterday that one of the principal impediments to the formation of Mutual Assurance Associations in this State resulted from their incapacity to act as a body corporate. Another obstacle arises from the fact that the law makes no provision by which individuals, associated in this manner, may limit their liabilities to any thing short of their whole private fortune. This should be otherwise. Any person should be allowed to inform those with whom he transacts business what security he gives for the fulfil-ment of his engagements; and if he does not deviate from the path he has designated, the law has no right to interfere in the matter. It is every man's business to look out for his own interests; and if, with his eyes open, he has entered into an engagement which has been honestly fulfilled, he has no right to call upon the law to remedy the effects of his indiscretion.

It is the same in case of a company or corporation. If they inform their creditors of the precise amount pledged for the fulfilment of their engagements, no matter how small the fund set apart for that purpose may be, the law has no business to interfere in the transac-tion farther than to prevent or punish fraud. What we contend for, therefore, is, that all persons associated for this purpose should be allowed, upon certain general conditions, to constitute themselves a corporate body, with power to limit their liabilities to any specified amount, and make any other regulations among themselves, provided due notice thereof be given to all the parties concerned. This is but extending the law of Limited Partnerships, with slight modifications, so as to embrace the subject of Insurance.

We hope ultimately to see every subject upon which human ingenuity or enterprise is exercised, placed in the same predicament. We believe there is no good reason why banking, as well as any other branch of business, should not be left to be regulated by the laws of trade, and why every reasonable facility should not be extended to persons engaging in that species of traffick. The object we hope eventually to accomplish, therefore, is, the enactment of a general "corporate partnership" law, enabling men to associate for every honest purpose, and when so associated, that they should possess most of the powers and privileges now conferred by special acts of incorporation.

It may not be deemed prudent, even by many of the disciples of the free trade school, to make this change immediately and all at once. They believe that the country is hardly prepared as yet to throw open the doors to universal freedom of competition in the business of banking,—that the small notes are not yet sufficiently curtailed, and that there is not yet the necessary amount of specie in the country.

But whatever difference of opinion there may be on this subject in regard to banking, we think there can be no reasonable objection to opening the door to practical free trade in the business of insurance. We say practical free trade, for we are well aware that there is no positive prohibition preventing any individual or company from engaging in this business; but such legal discouragements are thrown in their way, and such superior privileges given to incorporated companies, as to drive the former entirely out of the market. We destroy the equilibrium as effectually by adding to one scale of the balance as by taking from the other.

The object for which we are contending is one in which the whole state—the country as well as the city—feels a deep interest. Every little village in the interior ought to have its association for Mutual Insurance, the terms of which they should be allowed to fix at their own pleasure, and to suit their own convenience, or even caprice. They should have the power to form contracts of this nature without risking more than they severally choose. They should be enabled to enter into these engagements boldly, straightforward, and by daylight, without proceeding in a sly, stealthy circuitous track, by which one seems to evade the law with which he is unable openly to grapple. We ask of our legislators, therefore, the unrestricted power of managing our own private concerns. We are no longer infants—our leading strings are long since laid aside. We need no guardians to protect our interests from the effects of our own indiscretion. Give us the power of preventing or punishing injustice, and leave our own private interests to be watched over by ourselves. We shall make more vigilant and zealous sentinels than those whose fidelity is not secured by their interest. Yes, WE THE SOVEREIGN PEOPLE ASK OF OUR SERVANTS A RESTORATION OF THE POWER OF CONDUCTING OUR OWN AFFAIRS. We shall now see whether our good natured indulgence has emboldened our stewards to arrogate the functions of masters.

11

Leggett, The Restraining Law, and the Street of the Palaces

In the following extracts from the *New York Evening Post*, William Leggett departed from optimistic Jacksonian visions of American "Manifest Destiny" and "Exceptionalism." Whereas Jacksonian "Young American" nationalists believed that American military, economic, and cultural influence would inevitably tilt history's wheel in a positive direction, more sober voices such as Leggett's remained cautious. He argued that although democracy, republicanism, and the American Constitution were indeed all special products of history—to be guarded with all due force—Jacksonian America harbored a new form of corporate aristocracy perhaps even more dangerous than the creatures dominating the Old World. The New World monster sprang not from the easily identifiable personages of kings and emperors, but like mushrooms the new aristocracy sprouted from sources unknown and possessed powers not easily understood. The American power elite constituted itself through corporate personhood and feasted on an unending flow of bank credit, partial legislation, and tax revenues. The corporate aristocracy claimed legitimacy from the public's own constitutional arrangements, however, and no matter how medieval the origins of the corporation may have been, those particular corporations were chartered by the American people through their duly elected representatives. As Leggett sharply noted, however, the mere presence of democratic republicanism did not eliminate the power of the state. In fact, democracy seemed to strengthen greatly the health and well-being of state power, providing an even richer harvest for the now legally shielded moneyed class.

The New York State "Restraining Law" was one such example of a legal shield. The law forbade any nonauthorized institutions or individuals from issuing money and credit, essentially monopolizing the banking industry for chartered banks. In the *New York Evening Post*'s words, the law constituted "the creation of an Order of American Barons," which, as Leggett notes in the final article, could be easily identified after all: one must simply take a stroll down Wall Street.

New York Evening Post, 31 August 1836
"The Restraining Law and Its Abominations"[19]

—This vile blot upon our Statute Book, this tyrannous ordinance of the Chartered Money Power, this incredible outrage on the rights of the vast unprivileged majority of the inhabitants of this free state, is one of those monstrous violations of natural justice that would not exist but that their existence is denied, and which are denied existence, because they outshock belief. It is impossible that the people of New York have yet distinctly understood the provisions of this insulting statute. What! Can two millions of men called free, know that they are stigmatized by an insolent Oligarchy as too stupid to drive "the trade in money;" that they are ignominiously excluded from this simple traffick, and basely cheated of all participation in its profits? Will they submit to hang forever in menial dependence upon the haughty smiles of a Patrician Order? Will they consent that ten thousand stockholders shall rule this State, and through this State, the Union? Do they know that these ten thousand men have climbed so high that they fear not to look down and say to us, who are two hundred times their number, "Ye scurvy knaves, with one another you shall not lend, you shall not borrow, you shall not promise, you shall not trust, you shall in no wise deal in the thrice holy and mysterious trade of money. With one another, ye servile rout, the counter-changing craft is sacrilege, the traffick in paper promises is TABOO. If you have money, bring the vile dross to us. We will ease you of your fullness. But we warn you, let not your needy brother partake your abundance. Make us your almoners. Give us possession of the beggar's blessing, the supplicant's tribute, and the suitor's fee. If you would promise, promise us. We will make you keep your promises. You are not fit to trust each other in that kind. If you are in want, or in straits, or in dangers, come to us. Pay us salvage, and we will save you. But see that you help not one another. You are weak, and would let down the rate of usance. You are unskillful, and would ruin 'the trade in money.' If you have treasure that you would lay up, deposit it with us. With us it will be safe. You yourselves shall hardly tear it from our custody. But confide not your hard earnings with each other. You are base. You are stupid. You are faithless. We alone are to be trusted. This is our advice. Such is our command. Obey and you shall be fleeced so gently that you will not know it. Resist, and our strong men shall go into your houses and take forfeiture of your effects, and if you abide in your obstinacy, they shall strip you of all you have, and shall cast you out, you and your children, to want and beggary, if so it seems good to one of us, the Noble Order of Moneychangers by Special Patent from the State." If this is the language of exaggeration, some one can show us where. If this is not the literal translation of the Law, we should be glad to know what is. We appeal to the learned in legislative jargon if we have not rendered faithfully the meaning of the Statute of Restraint. Our version is less coolly insolent, because it is not in Christian English to utter such abominations without an honest shudder. We give the original at full length . . . If it is not . . . the creation of an Order of American Barons, the New York Times will tell us what is wanting to make the Patent of Nobility complete.

"1. No person unauthorized by law, shall subscribe to, or become a member of, or be in any way interested in, any association, institution or company, formed, or to be formed, for the purpose of receiving deposites, making discounts or issuing notes or other evidences of debt, to be loaned or put in circulation as money; nor shall any person, unauthorized by law, subscribe to or become in any way interested in, any bank or fund created, or to be created for the like purposes, or either of them. . .

3. No incorporated company, without being authorized by law, shall [similarly engage in banking.]. . .

5. All notes and other securities for the payment of any money or the delivery of any property, made or given to any such association, institution or company, that shall be formed for the purpose expressed in the first section of this Title, or made or given to secure the payment of any money loaned or discounted by any incorporated company or its officers, contrary to the provisions of the third section of this Title, shall be void.

6. No person, association of persons or body corporate, except such bodies corporate as are expressly authorized by law, shall keep any office for the purpose of receiving deposites, or discounting notes or bills, or issuing any evidences of debt, to be loaned, or put in circulation as money: nor shall they issue any bills or promissory notes or other evidence of debt as private bankers, for the purpose of loaning them, or putting them in circulation as money, unless thereto specially authorized by law.

7. Every person and every corporation, and every member of a corporation, who shall contravene either of the provisions in [this Title,] or directly or indirectly, assent to such violation, shall forfeit one thousand dollars."

New York Plaindealer, 10 December 1836,
"The Street of the Palaces"[20]

There is, in the city of Genoa, a very elegant street, commonly called, The Street of the Palaces. It is broad and regular, and is flanked, on each side, with rows of spacious and superb palaces, whose marble fronts, of the most costly and imposing architecture, give an air of exceeding grandeur to the place. Here reside the principal aristocracy of Genoa; the families of Balbi, Doria, and many others of those who possess patents of nobility and exclusive privileges. The lower orders of the people, when they pass before these proud edifices, and cast their eyes over the striking evidences which the lordly exteriors exhibit of the vast wealth and power of the titled possessors, may naturally be supposed to think of their own humble dwellings and slender possessions, and to curse in their hearts those institutions of their country which divide society into such extremes of condition, forcing the many to toil and sweat for the pampered and privileged few. Wretched indeed are the serfs and vassals of those misgoverned lands, where a handful of men compose the privileged orders, monopolizing political power, diverting to their peculiar advantage the sources of pecuniary emolument, and feasting, in luxurious idleness, on the fruits of the hard earnings of the poor.

But is this condition of things confined to Genoa, or to European countries? Is there no parallel for it in our own? Have we not, in this very city, our "Street of the Palaces," adorned with structures as superb as those of Genoa in exterior magnificence, and containing within them vaster treasures of wealth? Have we not, too, our privileged orders? Our scrip nobility? Aristocrats, clothed with special immunities, who control, indirectly, but certainly, the political power of the state, monopolise the most copious sources of pecuniary profit, and wring the very crust from the hard hand of toil? Have we not, in short, like the wretched serfs of Europe, our lordly masters, "Who make us slaves, and tell us 'tis their charter?"

If any man doubts how these questions should be answered, let him walk through Wall-street. He will there see a street of palaces, whose stately marble walls rival those of Balbi and Doria. If he inquires to whom those costly fabrics belong, he will be told to the exclusively privileged of this land of equal laws! If he asks concerning the political power of the owners, he will ascertain that three-fourths of the legislators of the state are of their own order, and deeply interested in preserving and extending the privileges they enjoy. If he investigates the sources of their prodigious wealth, he will discover that it is extorted, under various delusive names, and by a deceptive process, from the pockets of the unprivileged and unprotected poor. These are the masters in this land of freedom. These are our aristocracy, our scrip nobility, our privileged order of charter-mongers and money-changers! Serfs of free America! Bow your necks submissively to the yoke, for these exchequer barons have you fully in their power, and resistance now would but make the burden more galling. Do they not boast that they will be represented in the halls of legislation, and that the people cannot help themselves? Do not their servile newspaper mouth-pieces prate of the impolicy of giving an inch to the people, lest they should demand an ell? Do they not threaten, that unless the people restrict their requests within the narrowest compass, they will absolutely grant them nothing?—that they will not relax their fetters at all, lest they should next strive to snap them entirely asunder?

These are not figures of speech. Alas! We feel in no mood to be rhetorical. Tropes and figures are the language of the free, and we are slaves!—slaves to most ignoble masters, to a low-minded, ignorant, and rapacious order of money-changers. We speak, therefore, not in figures, but in the simplest and soberest phrase. We speak plain truths in plain words, and only give utterance to sentiments that involuntarily rose in our mind, as we glided this morning through the Streets of the Palaces, beneath the frowning walls of its marble structures, fearing that our very thoughts might be construed into a breach of privilege. But thank heaven! The day has not yet come—though perhaps it is at hand—when our paper money patricians deny their serfs and vassals the right to think and speak. We may still give utterance to our opinions, and still walk with a confident step through the Street of the Palaces of the Charter-mongers.

O'Sullivan, Introduction to the Democratic Review

John L. O'Sullivan founded the *United States Magazine & Democratic Review* in 1837 and issued his first volume in October of the same year. His mission—the purpose of the *Review*—was to proclaim and promote the genius of American culture and institutions. As such, O'Sullivan stocked his pages with robust and energetic defenses of democracy, republicanism, liberty, and the "manifest destiny" of free institutions and spontaneous order throughout human history. The bulk of the *Review*, however, was generally devoted to the advancement of American national culture. O'Sullivan patronized and sponsored the careers of literary luminaries, from Knickerbockers such as William Cullen Bryant and John Greenleaf Whittier to Young Americans such as Walt Whitman, Herman Melville, and Nathaniel Hawthorne.

In the introduction to the first issue, O'Sullivan unabashedly and directly declared his principles before the reading public. His vision of a democratic republic depended on the virtue of the voting public as well as of their elected officials and institutional arrangements. He argued for the critical role of local knowledge and the necessity that the majority temper its treatment of minorities with strict regard for universal, equal human rights. "The Voluntary Principle," O'Sullivan declared, was the singular, central, and guiding force of all democratic, republican theory. More than simply expressing their preference for one particular form of government, by embracing democracy and republicanism, Americans quite literally embraced the laws of nature. In the Old World, the vast majority of human beings remained shackled to the earth with the chains of feudalism and slavery, but in the United States, free men and women everywhere rose to dizzying heights of peace and prosperity. O'Sullivan pushed his argument further, declaring democracy and republicanism the "manifest destinies" inevitably awaiting all human societies as part of their natural historical developments. O'Sullivan and the early *Review*, therefore, propounded thoroughly and radically classical liberal theories of history, politics, and social development. With that introduction, O'Sullivan charted an important new course for American politics and culture, although, in ways modern readers can no doubt divine, his ideas in turn provided ad hoc and post hoc justifications for imperial conquest and the decidedly anti-liberal modern leviathan state.

"Introduction: The Democratic Principle, the Importance of Its Assertion, and Application to Our Political System and Literature"[21]

By John L. O'Sullivan

So many false ideas have insensibly attached themselves to the term democracy, as connected with our party politics, that we deem it necessary here, at the outset, to make a full and free profession of the cardinal principles of political faith on which we take our stand; principles to which we are devoted with an unwavering force of conviction and earnestness of enthusiasm which, ever since they were first presented to our minds, have constantly grown and strengthened by contemplation of them, and of the incalculable capabilities of social improvement of which they contain the germs.

We believe, then, in the principle of democratic republicanism, in its strongest and purest sense. We have an abiding confidence in the virtue, intelligence, and full capacity for self-government, of the great mass of our people—our industrious, honest, manly, intelligent millions of freemen.

We are opposed to all self-styled wholesome restraints on the free action of the popular opinion and will, other than those which have for their sole object the prevention of precipitate legislation. This latter object is to be attained by the expedient of the division of power, and by causing all legislation to pass through the ordeal of successive forms; to be sifted through the discussions of co-ordinate legislative branches, with mutual suspensive veto powers. Yet all should be dependent with equal directness and promptness on the influence of public opinion; the popular will should be equally the animating and moving spirit of them all, and ought never to find in any of its own creatures a self-imposed power, capable (when misused either by corrupt ambition or honest error) of resisting itself, and defeating its own determined object ...

Though we go for the republican principle of the supremacy of the will of the majority, we acknowledge, in general, a strong sympathy with minorities, and consider that their rights have a high moral claim on the respect and justice of majorities; a claim not always fairly recognised in practice by the latter, in the full sway of power, when flushed with triumph, and impelled by strong interests. This has ever been the point of the democratic cause most open to assault, and most difficult to defend. This difficulty does not arise from any intrinsic weakness. The democratic theory is perfect and harmonious in all its parts; and if this point is not so self-evidently clear as the rest is generally, in all candid discussion, conceded to be, it is because of certain false principles of government, which have, in all practical experiments of the theory, been interwoven with the democratic portions of the system, being borrowed from the example of anti-democratic systems of government. We shall always be willing to meet this question frankly and fairly. The great argument against pure democracy, drawn from this source, is this:

Though the main object with reference to which all social institutions ought to be modelled is undeniably, as stated by the democrat, the greatest good of the greatest number, yet it by no means follows that the greatest number always rightly understands its own greatest good . . . Majorities are often as liable to error of opinion, and not always free from a similar proneness to selfish abuse of power, as minorities; and a vast amount of injustice may often be perpetrated, and consequent general social injury be done, before the evil reaches that extreme at which it rights itself by revolution, moral or physical.

We have here, we believe, correctly stated the anti-democratic side of the argument on this point. It is not to be denied that it possesses something more than plausibility. It has certainly been, the instrument of more injury to the cause of the democratic principle than all the bayonets and cannon that have ever been arrayed in support of it against that principle. The inference from it is, that the popular opinion and will must not be trusted with the supreme and absolute direction of the general interests; that it must be subjected to the conservative checks of minority interests, and to the regulation of the more enlightened wisdom of the better classes, and those to whom the possession of a property test of merit gives what they term a stake in the community. And here we find ourselves in the face of the great stronghold of the anti-democratic, or aristocratic, principle . . .

In the first place, the greatest number are more likely, at least, as a general rule, to understand and follow their own greatest good, than is the minority.

In the second, a minority is much more likely to abuse power for the promotion of its own selfish interests, at the expense of the majority of numbers—the substantial and producing mass of the nation—than the latter is to oppress unjustly the former. The social evil is also, in that case, proportionately greater. This is abundantly proved by the history of all aristocratic interests that have existed, in various degrees and modifications, in the world. A majority cannot subsist upon a minority; while the natural, and in fact uniform, tendency of a minority entrusted with governmental authority is, to surround itself with wealth, splendor, and power, at the expense of the producing mass, creating and perpetuating those artificial social distinctions which violate the natural equality of rights of the human race, and at the same time offend and degrade the true dignity of human nature.

In the third place, there does not naturally exist any such original superiority of a minority class above the great mass of a community, in intelligence and competence for the duties of government—even putting out of view its constant tendency to abuse from selfish motives, and the safer honesty of the mass. The general diffusion of education; the facility of access to every species of knowledge important to the great interests of the community; the freedom of the Press, whose very licentiousness cannot materially impair its permanent value, in this country at least, make the pretensions of those self-styled better classes to the sole possession of the requisite intelligence for the management of public affairs, too absurd to be entitled to any other treatment than an honest, manly contempt. As far as superior knowledge and talent confer on their possessor a natural charter of privilege to control his associates, and exert an influence on the direction of the general affairs of the community, the free and natural action of that privilege is best secured by a perfectly free democratic system, which will abolish all artificial distinctions, and, preventing the accumulation of any social obstacles to advancement, will pen it the free development of every germ of talent, wherever it may chance to exist, whether on the proud mountain summit, in the humble valley, or by the wayside of common life . . .

It is under the word *government*, that the subtle danger lurks. Understood as a central consolidated power, managing and directing the various general interests of the society, all government is evil, and the parent of evil. A strong and active democratic government, in the common sense of the term, is an evil, differing only in degree and mode of operation, and not in nature, from a strong despotism. This difference is certainly vast, yet, inasmuch as these strong governmental powers must be wielded by human agents, even as the powers of the despotism, it is, after all, only a difference in degree; and the tendency to demoralization and tyranny is the same, though the development of the evil results is much more gradual and slow in the one case than in the other. Hence the demagogue—hence the faction—hence the mob—hence the violence, licentiousness, and instability—hence the ambitious struggles of parties and their leaders for power—hence the abuses of that power by majorities and their leaders—hence the indirect oppressions of the general by partial interests—hence (fearful symptom) the demoralization of the great men of the nation, and of the nation itself, proceeding (unless checked in time by the more healthy and patriotic portion of the mind of the nation rallying itself to reform the principles and sources of the evil) gradually to that point of maturity at which relief from the tumult of moral and physical confusion is to be found only under the shelter of an energetic armed despotism.

The best government is that which governs least. No human depositories can, with safety, be trusted with the power of legislation upon the general interests of society so as to operate directly or indirectly on the industry and property of the community. Such power must be perpetually liable to the most pernicious abuse, from the natural imperfection, both in wisdom of judgment and purity of purpose, of all human legislation, exposed constantly to the pressure of partial interests; interests which, at the same time that they are essentially selfish and tyrannical, are ever vigilant, persevering, and subtle in all the arts of deception and corruption. In fact, the whole history of human society and government may be safely appealed to, in evidence that the abuse of such power a thousand fold more than overbalances its beneficial use. Legislation has been the fruitful parent of nine-tenths of all the evil, moral and physical, by which mankind has been afflicted since the creation of the world, and by which human nature has been self-degraded, fettered, and oppressed. Government should have as little as possible to do with the general business and interests of the people. If it once undertake these functions as its rightful province of action, it is impossible to say to it thus far shalt thou go, and no farther. It will be impossible to confine it to the public interests of the commonwealth. It will be perpetually tampering with private interests, and sending forth seeds of corruption which will result in the demoralization of the society. Its domestication should be confined to the administration of justice, for the protection of the natural equal rights of the citizen, and the preservation of social order. In all other respects, the VOLUNTARY PRINCIPLE, the principle of FREEDOM, suggested to us by the analogy of the divine government of the Creator, and already recognised by us with perfect success in the great social interest of Religion, affords the true golden rule which is alone abundantly competent to work out the best possible general result of order and happiness from that chaos of characters, ideas, motives, and interests—human society. Afford but the single nucleus of a system of administration of justice between man and man, and, under the sure operation of this principle, the floating atoms will distribute and combine themselves, as we see in the beautiful natural process of crystallization, into a far more perfect and harmonious result than if government, with its fostering hand, undertake to disturb, under the plea of directing, the process. The natural laws which will establish themselves and find their own level are the best laws. The same hand was the Author of the moral, as of the physical world; and we feel clear and strong in the assurance that we cannot err in trusting, in the former, to the same fundamental principles of spontaneous action and self-regulation which produce the beautiful order of the latter.

This is then, we consider, the true theory of government, the one simple result towards which the political science of the world is gradually tending, after all the long and varied experience by which it will have dearly earned the great secret—the elixir of political life. This is the fundamental principle of the philosophy of democracy, to furnish a system of administration of justice, and then leave the business and interests of society to themselves, to free competition and association—in a word, to the VOLUNTARY PRINCIPLE . . .

This principle, therefore, constitutes our point of departure. It has never yet received any other than a very partial and imperfect application to practice among men, all human society having been hitherto perpetually chained down to the ground by myriads of Lilliputian fetters of artificial government and prescription. Nor are we yet prepared for its full adoption in this country—Far, very far indeed, from it; yet is our gradual tendency toward it clear and sure. How many generations, may yet be required before our theory and practice of government shall be sifted and analysed, down to the lowest point of simplicity consistent with the preservation of some degree of national organization, no one can presume to prophecy. But that we are on the path toward that great result, to which mankind is to be guided down the long vista of future years by the democratic principle,—walking hand in hand with the sister spirit of Christianity,—we feel a faith as implicit as that with which we believe in any other great moral truth . . .

We are not afraid of that much dreaded phrase, "untried experiment," which looms so fearfully before the eyes of some of our most worthy and valued friends. The whole history of the progress hitherto made by humanity, in every respect of social amelioration, records but a series of experiments. The American revolution was the greatest of experiments, and one of which it is not easy at this day to appreciate the gigantic boldness. Every step in the onward march of improvement by the human race is an experiment; and the present is most emphatically an age of experiments. The eye of man looks naturally forward; and as he is carried onward by the progress of time and truth, he is far more likely to stumble and stray if he turn his face backward, and keep his looks fixed on the thoughts and things of the past. We feel safe under the banner of the democratic principle, which is borne onward by an unseen hand of Providence, to lead our race toward the high destinies of which every human soul contains the God-implanted germ; and of the advent of which—certain, however distant—a dim prophetic presentiment has existed, in one form or another, among all nations in all ages. We are willing to make every reform in our institutions that may be commanded by the test of the democratic principle—to democratize them—but only so rapidly as shall appear, to the most cautious wisdom, consistent with a due regard to the existing development of public opinion anti to the permanence of the progress made. Every instance in which the action of government can be simplified, and one of the hundred giant arms curtailed, with which it now stretches around its fatal protecting grasp over almost all the various interests of society, to substitute the truly healthful action of the free voluntary principle—every instance in which the operation of the public opinion and will, fairly signified, can be brought to bear more directly upon the action of delegated powers—we would regard as so much gained for the true interest of the society and of mankind at large . . .

For Democracy is the cause of Humanity. It has faith in human nature. It believes in its essential equality and fundamental goodness. It respects, with a solemn reverence to which the proudest artificial institutions and distinctions of society have no claim, the human soul. It is the cause of philanthropy. Its object is to emancipate the mind of the mass of men from the degrading and disheartening fetters of social distinctions and advantages; to bid it walk abroad through the free creation in its own majesty; to war against all fraud, oppression, and violence; by striking at their root, to reform all the infinitely varied human misery which has grown out of the old and false ideas by which the world has been so long misgoverned; to dismiss the hireling soldier; to spike the cannon, and bury the bayonet; to burn the gibbet, and open the debtors dungeon; to substitute harmony and mutual respect for the jealousies and discord now subsisting between different classes of society, as the consequence of their artificial classification. It is the cause of Christianity . . . It is, moreover, a cheerful creed, a creed of high hope and universal love, noble and ennobling; while all others, which imply a distrust of mankind, and of the natural moral principles infused into it by its Creator, for its own self-development and self-regulation, are as gloomy and selfish, in the tone of moral sentiment which pervades them, as they are degrading in their practical tendency, and absurd in theory, when examined by the light of original principles.

But a more potent influence than any yet noticed, is that of our national literature. Or rather we have no national literature. We depend almost wholly on Europe, and particularly England, to think and write for us, or at least to furnish materials and models after which we shall mould our own humble attempts. We have a considerable number of writers; but not in that consists a national literature. The vital principle of an American national literature must be democracy. Our mind is enslaved to the past and present literature of England . . . There is an immense field open to us, if we would but enter it boldly and cultivate it as our own. All history has to be re-written; political science and the whole scope of all moral truth have to be considered and illustrated in the light of the democratic principle. All old subjects of thought and all new questions arising, connected more or less directly with human existence, have to be taken up again and re-examined in this point of view. We ought to exert a powerful moral influence on Europe, and yet we are entirely unfelt; and as it is only by its literature that one nation can utter itself and make itself known to the rest of the world, we are really entirely unknown. In the present general fermentation of popular ideas in Europe, turning the public thoughts naturally to the great democracy across the Atlantic, the voice of America might be made to produce a powerful and beneficial effect on the development of truth; but as it is, American writings are never translated, because they almost always prove to be a diluted and tardy second edition of English thought . . .

If the United States Magazine and Democratic Review shall be able, by the influence of example and the most liberal encouragement, to contribute in any degree towards the remedy of this evil, (as of the other evils in our institutions which may need reform,) by vindicating the true glory and greatness of the democratic principle, by infusing it into our literature, and by rallying the mind of the nation from the state of torpor and even of demoralization in which so large a proportion of it is sunk, one of the main objects of its establishment will have been achieved.

13

Leggett and Spooner, Abolishing Slavery without the State

The anti-slavery movement—although extremely humble in its origins and slow in its growth—steadily gained key converts in American intellectual and political life during the decades before the Civil War. As early as the 1830s, important journalists such as the *New York Evening Post*'s William Leggett provided broad ideological force to the moral and emotional arguments so well and so often articulated by movement abolitionists. Throughout the 1840s and 1850s, the subject of slavery became increasingly politicized, and many northerners found themselves personally confronted with "the Slave Power" for the first time. A turbulent, violent, and transformative period, the Jacksonian and Antebellum eras produced radical and piercing liberal critiques of slavery and proposals for decentralized, individualistic solutions to a seemingly intractable political problem. In the following documents we have two examples of fiercely anti-slavery northerners advocating and justifying not only slave rebellion but also white Americans' joining alongside their enslaved countrymen in a grand war for abolition.

Writing 21 years apart, William Leggett and Lysander Spooner both insisted that the institution of slavery is contrary to the natural law and all righteous and proper American traditions. Whereas Leggett spent most of his time lamenting the plight of the slave and sympathizing with slaves' personal or collective struggles for liberty, Spooner resolved to put ideology into practice. As one of John Brown's "Secret Six," a ring of conspirators and financial supporters, Spooner reacted to the infamous and hated Dred Scott decision (1857), which effectively nationalized the institution of slavery, by implementing his own private abolitionist filibustering operations into southern states to raise slave revolts. Although Brown's raid on Harper's Ferry (1859) failed to incite slave rebellions, Spooner's plan of action for spontaneously raised armies of moral crusaders, North and South, black and white, stands as a testament to the moral seriousness of slavery in radical liberal intellectual and activist circles. From the early days of Leggett's excommunication from the Democratic Party for his abolitionism to Spooner's demands for private war against slaveholders, anti-slavery served as a pivot point dividing the ranks of "thick," or unswervingly radical liberals, and the far more numerous ranks of "thin," or compromising moderates.

"Abolition Insolence"[22]

By William Leggett

Under this head, the *Washington Globe* copies, from a Boston newspaper, the following paragraph:

> "The insolence of some of the reckless agitators who attempt to excite the people by their mad practices, is insufferable. On the fourth, the American flag . . . was suspended from a cord extended from Concert Hall to the Illuminator office nearly opposite. In scandalous derision of this glorious emblem . . . a placard . . . was suspended by the side of the flag, bearing in large letters, on one side, 'Slavery's Cloak,' and on the other 'Sacred to oppression.' It remained only till it was noticed, when it was soon torn down. It is creditable to the assembled citizens who saw the scandalous scroll, that their insulted feelings were not urged to violent exasperation against the perpetrators of the outrage, and that the deed was treated with the contempt it deserved."

The insolence of the abolitionists, in the case here adduced, owed its insufferableness to its truth. While the people are told that the spirit of the federal compact forbids every attempt to promote the emancipation of three millions of fellow-beings, held in abject and cruel bondage, and that even the free discussion of the question of slavery is a sin against the Union, a "reckless disregard of consequences" deserving the fiercest punishment which "popular indignation" can suggest, we are forced to consider the emblem of our federal union a cloak for slavery and a banner devoted to the cause of the most hateful oppression. The oppression which our fathers suffered from Great Britain was nothing in comparison with that which the negroes experience at the hands of the slaveholders. It may be "abolition insolence" to say these things; but as they are truths which justice and humanity authorize us to speak, we shall not be too dainty to repeat them whenever a fitting occasion is presented. Every American who, in any way, authorizes or countenances slavery, is derelict to his duty as a Christian, a patriot, and a man. Every one does countenance and authorize it, who suffers any opportunity of expressing his deep abhorrence of its manifold abominations to pass by unimproved. If the freemen of the north and west would but speak out on this subject in such terms as their consciences prompt, we should soon have to rejoice in the complete enfranchisement of our negro brethren of the south.

If an extensive and well-arranged insurrection of the blacks should occur in any of the slave states, we should probably see the freemen of this quarter of the country rallying around that "glorious emblem" which is so magniloquently spoken of in the foregoing extract, and marching beneath its folds to take sides with the slaveholders, and reduce the poor negroes, struggling for liberty, to heavier bondage than they endured before. It may be "abolition insolence" to call this "glorious emblem" the standard of oppression, but, at all events, it is unanswerable truth. For our part, we call it so in a spirit, not of insolence, but of deep humility and abasement. We confess, with the keenest mortification and chagrin, that the banner of our country is the emblem, not of justice and freedom, but of oppression; that it is the symbol of a compact which recognizes, in palpable and outrageous contradiction of the great principle of liberty, the right of one man to hold another as property; and that we are liable at any moment to be required, under all our obligations of citizenship, to array ourselves beneath it, and wage a war, of extermination if necessary, against the slave, for no crime but asserting his right of equal humanity—the self-evident truth that all men are created equal, and have an unalienable right to life, liberty, and the pursuit of happiness. Would we comply with such a requisition? No! rather would we see our right arm lopped from our body, and the mutilated trunk itself gored with mortal wounds, than raise a finger in opposition to men struggling in the holy cause of freedom. The obligations of citizenship are strong, but those of justice, humanity and religion are stronger. We earnestly trust that the great contest of opinion which is now going on in this country may terminate in the enfranchisement of the slaves, without recourse to the strife of blood; but should the oppressed bondmen, impatient of the tardy progress of truth urged only in discussion, attempt to burst their chains by a more violent and shorter process, they should never encounter our arm, nor hear our voice, in the ranks of their opponents. We should stand a sad spectator of the conflict; and whatever commiseration we might feel for the discomfiture of the oppressors, we should pray that the battle might end in giving freedom to the oppressed.

A Plan for the Abolition of Slavery[23]

By Lysander Spooner

When a human being is set upon by a robber, ravisher, murderer, or tyrant of any kind, it is the duty of the bystanders to go to his or her rescue, by force, if need be.

In general, nothing will excuse men in the non-performance of this duty, except the pressure of higher duties, (if such there be,) inability to afford relief, or too great danger to themselves or others.

This duty being naturally inherent in human relations and necessities, governments and laws are of no authority in opposition to it. If they interpose themselves, they must be trampled under foot without ceremony, as we would trample under foot laws that should forbid us to rescue men from wild beasts, or from burning buildings.

On this principle, it is the duty of the non-slaveholders of this country, in their private capacity as individuals—without asking the permission, or waiting the movements, of the government—to go to the rescue of the Slaves from the hands of their oppressors.

This duty is so self-evident and natural a one, that he who pretends to doubt it, should be regarded either as seeking to evade it, or as himself a servile and ignorant slave of corrupt institutions or customs.

Holding these opinions, we propose to act upon them. And we invite all other citizens of the United States to join us in the enterprise. To enable them to judge of its feasibility, we lay before them the following programme of measures, which, we think, ought to be adopted, and would be successful.

1. The formation of associations, throughout the country, of all persons who are willing to pledge themselves publicly to favor the enterprise, and render assistance and support, of any kind, to it.

2. Establishing or sustaining papers to advocate the enterprise.

3. Refusing to vote for any person for any civil or military office whatever, who is not publicly committed to the enterprise.

4. Raising money and military equipments.

5. Forming and disciplining such military companies as may volunteer for actual service.

6. Detaching the non-slaveholders of the South from all alliance with the Slaveholders, and inducing them to co-operate with us, by appeals to their safety, interest, honor, justice, and humanity.

7. Informing the Slaves (by emissaries to be sent among them, or through the non-slaveholders of the South) of the plan of emancipation, that they may be prepared to co-operate at the proper time.

8. To encourage emigration to the South, of persons favoring the movement.

9. When the preceding preliminaries shall have sufficiently prepared the way, then to land military forces (at numerous points at the same time) in the South, who shall raise the

standard of freedom, and call to it the slaves, and such free persons as may be willing to join it.

10. If emancipation shall be accomplished only by actual hostilities, then, as all the laws of war, of nature, and of justice, will require that the emancipated Slaves shall be compensated for their previous wrongs, we avow it our purpose to make such compensation, so far as the property of the Slaveholders and their abettors can compensate them. And we avow our intention to make known this determination to the Slaves beforehand, with a view to give them courage and self-respect, to nerve them to look boldly into the eyes of their tyrants, and to give them true ideas of the relations of justice existing between themselves and their oppressors.

11. To remain in the South, after emancipation, until we shall have established, or have seen established, such governments as will secure the future freedom of the persons emancipated.

And we anticipate that the public avowal of these measures, and our open and zealous preparation for them, will have the effect, within some reasonable time—we trust within a few years at farthest—to detach the government and the country at large from the interests of the Slaveholders; to destroy the security and value of Slave property; to annihilate the commercial credit of the Slaveholders; and finally to accomplish the extinction of Slavery. We hope it may be without blood.

If it be objected that this scheme proposes war, we confess the fact. It does propose war—private war indeed—but, nevertheless, war, if that should prove necessary. And our answer to the objection is, that in revolutions of this nature, it is necessary that private individuals should take the first steps. The tea must be thrown overboard, the Bastile must be torn down, the first gun must be fired, by private persons, before a new government can be organized, or the old one be forced (for nothing but danger to itself will force it) to adopt the measures which the insurgents have in view.

If the American governments, State or national, would abolish Slavery, we would leave the work in their hands. But as they do not, and apparently will not, we propose to force them to do it, or to do it ourselves in defiance of them.

If any considerable number of the American people will join us, the work will be an easy and bloodless one; for Slavery can live only in quiet, and in the sympathy or subjection of all around it.

[The following note is to be addressed to some person at the South, and signed by the person sending it, giving his own residence.]

Sir:

Please accept, and exhibit to your neighbors, this copy of a document, which we are intending to distribute very extensively through the South, and which, we trust, will give birth to a movement, that shall result not only in the freedom of the blacks, but also in the political, pecuniary, educational, moral, and social advantage of the present non-slaveholding whites. Please let me hear, from you often, informing me of the progress of the work. Direct to me at _____

WE, the subscribers, residents of the Town of _____ in the County of _____ in the State of _____ believing in the principles, and approving generally of the measures, set forth in the foregoing "Plan for the Abolition of Slavery," and in the accompanying address "To the Non-Slaveholders of the South," hereby unite ourselves in an Association to be called the League of Freedom in the Town of _____ for the purpose of aiding to carry said plan into effect. And we hereby severally declare it to be our sincere intention to co-operate faithfully with each other, and with all other associations within the United States, having the same purpose in view, and adopting the same platform of principles and measures.

The Autobiography of Ferret Snapp Newcraft, Esquire

The Young America movement (fl. 1830s–1840s) transformed life in the United States by applying curiously American values, motifs, styles, and ideas to the literary and visual arts. John L. O'Sullivan's *United States Magazine & Democratic Review* stood at the vanguard of the Jacksonian culture wars, directing and developing the literary canon while it advanced a radical republican (or Locofoco) political philosophy. During time of vexing depression, Jacksonians fought tooth and nail to divorce the forces of bank and state while their Whig opponents easily assumed political advantages. In early 1838, little more than a year after widespread bank suspensions of specie payments and even flour riots in New York City, the *Review* published a "Full Exposition and Exemplification of 'The Credit System,'" in the form of a satirical autobiography.

In this sly and amusing commentary on the emerging American monetary system, one Ferret Snapp Newcraft describes his upbringing as a young captain of finance. Through his youth, he travels the countryside with his swindler father, learning the methods and ideology of graft. As a young man, Newcraft joins a ring of near-criminal stockbrokers, in which he is taught the finer points of speculation. Ferret remains captivated throughout his life by the idea of hatching the perfect pyramid scheme—establishing an unending stream of paper money and bank credit. By the end of this first of two selections from his "Autobiography," Newcraft determines that the fate of his grand project for endless (and laborless) wealth depends on his ability to influence politics. He buys his way into the legislature, where he pioneers the fine art of logrolling.

To the invention of logrolling, he adds lobbying. Through his dealings with fellow bankers, stockjobbers, and speculators, Newcraft purchases large amounts of western land and reaches the pinnacle of his career. His credit-induced boom to wealth and power, however, is popped by the ineffable radical Jacksonians, the Locofocos, and their outdated, religious fervor for hard currency and hard work. The stupidity of the people—their inability to see the perfection in his system of never-ending credit extension and their insistence that Jackson's Specie Circular be maintained—arrests the land boom and ruins Newcraft's bank as well as his investments. He and his compatriots, however, make sure to pay specie for their own notes before burning the remainder and suspending payments to small savers. Although Newcraft ends his autobiography with a lament over the Locofocos toppling his great dreams of "castles in the sky," he notes in mystification and amazement that through his entire life he managed to live very well on the fruits of credit while producing absolutely nothing. He confidently challenges the reader: Is that not a perfect system?

"Autobiography of Ferret Snapp Newcraft, Esq., Being a Full Exposition and Exemplification of 'The Credit System'"[24]

My family, though poor, was of great antiquity, and withal respectable, since I have often heard my father say, not one of his ancestors . . . degraded himself by following any regular occupation. The only tainted limb of the family tree was our grandfather, who was ignominiously bound apprentice to a cobbler; but thank Heaven, he ran away before he took a degree, and became distinguished as all our race have been, by "living by their wits"— an expressive phrase which distinguishes the happy few from the miserable many, who are justly condemned to live by the sweat of the brow, seeing they cannot live by the sweat of the brain . . .

As we rambled about from town to town—for my father seldom remained long in one place, on account, he said, of the envy and ill will he excited by the superiority of his wits—he would stop and call my attention to a fall of water, a little murmuring river, a particular point of land, or some other matter, and tell me what a capital speculation he could make out of it if he only had the money. In one place, he would erect a great manufactory; in another, make the river navigable; in a third, found a city; and in a fourth, cut a canal that would enrich the whole country. So far as I could judge, at that time, his sole dependence was on these castles in the air, which he never realized, except in the way of now and then persuading some poor dolt of a workingman, who had saved a little money, to embark it in some one of his speculations, which I confess almost always failed, for want, as my father said, of a proper credit system founded on paper-money. But though they failed, my father always managed to take care of himself . . .

"My son," said he, "what do you suppose constitutes the superiority of man over all other animals?"

I mustered up my scholarship, and replied, "His reason, sir."

"Good—you are right. It follows, then, that reason being his great characteristic, it was the design of Providence, that he should live by his reason—in other words, by his wits—and that, therefore, it is his bounden duty to make the most of them. Do you understand?"

"I think I do, sir. But he should not make use of his wits to deceive others. Justice—"

"Justice? Where did you get these queer notions, boy?"

"From nature, I believe, sir."

"Nature is a son of a—tinker!—and the sooner we turn it out of doors the better. This is the object of all education. The impulses of nature are the mere errors of ignorance and inexperience, and what philosophers call a knowledge of the world—which, by the way, is worth all other knowledge—consists solely in sharpening our wits, and preparing us to take advantage of the dullness of others . . . It is not only justifiable, but obligatory; for not to make use of the faculties bestowed on us by nature, or acquired by experience, would be flying in the face of our Maker. It would be a most criminal negligence . . . Is it not . . . the great duty of man [to] turn a penny, and make money as fast as he can?"

"But, sir, I think he ought to make it honestly."

"Pooh—you're a blockhead . . ."

This, and various similar conversations, together with the daily example of my father, and his perpetual turmoil about speculations, gave a radical turn to my mind, and fixed my destiny for life. I saw very clearly that mankind were condemned to labour, not for their own benefit, but that of others; and that inasmuch as the wits of a man were the noblest part of him, it was but just they should live at the expense of those democratic physical powers, which were undoubtedly intended for that special purpose.

One of the great resources of my father, who was a decided enemy to hard work, was the invention of labour-saving machines. I remember to have heard him boast that he had, during his life, taken out patents for a hundred and thirty-seven contrivances of this sort, many of which he sold out to the country farmers and village mechanics, for he had a most slippery tongue, and a keen wit . . . We lived comfortably three months on these inventions, at the end of which time the ignorant country people began to be so jealous of the superiority of my father's wits, that they threatened to tar and feather him, and subject me to the new patent scalding machine.

In short, the country was becoming rather warm for us, and my father determined to seek not only a wider sphere of action, but of impunity, in the principal city of that section of country which had hitherto been the scene of the triumphs of his wits . . .

Accordingly we departed for the great city to seek our fortunes in a more enlarged sphere of action. As we proceeded along, my father whiled away the time by pointing out a variety of excellent speculations . . .

"There, now," said he, as we passed the house of an honest farmer, "There is a fellow who might double the value of his farm, and live like a fighting cock, if he would only drain that great swamp, blow up that ledge of rocks, sprinkle a few hundred bushels of plaster over it, lay it down in grass, and stock it with the short horn breed."

I replied in the simplicity of my heart,

"I suppose sir, he has not the means of doing this."

"Ah! Ferret, there's the thing. The whole world is, as it were, standing still for want of means. There is not half enough money in the world to supply the new development of speculation; and the possibility of supplying this want so as to keep pace with the spirit of the age—do you understand me, boy?—is what employs my mind day and night. The difficulty of getting money has always appeared to me a great defect in the scheme of Providence, and were that only got over, man would be all but omnipotent. I believe this to be possible, and have a sort of dim conception working its way in my brain, which, if I can only bring it to maturity, will produce the greatest revolution that has happened in the world since the deluge, and relieve mankind from that cruel denunciation that he should earn his bread by the sweat of his brow . . ."

This conversation set my thoughts in motion. I pondered almost without intermission on the subject . . .

[Shortly after arriving in Ragamuffinville, Ferret is employed by an investment broker.]

I was told to look sharp, listen to every thing, and say nothing. Here was a noble school to awaken the powers of my mind, and the exercise of my wits. The head of the house, or rather the cellar, was one of the most profound men of his time, as a proof of which it is only necessary to state, that he began business with no capital but his wits, lived like a prince for several years, without ever being worth a dollar, and finally failed for some millions. Here was a sublime genius for you . . . "the great Archimedes who can move a world by putting his lever upon nothing.". . .

By degrees, he opened to me the mysteries of the shaving business, and displayed to my mind all the wonders of an invisible world, appealing to the imagination instead of the senses.

The glorious mysteries of kiting, race-horsing, and other occult matters connected with the sublime science of raising the wind; the manner in which the credit system is built up and sustained, without any thing but itself to stand upon; the masterly process by which any amount of ideal money may be conjured out of nothing, like the spirit from the cloud, and made to represent ten times the amount of the same sum if it were real; these and some other of the "great principles," which constitute the sublime of the new credit system, he could not present to me, for as yet they had no existence, except in the heated chaos of my mind, which, from the period in which I received this first practical insight into the great money, or rather credit, kingdom, continued to boil and bubble with the fever heat of grand conceptions, fighting their way from a faint embryo to a glorious maturity . . .

Suddenly, there was a great and increasing demand for money, for all the world had become borrowers, to invest in lots, in order to take advantage of the great rise in value a hundred years hence. The precious metals not being of a ductile nature, and incapable of expanding fast enough to suit these great exigencies, it became indispensable that some substitute should be found, more suitable to the spirit of the age, and the newly discovered wants of the community.

My master every day lamented to me the contracted sphere of operations to which his genius was confined, by what he called the "infamous Specie Humbug," meaning the stupid attachment mankind had inherited from the dark ages, to what they called a standard of value. "If I could only make money out of nothing," would he exclaim in a paroxysm of enthusiasm, "I would, in a short time, possess the world!"

I brooded on this idea from morning till night, and sometimes lay awake for hours, thinking on the glorious hope of its successful accomplishment. I often asked myself what was the basis of the value of every thing in the world, and at length came to the conclusion that it was the general estimation of mankind. I then proceeded to investigate the possibility of substituting an imaginary, for a real, value, and appealing to human credulity as its basis. Mankind, thought I, worship false gods, adopt false opinions, and arrive at false conclusions. Many believe the moon is made of green cheese; is it not possible to make them believe that what is worth nothing intrinsically, is just as good as a thing of inestimable value, provided it will exchange for just as much? What . . . was the intrinsic value of a fathom of Wampum, and yet, in old times, you could purchase a farm with it from the Indians. I forgot at that time that this Wampum was the product of labor, and therefore represented the value of all the labor bestowed upon it. . . .

I learned the art of evading the laws against usury, without subjecting myself to the penalty of their violation; I mastered all the mysteries of the business in which I was engaged; and in good time became such an adept that I could practically define to a hair the precise line which separated a lucky speculation from an act of downright swindling. I could tell to the utmost nicety, how far it was lawful to play on credulity and ignorance, and the extent to which deception might be carried without constituting a fraud. In short, I could see my way clear in the darkest transaction, and split a hair with my eyes shut.

I was gradually . . . admitted sometimes to a share in the profits when I had made a good hit, and soon found myself in possession of a snug little sum. With this . . . I commenced business on my own account, and considered my fortune as good as made, when, by his influence, I was admitted a member of the Board of Brokers, which . . . enjoys a monopoly of gambling.

In truth, it was carried on upon a great scale. Not a day passed that some one of us, who, perhaps, was not worth one-fiftieth part of the money, did not play stakes for thousands, and buy or sell what neither possessed, or what, in fact, had no existence. But every thing was done in the most gentlemanly manner, and all the members were strictly governed by the point of honor, which consisted in taking every possible advantage of each other. . . .

Being now in a prosperous and honorable situation, I began to sigh for the enjoyment of domestic felicity, as I could now afford myself that expensive luxury. I accordingly sought a partner, and being guided by prudence, as well as inclination, married a lady of a certain age, who had great family interest. Her father was president of a bank, and three of her uncles bank directors. This at once initiated me into the mysteries of the "Credit System," as it existed at that time.

I at once saw its defects, and my mind again reverted, with increasing force and vigour, to the question of a currency founded exclusively on public credulity. . . . I reflected, and believed in the possibility of perfecting the Credit System, so that it should consist solely of credit, without being adulterated by a single particle of real value.

The period was now come for realizing this long cherished vision of my imagination. I was rich in credit and paper-money. . . . I had also bank influence; and now set about acquiring political distinction as indispensable to my purposes. I turned a furious democrat, that party being then uppermost; attended every ward meeting, and made speeches in favour of Equal Rights; until, by degrees, I rose to be a member of the general committee for nominating members of Assembly. When this measure came up, there were so many candidates, and so great a diversity of opinions, that we settled the matter by nominating ourselves, and were triumphantly elected.

It was now that I grasped the reality of what I had so long anticipated. Before proceeding to the seat of government, I had projected a scheme for a bank, founded on the great principle of making money out of nothing; a self-constituted, self-existent, perpetual-motion bank-machine, entirely independent of any representative of real value, and which, like a spider, would spin its web for catching flies out of its own bowels. On opening my scheme to several of my confidential friends, who had submitted to the disgrace of being called democrats for a time, in order that they might make use of their support in the attainment of their object, they were delighted with it, most especially when they found that my bank required not a dollar for its specie basis. They eagerly joined me in a memorial to the Legislature, stating that there was a great necessity for an increase of capital in the great city of Ragamuffinville, and... to request a charter, conferring on them certain privileges, which, though the people were prohibited from exercising, were exclusively for their benefit. . . .

On my arrival, I found that almost every member of that honorable body had some scheme or other on the anvil for the public good. . . . I made it my first object to become acquainted with the individual interests of every member, and set about reconciling them all, if possible, . . . [or] unite them all, and thus produce perfect harmony. This plan was accordingly adopted, and produced the most beneficial consequences. Each member proceeded on the great and only just principle of reciprocity . . . and thus, the whole batch was carried triumphantly through our honorable body with only three dissenting voices, consisting of three members who had been guilty of the unpardonable negligence of coming thither without a single project for the public good. This was the origin of that great modern improvement in legislation, called log-rolling, of which I flatter my self I am the sole inventor. . . .

We began with engraving and filling up notes to the amount of twice our nominal capital, with which we paid the first instalment on our subscriptions for stock, the whole of which, with the exception of a few hundred shares—assigned to some members of the Legislature as a compliment for voting according to their consciences—was distributed among ourselves. . . .

Here then was the credit system brought to that perfection which I had long imagined possible, and now saw realized. It was the ideal representation of a pyramid reversed; nothing at the bottom, and a vast expansion of surface at the top. It was credit founded on credit, paper on paper, and promise on promise. It might, consequently, be extended to an infinite series, or at least so long as human credulity, that great beast of burden, could be brought to stagger under the blessing. . . .

Having thus achieved the grand desideratum of making money out of nothing, my next step was to turn the discovery to the greatest advantage by changing what was worth nothing for something of real value. The truth is, I could never entirely discard from my mind certain unpleasant intruding doubts of the stability of my system, and therefore resolved to make hay while the sun shone. Accordingly, I conceived another grand scheme for the employment of the surplus funds of our institution . . . a great public improvement, that is, a rail road of a few hundred miles in length.

The thing was kept perfectly snug, while, by means of the funds furnished by our Bank, which was capable of expanding like an empty bladder, we proceeded quietly to purchase all the land in the immediate vicinity of the line of the contemplated improvement. . . . We then once more commenced the system of log-rolling, to which I added another lever of my own invention, to wit, the agency of lobby members, and the law passed by a great majority; although sturdily opposed by an ignorant, old Dutch member, who insisted that the public good had come to signify nothing but private interest. . . .

As a sort of interlude to this, I became a purchaser of vast tracts of public land in the West, which I paid for in the notes of our bank, on which I expected to realize immense profits, and which, even though it fell in price, would still be worth more than our paper promises. . . . This is another great advantage of my newly invented Credit System, if not to those who receive, at least to those that pay. In this case, as I purchased of Uncle Sam, my conscience was quite easy, for in case the worst came to the worst, the old fellow could afford to lose the money.

I was now rolling in wealth; the idol of the brokers; the oracle of financiers; the controller of the stock market; . . . and the founder of cities, for I had laid out six of these on my new lands, or rather on the maps of my lands. . . . Nay, I don't know but I may in time become the founder of a great empire on the North Pacific, where I once established an Agency for buying muskrat and mink skins.

But alas! there is nothing perfect in this world. . . . I mean the mischievous and abominable principle of REACTION, the greatest enemy to the Credit System which has ever presented itself. Under the operation of this, it is pretended that the affairs of this world resemble the action of a pendulum, which the farther it is driven one way the farther it will recede on the other, thus ever returning to opposite extremes. . . .

I discovered the origin of all the dangers which now began to threaten my system in two great sources, namely, the "Specie Circular and the Specie Humbug." . . . The former interfered with the founding of my cities in the West, by striking at the root of my Credit System, which contemplated the entire extension of every thing but promises to pay instead of payments; and the latter was a serious obstacle to my plan of causing the people to give up their absurd prejudices in favour of silver and gold, by keeping the latter out of sight, until they should actually forget such things ever existed. I always considered specie as the great ally of ignorance and barbarism, and was convinced in my own mind that an extensive paper circulation representing nothing, and which nobody was obliged to redeem, was the sole agent of refinement and civilization. . . .

The dunderheaded people, I mean the big-pawed Farmers, and the hard-handed Mechanics and Labourers, began once more to recall to mind those demoralizing substitutes for paper-money, silver and gold, which are well denominated in the Scriptures the root of all evil. Certain mischievous fellows . . . began to write essays in some of the newspapers . . . full of the most disorganizing principles. They maintained the enormous heresy of Equal Rights; denounced Monopolies; denied that a promise was the actual substance of the thing promised, and cancelled the obligation; and dared to insinuate that a superstructure that had no foundation would be very likely to fall to the ground, the first storm it encountered. Nay, they had the hardihood to assert that of nothing, nothing could come, and thus struck at the very heart of my system.

In vain did I marshal my forces, consisting of editors of newspapers whom I had conciliated by my generosity, and who repaid me with gratitude; politicians whom I had linked body and soul with the existence of my system, and who lived and breathed in that alone; and legislators who had grown out of it like toad stools from rotten wood. In vain did I set on foot the cry of Loco Foco, Fanny

Wright, Robert Dale and Jack Cade; equally vain that I called on the people who owed more than they could pay; the people who sighed to make promises they could not fulfil, and all those who desired to live by their wits instead of their labour, to come forth and defend their possessions, their morals and their religion. All would not do. . . . and it became evident that the crisis of my great Credit System was at hand.

It behooved us, therefore, to make ready for the shock; and accordingly we proceeded to prepare ourselves for a run upon our Bank. We had only specie enough in our vaults to pay the postage of our letters. . . .

The reader will readily perceive that our Bank had actually no other capital than public confidence, or as the infidel Loco Focos, and Fanny Wright men . . . call it, public credulity. This was the perfection of my system. It is easy enough to found a Banking system on a specie basis, but to raise it upon credit alone, I consider the triumph of financiering.

Our first act, in order to meet the unreasonable demands of the senseless people who held our notes . . . was to discharge a great duty to ourselves. Charity begins at home. . . . So we unanimously decided to liquidate our own obligations by cancelling all our respective notes, given as security for the capital stock. Our next act was, to cancel the certificates of stock pledged by ourselves as collateral security for the stock; and our third to throw both notes and certificates into the fire. Thus at once were cancelled all our responsibilities in the most satisfactory manner.

The bank which . . . originated in nothing, returned to its original element of nothing, and all parties were perfectly content, except those eternal and disorganizing grumblers, the Loco Focos and Jack Cade men . . . who came with their hands full of our notes to demand payment, and began to talk of tarring and feathering. But the Mayor had providentially ordered out the military to overawe these unreasonable villains. . . . I dare say some of them suffered considerably by the loss of a pitiful sum, unworthy the notice of the great inventor of the Credit System, but I have since quieted my conscience by subscribing liberally to soup-houses, and thus fairly quit scores with these wretched, irreligious, demoralized beings.

This equitable adjustment of our affairs placed me on the very pinnacle of prosperity. I had paid all my debts to the people, and might now have sat down in the enjoyment of a quiet conscience amid unbounded wealth, but the truth is, I longed for [more]. . . .

When in consequence of the "suspension" of our Bank, I had got rid of all my responsibilities in the most satisfactory manner, and felt myself perfectly independent of panic and pressure, my worthy friend came to me one day with a proposition to sell a tract of new land, comprising three millions of acres, and several large towns in perspective. This tract I had originally sold him at a pretty considerable profit, and now thought it would be a capital operation to purchase back again under the depression of the panic which I was convinced would blow over again and be followed by a corresponding reaction of prices.

My worthy friend was excessively alarmed. . . . I took advantage of his apprehensions, and finally purchased back my land at somewhat less than half of what I received for it, paying him cash in hand. The poor creature went away highly delighted, and

what is not common on such occasions, both parties were perfectly satisfied. He rejoiced in selling, and I in purchasing, what I
was assured would enrich me a few hundred thousands in the end.

This would undoubtedly have been the case if it had not been
for the obstinate ignorance and stupidity of our outlandish
Government, which about this time began a series of diaboli-
cal experiments which played the very mischief with my Credit
System, and gradually undermined its only support, namely, the
public credulity. It undertook to refuse my bank notes in payment
of the public lands, which operated against my system like a two-
edged sword, right and left. It injured its credit and depressed the
price of lands, by demanding payment in specie. . . .

It embarrassed me, terribly, and was the commencement of the
downfall of one of the greatest estates ever acquired by a single man
in the United States. People when they found themselves obliged
to give real value . . . began to calculate the cost, etc., which they
never did before, when they paid in promises. . . . Land began to
descend rapidly, and like a wagon running down hill, the nearer it
got to the bottom the faster it went. Not content with aiming this
blow at the national prosperity, this outlandish Government not
long afterwards proposed the "Infamous Scheme" of a divorce of
Bank and State, which completed my downfall.

"Infamous Scheme," indeed. . . . It was in fact a base conspiracy
against my system, and accordingly all the really honest patriots
raised a hue and cry the moment it made its appearance. . . .

The blunders of this outlandish Government had arrested
the glorious career of speculation, which like a top the moment
it ceases to whirl round, falls to the ground. I had risen with

speculation, and I fell with speculation. I had lived for years in the anticipation of a rise in the value of every thing on the face of the earth, except paper-money, and as soon as prices declined I became. . . a lame duck. . . .

I had for more than fifteen years lived in the greatest luxury and splendor; I had spent in that time upwards of two hundred and fifty thousand dollars; I had held property to the amount of between two and three millions, and yet when I came to investigate my affairs critically, I found that at no period of my prosperity had I ever been worth a dollar in the world! In short, I had been over head and ears in debt every moment of that time. . . .

This is the great beauty of my system. It works by an infinite series, as it were, and there is only one trifling thing wanting, namely, that there should be all debtors, and no creditors, in the world.

I don't despair of bringing this about, when, as will certainly be the case a couple or three years hence, our ignorant outlandish Administration is replaced by my disciples of the Credit System. Then shall we see the age of Internal Improvements, unexampled exquisite refinement, and unlimited public prosperity, for then will every body owe and nobody pay; then will the wealth of the nation, like that of England, be demonstrated by the amount of its debt; then will the true Agrarian principle be in practical operation, for a man who borrows a hundred thousand dollars will be as rich as the one that lends it; and then there will be no occasion for a bottom to the sea, for the whole world will be adrift on its surface. . . .

P.S. On my retirement from the presidency of my bank, the Directors unanimously voted me a service of plate, worth twenty thousand dollars; and that my father, to whose lessons I am indebted for every blessing I have enjoyed or anticipated, has lately been appointed by the Federal Common Council of Ragamuffinville, Chairman of the Finance Committee, on account of his great talent at "raising the wind," which is now the principal employment of our States and Corporations.

15

Extracts from the Private Diary of a Certain Bank Director

As a high school student studying Advanced Placement American history, I became fascinated by the idea that Jacksonian Americans got so worked up over the subject of national banking. Sure, I was mildly interested in such things, but practically no one else was. How, then, did such a mundane and arcane subject so seize the minds, imaginations, passions, and fears of two or three generations of 19th-century Americans? For their part, Jacksonians, too, found the subject at least mildly interesting and often electrifying. To Jacksonian Democrats, the Bank of the United States often represented the worst of all modern evils, the most perilous of threats to American freedom and republican destiny. It was a species of Old World monopoly (run in part by and for foreign investors) shoehorned into the American constitutional, republican order, spawning aristocratic bubble-lords and -ladies all over the country. To Jacksonian Whigs (pardon the odd expression), the bank was a perfectly logical, time-honored method of modern statecraft. In fact, many believed it was the crowning touch on a history of conservative monetary and fiscal policies; a constraint on the issue-happy state banks and the flagship engine of internal improvement.

Despite the Whigs' long-term ideological staying power, the Democrats dominated both the cultural and the political battles of the Jacksonian era. Jackson and Van Buren were successful in their bank war, converted the Treasury into an independent holder of government funds, and managed to reunite their party through bitter divides at the state and local levels during it all. Invigorated by a decade of political successes and inspired by what seemed to be a rising tide of thoroughly democratic and republican American culture, intellectuals such as John L. O'Sullivan and his *Democratic Review* published lively satires of their Whig enemies and cashed in on the cultural appeal of the banking subject. The following is the first portion of one such wry commentary on the daily lives of America's new mushroom aristocracy of high finance.

Our narrator (one Mr. Graball) explained in particular the difficulties of maintaining sufficient specie to meet the depositor's demands and his bank's persistent shortage of hard currency. In his quest to fill the vaults and balance his accounts, Graball becomes convinced that specie is in fact worth whatever people deem it to be worth, and therefore virtually anything can count toward a bank's specie reserves—including IOUs written on the spot by the bank's directors. Through linguistic alchemy, Graball thus converts his personal guarantee into real assets.

In the second half of the story, his intellectual idol departs from the local church for a preaching (and drinking) binge, leaving Graball and the rest of the flock in the hands of a rather different temperament. The new "priest" insists that institutions do not nullify the laws of ethics, and theft by any other name remains theft. The narrator spends most of his diary space defending his business affairs, his personal charity, and his public ethics. Later confronted by a Locofoco, however, Graball is once again shaken at the notion that he has dishonestly and immorally leached a lush life out of his fellow beings. The Locofoco suggests that ethics is singular and cannot be divided into "theoretical" and "practical," "private" and "public." Put simply, individuals are called on to be good, virtuous people in all their dealings; the Locofoco "never heard of Adam Smith or J. B. Say's keeping a huckster-shop." Our heroic bank director, however, flees the devilish Locofoco, retreating to Dr. Diddler and his church, where he is "comforted and edified as usual."

"Extracts from the Private Diary of a Certain Bank Director"[25]

Unsigned Contribution to the Democratic Review

Monday. Had just finished my breakfast, when Mr. John Jones called at my dwelling, to beg I would use my influence with our board, to prevent a note of his from being thrown out. Mr. Jones pleaded very hard—said his credit would be ruined if this note were not discounted. He proved to me very satisfactorily that he owns twice as much as he owes, and is only pressed for a little ready money. Assured Mr. Jones that I would do all in my power to serve him. When the board met, and Mr. Jones's note came under consideration, I mentioned that I had great respect for the offerer, who was one of my most particular friends, and one for whom I would go all lengths that I could, with propriety, to serve. But, as a member of a directory to which the little property of orphans and widows was intrusted, I felt it my duty to state that I had undoubted information that my friend's credit was at this moment in a very ticklish condition. Did not doubt, however, but he would ultimately pay every body, and have something handsome left . . . Mr. Snatchpenny, chairman of the discount committee, said that, as I was a particular friend of Mr. Jones's, I would probably be willing to guarantee the bank from loss. Astonished at such a proposition, and frankly told Snatchpenny as much. Friendship is one thing—business another. Sorry to say that, notwithstanding all my endeavors, the board threw out Jones's note. However, we had no sooner adjourned, than I went to the first teller, and took up the amount on a memorandum check of my own.

As I passed out of the bank door, found Jones waiting on the steps in great anxiety. Told him of my bad luck in as circumspect terms as possible; but the poor fellow was near sinking to the earth. Did all I could to comfort him, but he refused to be comforted. He spoke of his wife and children, and of the loss of all his earnings and savings, the result of many years of toil and trouble. Could not bear to see him so distressed, and therefore told him that, though exceedingly pressed for money myself, I would speak in his behalf to a friend of mine . . . Referred him accordingly to Mr. Sharpsucker, my private broker, taking care to have first an interview with Sharpsucker to be sure that my benevolent intentions should not be frustrated.

In the afternoon met Jones, and found him very grateful. Was sorry to learn from him, however, that Sharpsucker had himself to borrow the money, and therefore could not let him have it at less than three per cent a month. But this, as Jones himself says, is a trifle in the present condition of his affairs.

I have done a good day's work. I have done my duty to the bank, to myself and family, and to my friend.

Tuesday. In the evening there was a social little party of one or two hundred friends at my mansion. Among them there was our beloved pastor, the Rev. Dr. McThwackem, with whom I had a most interesting conversation. As the Doctor was once Professor in a University, and as he is as distinguished for his erudition as he is for his piety, I took occasion to ask him the exact meaning of the word *specie*, and was pleased to learn from him that the popular use of the word is entirely unauthorized by any classical authorities. The true word, the Reverend Doctor says, is species. . . . As language deteriorated, men began to speak of species of coin, as philosophers sometimes spoke of species of things; but not knowing exactly what philosophers meant by species of things, the vulgar herd misapplied the term, and further corrupted speech by an ellipsis "of coin," and dropping the final s in "species." To a man of true classical taste, the Reverend Doctor said, nothing could be more offensive than a word thus extruncated and misapplied, and in this I perfectly agree with him. . . .

Nothing could be more lucid than the reverend gentleman's illustrations; and his arguments were perfectly conclusive.

This encouraged me to ask him the true meaning of the word *bullion*. . . . The French word *billon*, a kind of base metal or base coin, was evidently related to it; but it was altogether too base a word to have an etymon in respectable Greek or Latin. Its root, if to be found anywhere, was, perhaps, to be found in *bulla*, a word of the corrupt Latin of the middle ages, which word might be rendered into English by either *ball* or *bubble*. . . . "I never hear the word mentioned without experiencing the most painful emotions. The Popish edicts take their name of *bulls* from a little ball of gold attached to each, called *bulla* in monkish Latin. Hence the English word *bullion*. The bare sound makes me tremble, for it immediately causes my mind to revert to the little balls of gold attached to the Popish bulls, thence to the contents of those bulls, and thence to the horrible designs many entertain of subverting our Protestant liberties by bringing in the Pope, and it may be the Pretender also."

Well may you tremble, my beloved pastor. The evident intention of the hard-money men is to bring us back to the condition of the dark ages.

Wednesday. I was early at bank this morning, for this is the day for preparing our annual return to the Legislature. Cashier in trouble,—circulation above a million—gold and silver coin in vaults of too small an amount to be mentioned except to particular friends. Asked cashier if he could not borrow from other banks for the day, to be paid back to-morrow. Said he had already borrowed as much as he could from every bank and broker for five miles round, and that to get what he had got, he had been obliged to promise to pay back to-day instead of to-morrow, and also to lend every pistareen he had to three several banks in succession, before three o'clock this afternoon. How very embarrassing these returns to the Legislature sometimes prove! . . . One of the board suggested that the notes of other banks on hand, and sums due from other banks, being as good as specie, might be put down as specie. Cashier said . . . [that] as a conscientious man, he should not like to swear to such an account. Mentioned to cashier my conversation of last evening with his beloved pastor and mine. The whole board loud in their praise of the Rev. Dr. McThwackem's piety and patriotism; but cashier, though perfectly satisfied that there is a Popish plot at the bottom of the schemes of the hard-money men, a little dubious as to the true meaning of the word specie. Said, however, that if he could be convinced that specie meant much the same as specious and speciously, he could make out a very fair account, for then he could include the memorandum checks of the directors among the specie.

Sent for Webster's large dictionary, and read to cashier . . .

Cashier perfectly satisfied, except as to whether species and specie were not different words; therefore read to him a part of what Webster says under the eighth head, namely,

"In modern practice this word is contracted into specie."

Cashier convinced, and at the same time delighted. Says he shall never more have any difficulty in making up his annual returns. Memorandum checks are the real specie; for, if they are not "a special idea," they are certainly "an appearance to the senses,—a visible or sensible representation—a representation to the mind—a show—a visible exhibition"—of something.

Mr. Snatchpenny proposed that, to make the specie in our bank a round half million, we should each take up an additional amount on memorandum checks, allowing the cashier to share equally with the directors. Nothing could be fairer, and the conscientious scruples of the cashier being entirely removed, he went immediately before a magistrate and made oath to the return, agreeably to the provisions of our charter.

Thursday. My son Jack, who has just come from college, put into my hands the Democratic Review for May. Was highly gratified with the autobiography of my most worthy friend, Ferret Snapp Newcraft, Esq. Mr. Newcraft hardly does himself justice in this brief memoir. I hope he will publish fuller reminiscences of his life and times, for the benefit of his children, and of mine. It is true, he was not quite free from faults; and I always thought that, as he himself says, "the distinction between making a great speculation and 'taking in' a fellow creature, was never precisely clear to his mind."

Thanks to McThwackem's excellent instructions, I can perceive distinctions where Newcraft never could. McThwackem splits hairs with so much dexterity, that they never break off in the middle. . . .

I do like McThwackem, I only wish he would drop the ugly prefix to his name, and become a native.

Friday. Great outcry among the merchants, because our bank and the other banks cannot grant them facilities, in consequence of the directors and a few others monopolizing the funds of public institutions for their private speculations. Of all stations in society it appears to me that that of director of a bank is the most thankless. The officers of Government are all paid for their services, and the officers of banks, presidents and cashiers excepted, are not paid. Even the small emoluments we get in an indirect way seem to be grudged to us, though these have never, in my won [sic] case at least, amounted to more than fifty thousand dollars in any one year. Yes, these little gains excite envy, and this at a time when we are doing all in our power to make dollars as plenty as black-berries. . . .

The merchants and the rest of the community have, indeed, abundant cause of complaint, but then it is of the government, not of the banks. If the government would only cease its war on the banks, we could make money so plenty that there would be not only enough to promote our own speculations, but also to grant the merchants the facilities they require. . . . If there were no banks, commerce would be a humdrum affair, whereas it is now almost as exciting as a game at rouge et noir, and almost as uncertain. If there were no banks every man would have to be content with his own earnings, and there would be no capital to the Corinthian column at all, nothing but a plain Doric shaft. If there were no banks there would be no means of acquiring even a competency, except by labor, agricultural, mechanical, mercantile, or professional, all slow and hard ways of becoming rich. Banking affords a quick and easy road to wealth,—if not to the whole nation at least to a part of it. By its means I have myself, besides living tolerably like a gentleman, acquired a snug little fortune of two hundred thousand dollars in the short space of ten years, and I am morally certain that if I had been obliged to work for it I never should have been worth the one-half part of that many cents.

Saturday. Entered into a combination with a number of friends to depress the price of certain articles by refusing to the holders of them all kind of facilities, and pressing on them for the prompt discharge of their obligations. As the scheme was an extensive one, requiring a number of persons to carry it on, and profound secrecy to bring it to a successful issue, it was several times in danger of miscarrying. But our power was so great, and the necessities of the merchants who held the articles were somehow so urgent, that we bought them all up pretty much at our own price. We have now only to increase our issues, and we shall be able to sell these articles at such rates as we may choose to ask. In that case my two hundred thousand dollars will become four hundred thousand. I prefer going on in this snug way to dashing out as Newcraft did. He always appeared to me to go ahead too fast.

At a special meeting of our board, held to-day, Mr. O'Squeezem made a long speech, in which he dwelt at great length on some very plain truths, such, for example, as that gold and silver in the vaults of a bank are a dead weight to a bank, and of no use to the community—that there is a continual risk of the metals being stolen—that memorandum checks are the real specie, &c. &c.; and finally wound up with a proposal to rid the bank of the gold and silver with which it was encumbered, by giving his own memorandum checks for it.

O'Squeezem is all for self. Now, if there is any one vice I do dislike, it is selfishness. I therefore opposed him most manfully; but I had not spoken more than half an hour before another director proposed that each member of the board should have an equal share of the gold and silver. In this form there was something like fairness and justice in the proposal; and I withdrew my opposition, for the moment, that the cashier might give some necessary information.

Cashier expressed his desire to do all in his power to favor the wishes of the board, but stated frankly that the adoption of the resolution in its present form would expose him to considerable inconvenience, and he doubted if all the gold and silver at present in the vaults of the banks, would be much of an object to the directors, if equally divided among them. Mr. O'Squeezem remarked that the amount, when the annual return was made up, appeared to be considerable. Cashier said that appearances were frequently deceitful. . . . He hoped that whatever was done, the board would leave him enough gold and silver coin to pay postages. The tyrannic requisitions of the Government under which we live made this indispensable. The remark of the cashier in regard to postages almost decided me, and a few words I had with him apart, left me no longer in doubt as to the course I should pursue. I opposed the proposition in its modified form with as much energy as I had resisted it in its original shape. . . .

O'Squeezem sneeringly remarked that Deacon Graball ought to be at his prayers—that he was becoming a convert to the Specie Humbug—a defender of the Specie Circular, &c. These revilings affected me not. I look on all kinds of paper money except what is founded on a metallic basis as a DOWNRIGHT FRAUD on the community. Whether the basis is large or small, is not of much moment. Such is the excellent nature of paper credit, that a single dollar in metal may serve for any number of dollars in paper.

Sunday. Brother McThwackem has gone to a watering place, partly to recruit his health, partly to look after some rail road, and other speculations in which he and I are jointly interested—and partly to try if he cannot be of some spiritual benefit to the poor, light-headed mortals who usually flock to these scenes of gaiety. Through some strange mistake he left to fill his pulpit a stupid country parson, or I should rather say priest, for if his sermon did not savor of popery I know not what popery is. It was all works—works—works! Not one word about the precious doctrines of grace! I doubt if the man be not a Jesuit in disguise, smuggled into the church by the hard-money men with intentions best known to themselves. His text was "THOU SHALT NOT STEAL;" and, in the course of his remarks, he drew a strongly marked line between what he was pleased to call conventional and essential honesty. There were, he said, many practices which, though strictly compatible with the former, were at utter variance with the latter. Taking advantage of men's ignorance and necessities in driving a bargain, was, he said, just as bad in the eyes of reason and religion, as taking advantage of their physical weakness and robbing them on the high way. It was no matter whether this was done according to the forms of law or contrary thereunto. What was wrong in itself, mere human enactments could never make right. . . . If a multitude of men were thus treated, it only added to the enormity of the offence. . . .

If I use the power which circumstances or my superior intelligence gives me to increase my wealth, I am only acting according to the dictates of nature. That is morally right which is conformable to the law of the land. It is the law of the land which, in fact, determines what is right in a civil sense, and therefore in a moral sense. If the law is wrong I am not in fault. I did not make the law.

Went in the evening to hear Dr. Diddler, and heard a truly great and glorious discourse. It was all gospel and no law—all faith and no works.

Monday. An old friend . . . called on me this morning . . . and from some of his remarks I fear he is infected with the new-fangled notions of the day. The doctrines of legal righteousness are making strange havoc among professors. . . . He reminded me that about twenty years ago when I was much embarrassed [i.e. poor], he had not pressed for the payment of a debt of five thousand dollars I then owed him, but suffered the claim to lie over. With some little difficulty I recollected the fact, but I did not think it very Christian-like in him to call it up at this late day. A favor ceases to be a favor if gratitude is required in payment. He said that he had met with many reverses since that time—an ample estate had been reduced to nothing—and all the efforts he had made in the South and West to retrieve his fortunes had proved unsuccessful. Understanding that I was possessed of boundless wealth—of a tract of three millions of acres of land, and six town plots, in the Western country, besides stocks and various other property in the East, he now ventured to hope I would discharge his claim— the interest he would give in if I would pay the principal.

Such effrontery I never before met with. The debt is barred by the statute of limitations, and has been these thirteen or fourteen years.

Mr. Downright said law was not every thing—there was such a thing as equity. So there is, I admit, but I have had the misfortune to fail three times in the course of my life, and the aggregate of my old debts (if debts they can be called) is between two and three millions of dollars. It is utterly impossible for me to pay all, and nothing could be more clearly inequitable than for me to pay one of my creditors and not the others.

Finding by further conversation that Downright was in great distress I gave him a check for fifty dollars, writing charity on one corner of it, as is my practice when I make donations, in order that I may keep my accounts square, and know exactly how much I give in each year for benevolent purposes. Downright refused to receive the check unless this word was erased; and so finding him both poor and proud, I took it back, leaving him to suffer the consequences of his folly. People ought to learn to conform to their circumstances.

In regard to the three millions of acres of Western land, I must remark that they are not exactly mine, though they will, I hope, nay trust, be mine. It is Newcraft's tract which he has transferred to me on certain conditions, and which I am to restore to him in certain contingences, which I shall take good care shall never occur. Newcraft thinks himself a man of business. And so he is, but others are men of business as well as he.

Tuesday. Beset during the whole day by a crowd of vulgar mechanics, to whom, during the late high prices, I had sold, or let on ground rent, some hundreds of lots in the city and the many new and important towns and villages that were then rising up around us on every side. The company of this class of people is always disagreeable, but I had to endure it. On a great number of these lots they have erected substantial buildings, but owing to the pressure of the times, (produced entirely by the doings of the Government,) these buildings rent at very reduced rates, and such of the lots as remain vacant will sell for but a small part of their original cost. Made the best arrangement with these people that I could, both for themselves and for myself. I cannot enter into particulars. It is enough to say that there is a fair prospect of my getting back one-half of my lots with good houses upon them, and the mechanics who built them will be rid of all incumbrances—for property is always an incumbrance to this kind of people. I fear, though, I shall have to sue some of them to get my just dues, and this will be very unpleasant and somewhat expensive.

Was bored for a whole hour by that eccentric old mortal, Judge Johnson of West-Quoddy Head. He maintained that I and Snatchpenny and O'Squeezem, and the other directors of the great bank of Bubble-opolis, are conducting our affairs on false principles. He said that the proper business of a bank is granting facilities to merchants by discounting business paper, and that to this we ought to confine ourselves. He averred that a banks dealing in cotton was only a kind of wholesale pawnbroking. He said that the bank of West-Quoddy Head, of which he is a director, never discounts any thing but business paper, and has in consequence not made one bad debt in twenty-five years.

I cannot subscribe to such views. Banks, so far as my observation goes, are not established by people who want to lend money, but by people who want to make money. We pay heavy sums to the State for our privileges, first in the shape of a bonus and next of an annual tax. And it is strange, indeed, if after this we are not to be allowed to use our privileges for our own exclusive benefit. But I must confess that I see a great deal of ignorance of the proper principles of modern civilized financiering still prevailing even among those who ought to know better. When I see, as I must say I do pretty often, men enjoying the advantages of position, and the opportunities of knowledge, of bank directors, neglecting to take the gifts the Gods provide them, and clinging to the absurd antiquated notions which our glorious science has exploded, and which those pestilent Loco-Foco destructives are trying to revive,—I can scarcely conceal my contempt for such ignorance and stupidity.

Wednesday. It seems as if my troubles were never to end. Today I was tormented by groups of old men, and old maids, and old widows, and some young ones among them, to whom I had sold stocks when they were high. Stocks have fallen now, and these foolish people really seem to think I am to blame. I told them that the fall of stocks was altogether owing to the infamous Specie Circular, and the odious Sub-Treasury, and thus satisfied some of them. With the rest I did the best I could—that is, I bought back their stocks at such prices as I was able and willing to give. Some of them said I was rather buying them back at such prices as they, from stress of circumstances, were forced to take. But what is this but the usual course of trade? All questions of price are questions of power—of power on the side of the seller to get as much as he can, and of power on the side of the buyer to give as little as he can.

I was truly grieved at the conduct of many professing Christians, both among the mechanics who visited me yesterday and the motley group that filled my office to-day. Downright infidels— very heathen—could hardly have displayed less resignation under reverses of fortune. There was one old father in particular, a man seventy-five years of age, and a member of the church from his youth, who seemed as if he would go frantic under his losses. . . . The old man said he knew not how, with what was left, he should be able to support himself, his aged and bed-ridden wife, and three small grandchildren, who had, within the last six months, lost both father and mother.

Thursday. Good news at last. The odious Specie Circular is repealed! I know not at which most to rejoice, whether at the Governments being compelled to bow to the banks, or to the power now given to us to raise prices as high as we please. One joy is enough for one day, and the prospect of the rise of prices is quite sufficient of itself to make me forget all my past troubles. Now for the sale of the lots and houses that were transferred to me on Tuesday, and for the stocks I bought on Wednesday. And now I shall be able to do something handsome with my three million acres of Western lands and my six town plots. I may as well call them mine, for I have so arranged matters that Newcraft can never get them from me.

Of all means of advancing the wealth of a country there is none like banking. Agriculture, manufactures, and commerce, are well enough in their place; but they all sink into insignificance when compared with this modern mode of acquiring wealth—or rather of producing, for I will maintain that the two terms are synonymous. By our banking operations, between 1834 and 1836, we gave value to many pieces of property which never had any value before, and which will never have any value again. The pine lands of Maine attest our power, as do also the cabbage gardens in the neighbourhood of New York, and the lands ten feet under water in the new State of Arkansas. An able writer estimates all the landed property in the United States as having been worth four thousand millions of dollars in 1834, and six thousand millions in 1836. By our banking operations we added half as much to the value of real estate in two years as all the industry of the country had been able to give to it in two hundred years. And if the Government had not interfered with its despotic and atrocious experiments, who knows but that we might, in two years more, have made the real estate of the country worth sixty thousand millions!

Now this obstacle is happily removed, confidence will be restored, and we shall go on increasing in wealth. Some say this will be only in appearance. Let it be so. What is there that is truly real in this world of vanity and show? Every thing depends on our conceptions of things, and if a man can only fix it firmly in his fancy that he is worth six millions of dollars, he may enjoy just as much happiness as if he really possessed this amount of solid wealth. If he had the whole sum in silver dollars he could not eat them or drink them; neither could he eat or drink what they could procure. A man's personal wants are very few, and easily supplied; but most men have cravings to which it is not easy to set limits. And I will affirm that there is no way in which all men's cravings, or even the cravings of any great number, can be satisfied, unless it be by banking, or some similar contrivance. It is, in the nature of things, absolutely impossible that all men, or that any great number of men, should be very rich; but by the rise of prices, produced by plentiful issues of paper money, a great many may be brought to believe that they are very rich, and thus enjoy as much satisfaction as if they really abounded in wealth. Happiness resides in the mind. All philosophers agree in this.

Friday. Great jubilation at a meeting of our friends to-day; but Satan came among us in the guise of a Loco-Foco, and a more appropriate shape he could not have assumed. Loco-Foco said much about the importance of a fixed standard of value—that it would be as absurd to be always changing the size of the bushel, or the length of the yard stick, as to be always changing the value of the dollar, &c. Talked, also, much about justice, and equity, and honesty, and all that sort of thing. The devil can, you know, quote scripture to serve his purpose. Told Loco that all he had said was very true in the abstract; but he was a mere theorist. I was a practical man. Loco asked me if I knew the meaning of the word "theory." Told Loco that if I did not, my friend Doctor Diddler did. Loco asked what I meant by "a practical man." He had never heard of Adam Smith or J. B. Say's keeping a huckster-shop. Made no reply to Loco, but thought within myself that "a practical man" is one who has failed in business at least twice, and owes at least twice as much as he can ever pay.

Changed the subject by telling Loco that the "Specie Circular" was "a humbug." Loco said modestly that perhaps the paper money system was "a humbug. . . ."

Saturday. Well, this is most outrageous. The old Specie Circular is repealed; but here comes a new Specie Circular close on its heels. Our tyrannical Government is not content with redeemable paper, but will have it actually redeemed at stated periods! This is a downright farce.

Redeemable paper, every one knows, is just as good as gold and silver. Having it redeemed is sinking bank notes to a level with the notes of private traders. The very means by which banks make their profits are by issuing a great many notes which, though always payable, are never paid. However, we have obtained one great and open triumph over our abominable Government, in the repeal of the old Specie Circular; and, as for the new, if we do not make that a dead letter my name is not Graball. Government is at Washington. The collectors are all along shore; and the receivers all over the prairies. They are not as stupid as the Administration. They know where their own true interest lies.

Sunday. Really the Church is as much in need of reform as the State. McThwackem is still at the watering place, and his pulpit was supplied by, if possible, a more intolerable proser than we had last Sunday. His text was, "Ye cannot serve God and mammon." He said that to be idolaters men need not bow down before images of wood and stone. There were false gods still more to be dreaded—idols of the mind, for, whatever a man did in heart regard as his Supreme Good was, in reality, the god he worshipped. . . .

In the evening went to hear Dr. Diddler, and was comforted and edified as usual.

16

O'Sullivan's Great Nation of Futurity

In 1837, John Lewis O'Sullivan and his brother established The *United States Magazine and Democratic Review* in Washington, D.C., and it soon became one of the most important periodicals in American history. By late 1840, the brothers moved the magazine to New York City. The move marked a significant shift in American life. Throughout the 1830s and 1840s, New Yorkers gradually wrested cultural preeminence from Puritanical and relatively stagnant Boston, enshrining New York City as the de facto capital of American life. In politics, economics, and now the arts, New York City and its radical cutting edge of Locofoco Democrats and visionary artists led their fellow Americans into the brave new world of the mid-19th century: a period in which railroads connected continents and telegraphs converted ideas into electric signals allowing for instantaneous communication.

John L. O'Sullivan and his *Democratic Review* gained fame, notoriety, and influence by spearheading the movement to produce an authentically American national culture distinct from European antecedents. Publishing now-canonical authors like Whitman and Hawthorne as well as editorials written by O'Sullivan himself, the *Democratic Review* trumpeted the concept of "Manifest Destiny" cast in a decidedly radical liberal direction. The wider New York cultural movement identified itself with the phrase "Young America," sharply contrasting the United States, which O'Sullivan called "The Great Nation of Futurity," with the monarchies, aristocracies, and corporate-plutocracies proliferating throughout the Old World. O'Sullivan and his fellow Young Americans were far from perfect, and by no means were they equivalent to modern libertarians, but their visions and concepts of republicanism, democracy, and the United States constituted one of the most virulent and influential strains of liberal thinking in the entirety of 19th-century America.[26]

"The Great Nation of Futurity"[27]
By John L. O'Sullivan

The American people having derived their origin from many other nations, and the Declaration of National Independence being entirely based on the great principle of human equality, these facts demonstrate . . . our disconnected position as regards any other nation; that we have, in reality, but little connection with the past history of any of them, and still less with all antiquity, its glories, or its crimes. On the contrary, our national birth was the beginning of a new history, the formation and progress of an untried political system, which separates us from the past and connects us with the future only; and so far as regards the entire development of the natural rights of man, in moral, political, and national life, we may confidently assume that our country is destined to be the great nation of futurity.

It is so destined, because the principle upon which a nation is organized fixes its destiny, and that of equality is perfect, is universal. It presides in all the operations of the physical world, and it is also the conscious law of the soul—the self-evident dictate of morality, which accurately defines the duty of man to man, and consequently man's rights as man. Besides, the truthful annals of any nation furnish abundant evidence, that its happiness, its greatness, its duration, were always proportionate to the democratic equality in its system of government.

How many nations have had their decline and fall, because the equal rights of the minority were trampled on by the despotism of the majority; or the interests of the many sacrificed to the aristocracy of the few; or the rights and interests of all given up to the monarchy of one? These three kinds of government have figured so frequently and so largely in the ages that have passed away, that their history, through all time to come, can only furnish a resemblance. Like causes produce like effects, and the true philosopher of history will easily discern the principle of equality, or of privilege, working out its inevitable result. The first is regenerative, because it is natural and right; the latter is destructive to society, because it is unnatural and wrong.

What friend of human liberty, civilization, and refinement, can cast his view over the past history of the monarchies and aristocracies of antiquity, and not deplore that they ever existed? What philanthropist can contemplate the oppressions, the cruelties, and injustice inflicted by them on the masses of mankind, and not turn with moral horror from the retrospect?

America is destined for better deeds. It is our unparalleled glory that we have no reminiscences of battle fields, but in defence of humanity, of the oppressed of all nations, of the rights of conscience, the rights of personal enfranchisement. Our annals describe no scenes of horrid carnage, where men were led on by hundreds of thousands to slay one another, dupes and victims to emperors, kings, nobles, demons in the human form called heroes. We have had patriots to defend our homes, our liberties, but no aspirants to crowns or thrones; nor have the American people ever suffered themselves to be led on by wicked ambition to depopulate the land, to spread desolation far and wide, that a human being might be placed on a seat of supremacy.

We have no interest in the scenes of antiquity, only as lessons of avoidance of nearly all their examples. The expansive future is our arena, and for our history. We are entering on its untrodden space, with the truths of God in our minds, beneficent objects in our hearts, and with a clear conscience unsullied by the past. We are the nation of human progress, and who will, what can, set limits to our onward march? Providence is with us, and no earthly power can. We point to the everlasting truth on the first page of our national declaration, and we proclaim to the millions of other lands, that "the gates of hell"—the powers of aristocracy and monarchy—"shall not prevail against it."

The far-reaching, the boundless future will be the era of American greatness. In its magnificent domain of space and time, the nation of many nations is destined to manifest to mankind the excellence of divine principles; to establish on earth the noblest temple ever dedicated to the worship of the Most High—the Sacred and the True. Its floor shall be a hemisphere—its roof the firmament of the star-studded heavens, and its congregation an Union of many Republics, comprising hundreds of happy millions, calling, owning no man master, but governed by God's natural and moral law of equality, the law of brotherhood—of "peace and good will amongst men."

But although the mighty constituent truth upon which our social and political system is founded will assuredly work out the glorious destiny herein shadowed forth, yet there are many untoward circumstances to retard our progress, to procrastinate the entire fruition of the greatest good to the human race. There is a tendency to imitativeness, prevailing amongst our professional and literary men, subversive of originality of thought, and wholly unfavorable to progress. . . .

This propensity to imitate foreign nations is absurd and injurious. It is absurd, for we have never yet drawn on our mental resources that we have not found them ample and of unsurpassed excellence; witness our constitutions of government, where we had no foreign ones to imitate. It is injurious, for never have we followed foreign examples in legislation; witness our laws, our charters of monopoly, that we did not inflict evil on ourselves, subverting common right, in violation of common sense and common justice. . . . Taught to look abroad for the highest standards of law, judicial wisdom, and literary excellence, the native sense is subjugated to a most obsequious idolatry of the tastes, sentiments, and prejudices of Europe. Hence our legislation, jurisprudence, literature, are more reflective of foreign aristocracy than of American democracy.

European governments have plunged themselves in debt, designating burthens on the people "national blessings." Our State Legislatures, humbly imitating their pernicious example, have pawned, bonded the property, labor, and credit of their constituents to the subjects of monarchy. It is by our own labor, and with our own materials, that our internal improvements are constructed, but our British-law-trained legislators have enacted that we shall be in debt for them, paying interest, but never to become owners. With various climates, soils, natural resources, and products, beyond any other country, and producing more real capital annually than any other sixteen millions of people on earth, we are, nevertheless, borrowers, paying tribute to the money powers of Europe.

Our business men have also conned the lesson of example, and devoted themselves body and mind to the promotion of foreign interests. If States can steep themselves in debt, with any propriety in times of peace, why may not merchants import merchandise on credit? If the one can bond the labor and property of generations yet unborn, why may not the other contract debts against the yearly crops and daily labor of their contemporary fellow citizens?

And our literature!—Oh, when will it breathe the spirit of our republican institutions? When will it be imbued with the God-like aspiration of intellectual freedom—the elevating principle of equality? When will it assert its national independence, and speak the soul—the heart of the American people? Why cannot our literati comprehend the matchless sublimity of our position amongst the nations of the world—our high destiny—and cease bending the knee to foreign idolatry, false tastes, false doctrines, false principles? When will they be inspired by the magnificent scenery of our own world, imbibe the fresh enthusiasm of a new heaven and a new earth, and soar upon the expanded wings of truth and liberty? Is not nature as original—her truths as captivating—her aspects as various, as lovely, as grand—her Promethean fire as glowing in this, our Western hemisphere, as in that of the East? And above all, is not our private life as morally beautiful and good—is not our public life as politically right, as indicative of the brightest prospects of humanity, and therefore as inspiring of the highest conceptions? Why, then, do our authors aim at no higher degree of merit, than a successful imitation of English writers of celebrity?

But with all the retrograde tendencies of our [institutions], still they are compelled to follow the mighty impulse of the age; they are carried onward by the increasing tide of progress; and though they cast many a longing look behind, they cannot stay the glorious movement of the masses, nor induce them to venerate the rubbish, the prejudices, the superstitions of other times and other lands, the theocracy of priests, the divine right of kings, the aristocracy of blood, the metaphysics of colleges, the irrational stuff of law libraries. Already the brightest hopes of philanthropy, the most enlarged speculations of true philosophy, are inspired by the indications perceptible amongst the mechanical and agricultural population. There, with predominating influence, beats the vigorous national heart of America, propelling the onward march of the multitude, propagating and extending, through the present and the future, the powerful purpose of soul, which, in the seventeenth century, sought a refuge among savages, and reared in the wilderness the sacred altars of intellectual freedom. This was the seed that produced individual equality, and political liberty, as its natural fruit; and this is our true nationality. American patriotism is not of soil; we are not aborigines, nor of ancestry, for we are of all nations; but it is essentially personal enfranchisement, for "where liberty dwells," said Franklin, the sage of the Revolution, "there is my country." . . .

Yes, we are the nation of progress, of individual freedom, of universal enfranchisement. Equality of rights is the cynosure of our union of States, the grand exemplar of the correlative equality of individuals; and while truth sheds its effulgence, we cannot retrograde, without dissolving the one and subverting the other. We must onward to the fulfilment of our mission—to the entire development of the principle of our organization—freedom of conscience, freedom of person, freedom of trade and business pursuits, universality of freedom and equality. This is our high destiny, and in nature's eternal, inevitable decree of cause and effect we must accomplish it. All this will be our future history, to establish on earth the moral dignity and salvation of man— the immutable truth and beneficence of God. For this blessed mission to the nations of the world, which are shut out from the life-giving light of truth, has America been chosen; and her high example shall smite unto death the tyranny of kings, hierarchs, and oligarchs, and carry the glad tidings of peace and good will where myriads now endure an existence scarcely more enviable than that of beasts of the field. Who, then, can doubt that our country is destined to be the great nation of futurity?

17

Whipple, Memoirs of Elleanor Eldridge

Frances Whipple, later Frances Harriet Whipple Green McDougall, was born in 1805 to a star-studded, quintessentially American family which included local Rhode Island heroes like Abraham Whipple (1733–1809), who led the burning of the *Gaspee* in 1772, and some of Roger Williams' earliest and closest associates. As a single, fiercely independent young woman, Frances supported herself through odd jobs, educated herself by reading widely in literature and philosophy, and built a place for herself within a swiftly changing American economy, culture, and society until her death in 1878.

The 19th century was the first great era of reform movements, and Frances Whipple remained a constant participant in a wide variety of "isms," from Spiritualism and Dorrism to Abolitionism and Republicanism. Whipple championed each of these causes and more throughout her long life of teaching, writing, speaking, and even spirit mediumship. Frances carried her radical ideas with her wherever she went, New York to California, and her body of work pushed American life in radical directions as Americans like Frances discovered who they were and where they fit into the ever-transforming world around them.

Frances Whipple's most significant early contributions to what she saw as a "New Age of Reform" were in the fields of feminism and abolitionism, both of which were often indistinguishable movements. After attaining some stature as a local writer of short pieces for the literary magazine *Original*, a Rhode Island women's benevolent society charged her with writing a fundraiser book for the relief of Elleanor Eldridge. Elleanor was a free African American resident of Providence recently embroiled in a legal battle for her home and property, virtually bankrupted by the legal fees incurred. To offset these costs, Whipple authored *The Memoirs of Elleanor Eldridge* and *Elleanor's Second Book*, both of which sold tens of thousands of copies and which publishers reprinted 16 times into the 1970s. The books were astonishing successes and helped make Elleanor Eldridge a folk hero of African-American feminism. Frances Whipple became a Rhode Island literary legend, which positioned her well to agitate the related issues of suffrage and slavery.[28]

In the following selections, Whipple describes the history of Elleanor's struggles in the Rhode Island land courts and lays ultimate blame at the intersection between unvirtuous public opinion (in this case, northern racism and sexism) and institutions enabling the exploitation of powerless minorities. Racism, sexism, and government—ideas and institutions—working in tandem, created and fostered Elleanor's long train of hardships.

Memoirs of Elleanor Eldridge, Excerpts[29]

By Frances Whipple

About sixteen years ago, Elleanor, having six hundred dollars on hand, bought a lot, for which she paid one hundred dollars, "all in silver money," as she has herself assured me. She then commenced building a house, which cost seventeen hundred dollars. This house was all paid for, with no encumbrance whatever. After it had been built three or four years; she built an addition on the east side, to live in herself; and subsequently one on the west side, to accommodate an additional tenant.— This house rented for one hundred and fifty dollars per anum. About this time there were two lots of land for sale, of which Elleanor wished to become the purchaser. Not having money enough she hired a gentleman of Warwick, two hundred and forty dollars.— For this she was to pay interest at the rate of ten per cent: and, by agreement, so long as she could do so, she might be entitled to keep the money; i.e., she was to pay the interest, and renew the note annually.

Elleanor had completed her house, which with its two wings, and its four chimneys, wore quite an imposing aspect; and in the honest pride and joy of her heart, she looked upon it with delight; as well she might do, since it was all earned by her own honest labors, and afforded the prospect of a happy home, and a comfortable income in her old age. Attached to this house, and belonging to a Mrs.— was a gangway which Elleanor wished very much to obtain possession of, as she was entirely cut off from out door privileges, without it. She had hired it for five years; and . . . she finally determined to do so; although, by doing so, she was obliged to involve herself considerably. This house had been built by Mr. C, who, being unable to pay for it, had given a mortgage of the premises. At this time Elleanor had five hundred dollars in her possession, which she had been wishing to dispose of to the best advantage. She finally came to a bargain with Mr. C, agreeing to give two thousand dollars for the house. She paid the five hundred dollars down; and then gave a mortgage on the house to Mr. Greenold, for fifteen hundred dollars. This was to be paid in four years; which, if she had received the least indulgence, she might easily have done; or rather if she had not, in her own honesty of heart, been led to confide in the promise of one, who had more regard for his purse, than for his honor, or his Christian character, as we shall soon see.

[On a trip to Warwick, Elleanor becomes violently ill and confined to the bed at a roadside inn.]

Her brother went to the land-lady, and requested permission to remain through the day, as his sister was too ill to proceed. From this circumstance— this trifling fact—sprang all the subsequent troubles of Elleanor. It so happened that there were two persons from Providence, within the hearing of George Eldridge . . . and as they had some knowledge of his sister, they made their report, when they returned to Providence. This, her being very sick, like a gathering snow-ball, grew as it went the rounds of gossip, into exceedingly dangerous illness—the point of death; and finally, by the simple process of accumulation, it was resolved into death itself. Who could have foreseen results, so disastrous as those which followed, could have been occasioned by such a trifle? The reader will subsequently find, how all Elleanor's troubles sprang from the wanton carelessness of those, who so busily circulated the story of her death. "What mighty oaks from little acorns grow;" and, what a lesson of caution should be drawn from this simple fact, and its consequences. How careful ought we to be to speak nothing but the truth, even in regard to the most trifling circumstances; and not only so, but to be well assured that what we suppose to be true, is truth, before we receive it as such.

Chapter IX.

. . .

As soon as the news of their arrival had gone about, the gentleman who had laid an attachment on Ellen's property, in order to procure the liquidation of the two hundred and forty dollar note before alluded to, came directly to see her; and that too altogether of his own accord. This gentleman was not the original creditor; who had deceased, leaving his brother as his sole heir.

The gentleman told Ellen what he had done; at the same time saying, that he should never have done it, had he not been told that she was dead. "But" said he, "I am glad you have returned, safe and well; and though I want the money, I will never distress you for it."

Ellen had the simplicity to believe this, because the man—perhaps I ought to say gentleman—was a member of a church; and was called a Christian. Poor, simple-hearted, honest Ellen: she did not know then that she had met "the wolf in sheep's clothing."

Chapter X.

Elleanor had given Mr.— a conditional promise that she would raise a hundred dollars for him in April; but it so happened that she could not procure the money; and, relying on his promise of indulgence, which his honor as a gentleman, and his Christian character, alike conspired to strengthen; while, at the same time, his great wealth, or entire independence, placed him altogether above any temptation to uncharitableness.

In about a week she returned to Providence, satisfied that in the withdrawal of his suit, Mr.— had fairly "buried the hatchet," she commenced her summer's work with renewed vigor.

In order to make all secure before leaving town, Ellen paid up all that was due on the mortgage: but she did not pay Mr.— because she could not do so without great loss, and difficulty; and concerning this she felt no uneasiness, because there had been an express understanding between herself and the deceased Mr.—, that she should have the money so long as she could pay the interest of ten percent on the note: and besides her well-known character for integrity and industry, seemed to secure the promise of indulgence, which had been voluntarily given.

Ellen's last step was to go round among her families, and request them to be careful and prudent in all things, making no disturbance, and committing no trespass; and she assured them that if she heard any complaint from her neighbor, she should turn out the offenders, as soon as she returned.

Intent only upon her new duties, Elleanor then entered zealously into the service of Mrs. T.; and with that lady, and her family, left town for Pomfret, a distance of only thirty miles. The sickness of Mrs. T. and that of her family, rendered our heroine's activity and skill of peculiar value.

In about two months, the family of Mrs. T. having recovered, and the cholera panic having somewhat subsided, that lady determined to return to Providence. On arriving in the city, she stopped at the Franklin House, still retaining Ellen in attendance. The next morning after their arrival, a lady came in and told Mrs. T.—that the property of Elleanor was all attached, and sold; and to the latter, the sad intelligence was speedily announced; but she found it very difficult to believe a story, at once, so entirely opposed to all her convictions of right, and so fraught with distress and anguish to herself; yet, upon enquiry, she found that one half the truth had not been told.

Mr.—, of Warwick, had attached and sold property, which a few months before had been valued at four thousand dollars, for the pitiful sum of two hundred and forty dollars. Why he wished to attach so large a property, for so small a debt, is surprising enough; since Elleanor had then in her possession two house lots, and the little house and lot at Warwick; either of which would have been sufficient to liquidate the debt. There seems to be a spirit of wilful malignity, in this wanton destruction of property, which it is difficult to conceive of as existing in the bosom of civilized man.

One after another, all the aggravating particulars came to the knowledge and notice of Ellen. In the first place, the attachment, as we have before said, was entirely disproportioned to the debt; which the general good character, integrity, and property of the debtor, rendered perfectly secure. In the second place, the sheriff never legally advertised the sale, or advertised it at all, as can be learned. In the third place, the auctioneer, having, doubtless, ascertained the comfortable fact, that the owner was a laboring colored [wo]man, who was then away, leaving no friend to protect her rights, struck it off, almost at the first bid; and at little more than one third its value; it being sold for only fifteen hundred dollars, which was the exact amount of the mortgage. In the fourth place, the purchaser, after seeing the wrongfulness of the whole affair, and after giving his word three successive times, that he would settle and restore the property for a given sum, twice meanly flew from his bargain, successively making larger demands.

Chapter XII.

Thus, as we have seen, was Ellen, in a single moment, by a single stroke of the hammer, deprived of the fruits of all her honest and severe labors—the labors of years; and, not only so, but actually thrown in debt for many small bills, for repairs and alterations on her houses, which she had the honor and honesty to discharge, even against the advices of some of her friends, after the property by which they had been incurred had been so cruelly taken away. Elleanor has traits of character, which, if she were a white woman, would be called Noble. And must color so modify character, that they are not still so?

On visiting the premises, sad, indeed was the sight which the late owner witnessed.— The two wings of her first house, which she had herself built, with their chimneys, had been pulled down: and it seemed as if the spirit of Ruin had been walking abroad. All her families had been compelled to leave, at a single week's notice; and many of them, being unable to procure tenements, were compelled to find shelter in barns and out-houses, or even in the woods. But they were colored people— So thought he, who so unceremoniously ejected them from their comfortable homes; and he is not only a professed friend to their race, but an "honorable man."

Mark his excuse. How noble—how manly it was! He told Ellen he was very sorry for what he had done; but that he never should have done it, if the lawyer had not advised him to. He must have been a man of stern principle—of sterling independence, to perpetrate such an act, because his lawyer advised him to. I pity the man whose invention is so poor—so miserable, that he could not fabricate a better falsehood.

After a time, a ray of hope dawned on the dark path of Ellen. She consulted Mr. Greene, the State's attorney, and found that she might bring forward a case of "Trespass and Ejectment," against the purchaser of her property. She had hope to repudiate the whole sale and purchase, on the ground of the illegal or non-advertisement of the sale. This case was brought before the Court of Common Pleas, in January, 1837.

Of course, the whole success of it turned on the point of the sheriff's oath, in regard to the advertisement. When the oath was administered, the sheriff appeared strangely agitated, and many, then present in court, even the judge, thought it was the perturbation of guilt. Nevertheless he attested upon oath, that he had put up the notification in three public places;—viz. at Manchester's tavern bar-room, on the Court House done in time of Court, and on Market Square. There were three men who came prepared to take their oath, that the notice was never put up at Manchester's; thus invalidating that part of his testimony; but it was found that the oaths of common men could not be taken against that of the High Sheriff. So the case was decided against the plaintiff.

Ellen's next step was to hire two men, whom she fee'd liberally, to make enquiries throughout the city, in regard to those notifications. They went about, two days, making all possible search for light in regard to the contested notifications, calling upon all those who frequented public places. But no person could be found, who had either seen them, or heard of their being seen. A fine advertisement, truly! And here, let me ask, why was not this sale advertised in the public papers?— The same answer that has been given before, will suffice now. The owner of the property was a laboring colored woman. Is not this reply, truth as it is, a libel on the character of those who wrought the work of evil?

Elleanor then brought an action against the sheriff, tending to destroy his testimony in the late case; and on the very day when it was to be laid before the court, Mr.—, the purchaser, came forward and told Ellen's attorney, that he would restore the property for twenty-one hundred dollars, and two years' rent. Ellen then withdrew her case, and set herself about procuring the money. This she raised; and it was duly tendered to Mr.—. But mark his regard for his word.— He then said that Ellen had been so long in procuring the money, that he must have twenty-three hundred dollars.

The additional two hundred dollars were then raised, but the gentleman, in consequence of repairs and alterations, which he could have had no right to make, and require pay for, as the case stood, next demanded twenty-five hundred dollars, with six months' rent.

The suspended action had, in the mean time, been again brought forward; and was to have been tried before the Circuit Court.

But so anxious was Ellen again to possess the property, that she once more withdrew her action, and came to the exhorbitant terms of Mr.—. She again hired the additional two hundred dollars; and finally effected a settlement. This conduct, on the part of the purchaser, requires no comment; for its meanness, not to say dishonesty, is self-evident in the simplest statement of the facts themselves. But this is not all. The sheriff had informed Mr.—, that he could sue Elleanor for house rent, as her goods had never been removed from the tenement she had occupied. This he actually did, and laid an attachment on her furniture, which was advertised to be sold at public auction: and it would have been, had not a gentleman who had the management of her business, gone forward and settled with Mr.—.

The whole affair, from beginning to end, in all its connections and bearings, was a web of iniquity. It was a wanton outrage upon the simplest and most evident principles of justice. But the subject of this wrong, or rather of this accumulation of wrongs, was a woman, and therefore weak—a colored woman —and therefore contemptible. No man ever would have been treated so; and if a white woman had been the subject of such wrongs, the whole city—nay, the whole country, would have been indignant: and the actors would have been held up to the contempt they deserve! The story would have flown upon the wings of the wind to the most remote borders of our land. Newspaper editors would have copied, and commented on it, till every spirit of honor, of justice, and of chivalry, would have been roused. At home, benevolent societies would have met, and taken efficient means to relieve the sufferer; while every heart would have melted in kindness, and every bosom have poured out its sympathy. Is this wrong the less a wrong, because the subject of it is weak and defenceless? By the common laws of honor, it is cowardice to strike the unarmed and the weak. By the same rule, he who injures the defenceless, adds meanness to crime.

Are there none to feel for her? Are there none to sustain, and encourage her? Thank God!—there are already a few. . . . Then will not every reader of this little book, recommend it to the notice of the humane, and endeavor to promote its sale; not for its own sake, but for the sake of her, who depends upon its success, for deliverance from the difficulties in which she is involved. Ellen has yet a large debt to liquidate, before her estate is freed from its incumbrance. With a little timely help, together with her earnings, she may be able to do this.

18

Gemmel, Two Years in Van Dieman's Land

James Gemmel was your average mid–19th century Young American: he was an idealistic, romantic revolutionary whose vision disastrously exceeded his real power and influence. During the heady, radical days of the Jackson-Van Buren administrations, the most restless and hopeful of Democrats gathered together across the northern border to agitate republican revolution in Canada. The Canadians, for their part, did not rise to match the Americans' fury. Although there was indeed a flurry of relatively small battles between William Lyon Mackenzie's rebel forces and British-Canadian militiamen, the American filibusters constituted the largest corps of individuals in support of Canadian independence during the years of rebellion, 1837–1839. Insisting on trying their own luck at whipping the British, a few particularly brave (or foolhardy) companies actually invaded Canadian territory to meet battle. Unsurprisingly to virtually all observers, British forces easily prevailed and meted out swift, unyielding military justice to the American prisoners. James Gemmel, among many dozens of others, was sentenced to transportation and prison labor in British Australia. In the document that follows, Gemmel describes to his audience the conditions of life aboard the convict ships and within the colony and the details of his fortuitous escape home to New York. Gemmel published his account of "Van Dieman's Land" (Tasmania) in Levi Slamm's New York *Daily Plebeian* and in books circulated to eager Locofoco, Democratic readers.

Those looking to Gemmel to reinforce Americans' gradually increasing feeling of imperial rivalry with Great Britain must have come away from his book sorely lacking, however. James Gemmel, for all his youthful filibustering gusto for revolution, concluded his narrative with a plea for prudent inaction. "But let us avoid all frontier movements," he implored readers; "the best weapon . . . with which to revolutionize the world, is surely a strict adherence to that wise, just, and honest policy, which carries in its train prosperity and peace."

"Two Years in Van Dieman's Land" [30]

By James Gemmel

Mr. Editor:—The superintendent of the convict station on which I was employed last year, appointed me an overseer, a sort of spy upon my fellow prisoners, and insisted on my acceptance of that unpleasant office. To decline was to incense him, yet I flatly refused it, and was therefore immediately sent to the treadmill a month—very fatiguing for the legs it surely is, and the vile wretches whose company one is compelled to keep, double the punishment; I was next placed in the Bridgewater chain gang for two months, and kept standing in the water handling stones and building piers.

Linus W. Miller, the young law student from Chautauque County, made a bold defence at Niagara, when on trial for his life, though but 18 years of age. I presume that this boldness did him much injury with Sir John Franklin, for he was an object of special persecution on the island.

At length he joined [other prisoners] in a vain attempt to escape. They jumped into an open boat, and without rudder or compass, went out to sea, hoping that some vessel might be near that would aid their views. A storm overtook them—they were driven on the rocks on a desert island—their boat was smashed to pieces—and two weeks after that, they were found nearly famished, and carried back to Hobart Town.

When they were missed, the whole island was in an uproar. It was feared that they had got arms and joined the Bush Rangers . . . who, well armed and very resolute, keep the woods, and set the colonial authorities at defiance.

Miller and his comrades had no jury trial—two justices condemned them for two years to the coal mines at Port Arthur, a sentence the next in severity to the gallows—and there they were when I escaped.

It was to this place of torment, that Mr. Frost, late Mayor of Newport, with Williams and Jones, his comrades concerned in the Welsh outbreak, were sent, though some of the ablest lawyers and judges in England had declared their conviction and sentence to be at variance with law. They were at first treated better than the other wretched beings there, but bad is the best usage at Port Arthur, so they also put out to sea in a whale boat, were pursued, taken, and Williams was put in irons—in the day time he was made fast to a long and heavy chain fastened to an iron ring in the wall, and kept at hard labor stone-breaking, and Frost and Jones found their condition much changed for the worse. The editors were friendly to these Welshmen, but they could learn little and effect nothing. I am satisfied that in England they have no correct idea of Frost's sufferings; his letters dare not tell the truth. A convict or person in my situation would have been severely punished had we been seen talking to a free emigrant, or to any one not of our class and station. I have seen captive Americans flogged and sent to confinement on bread and water, for receiving a little tobacco or a slice of bread from a stranger, and for speaking to strangers. Our rules were printed, and, as enforced, no man could live up to them. . . .

After our arrival in England we were for some months on board the York Hulk, off Portsmouth. We were there taken into a square crib called a wash house, stripped naked, put into a big tub and well scrubbed by two convicts, our hair sheared quite close, and we attired in the convict garb. Grant and Miller came down with a gang of horrid looking wretches from Newgate, were sent to work, planned how to escape, but were informed on by Jacob Beemer, the Judas of the party, now a constable in Van Dieman's Land.

Elijah Woodman, of Maine, drew up a memorial, in the shape of a round-robin, addressed to Sir John Franklin, in July, 1840, setting forth that fellows guilty of the foulest and most revolting crimes, were our overseers—that many of us had to work long and hard barefooted, with wretched food and worn out garments, toiling whether it rained or whether we were in a burning sun, with no place to dry ourselves when wet and weary, till the bell called us to be locked up in our prisons at night. Sir John was incensed, mustered us, called us mutineers, ordered us to be dressed in magpie clothing—one leg and arm black, t'other yellow—with a military guard to shoot us down if disobedient. We were then sent to the worst station on the island, at Green Pond. There, however, we found a friend in the Hon. Capt. Erskine, son to Lord Chancellor Erskine, and brother to the Ambassador from England, who had married an American lady. This noble youth won the affections of us all by listening to our complaints when cruelly used, and doing justice on the felons who had maltreated us. His heart was full of kindness and humanity, but his conduct gave offence as being at variance with the policy Sir John Franklin had been directed to pursue, and the station was soon broken up.

On the 14th of last February, those of the captives not ordered to Port Arthur, were to have tickets by which they would be enabled to labor for their living, each man having a certain township far in the interior, beyond which if he dared to go, severe punishment would follow.

These townships extend perhaps ten miles by five, and contain, on the average, perhaps thirty landowners, who will unite to pay the poor captive just what they please, as he can go nowhere else; and if he demand a settlement, they may assert that he was saucy; and, any two of them being magistrates, can send him to the chain gang for a year, or otherwise coerce him. Redress is a thing not to be thought of. I have seen enough of this. If I were now a Van Dieman's-Land "relief captive," I would gladly exchange for slavery in Virginia, as far preferable.

Chandler and Waite are the exception to these remarks. They are much respected, and have been allowed to set up a blacksmith and wheelwright's shop; John Grant, of Toronto, being their hired assistant.

It is impossible for me fully to describe the state of society in Van Dieman's Land. Nine-tenths of the people are convicts. The men are bad enough. Some of their crimes are so revolting that I forbear to name them; and as for the London prostitutes, they are there in thousands, and infinitely worse than the worst of the men.—Virtue itself would soon be contaminated in such a polluted atmosphere. There are no distilleries but money is plentiful, and Van Dieman's Land is the most remarkable place for drunkenness I ever saw. The American and Canadian prisoners established temperance societies, at which sons of our ablest men lectured, and a very few of the English convicts joined us.

The law is administered in a very summary and severe manner. Sir George Arthur would sometimes sign eleven death warrants in a morning, and see them executed too. His severity was no doubt the reason why he was sent next to Canada, and is probably the cause of his promotion to the government of Bombay.

In April, 1841, Governor Franklin caused the American captives to be assembled, and made a speech to them. I think the pith of it was to this effect:—

He had received a letter from Secretary Lord John Russell, saying that our release rested entirely with the Governor General of Canada, who, if he could arrive at the conclusion that our return would not endanger the public safety, and prove the signal for renewed troubles on the frontier, might permit us to return home, but that so far as the condition of Canada was yet known to the government of England, our return was considered highly dangerous; that there was but little probability that we should ever be permitted to leave the island; and that his instructions were not to allow any of us a free pardon. He added, that as American vessels visited Launcestown and Hobart Town, he would keep us all in the interior, even after our first two years expired; that we might hope to be taken off by the sympathy of American seamen, but that if such a case should arise, the British and American governments being on the best possible terms, we would be demanded of the United States authorities, given us, brought back, and receive a most exemplary punishment. As for Linus Wilson Miller, he would keep him in the coal mines, if he retained that government, to the last hour of his life, as a warning and example to others.

My object is to state plain facts, [I leave to] better informed men the task of applying them; but I may venture to remark, that it would surely be better for England to govern gently in Canada, and thereby gain the affections of the people, than to be careless there, and keep some hundreds of honest, well meaning men, who sought to get or give relief from a government acknowledged by the authorities of that nation to have been very wicked, 18,000 miles from their homes[,] miserable, and among the most degraded of God's creation, under the pretext that their release would involve a million and a half of colonists in revolt.

So far as prudence will permit, I will not state the particulars of my escape.

Mr. Norries, a police magistrate, and formerly butler to Sir George Arthur, had received a large tract of land, which he was anxious to clear. I persuaded him that I could build a stump machine if I had the model from Mr. Woodman, of Maine, who lived beyond Hobart Town; and such was his anxiety, that he gave me a passport to that place, in which the ship that brought me, the places where I was born and tried, with my complexion and height, the color of my hair, eyes, cheeks, and eyebrows, the shape of my nose and chin, and size of my mouth, were faithfully inserted. . . .

This passport (which I yet have) was in direct contempt of the public orders of the British government; accordingly, the moment I exhibited to Mr. Gunn, the superintendent, a letter from several of the prisoners, asking for their own clothes, that shrewd Caledonian suspected my design, arrested and gave me in charge to an armed constable, I being still attired in the conspicuous magpie garb in which I had reached the capital. I was ordered to be taken back into the interior immediately, was handcuffed, and being accompanied by several male and female criminals thither bound, set out on my weary journey. At noon the constable took off my handcuffs, that I might eat, when I seized his musket, declared I was off for the bush, and disappeared. In the night I left my hiding-place, crept into Hobart Town, told some whole-souled American tars my unfortunate history, and they required no coaxing to perform the part of honest men. The victim of oppression found deliverers, and entertains no fears whatever that John Tyler, President of the

United States, will send him back again, but would rather hope that the friendly aid of this great nation, through its Executive, will soon effectually relieve those who yet groan in bondage, and restore them to their free and happy homes.

The American prisoners were not all put in cross-irons at first; but for one cause or other, the most of them were in the long run thus accommodated.

I joined the insurgents behind Toronto, of my own free will, and had long been anxious for such a movement. Sir George Arthur visited us occasionally while we were under sentence of death, and when he told me I had been deluded by Mackenzie, I replied that it was not so—that we were in the right—that if ever there was a just cause it was ours—and that I had weighed the matter and was sincerely sorry we had failed. Sir George's behavior to us was polite and affable. Of the justice of our cause, I have never since entertained nor expressed a different opinion; but this is not the time and place to discuss that question.

I was behind Toronto with the insurgents the first night, Monday—was in the Tuesday night's skirmish in the suburbs—took Sheriff Jarvis's fine blood mare, which Mackenzie rode until all was over on Thursday. I also brought in the Captain of Sir Francis's Artillery, of which we had none ourselves, nor even a bayonet—was of the small party on Wednesday who went and took the mails and carriages—and in the final fight at Montgomery's on Thursday. I parted with Mackenzie when he and Colonel Lount separated, (after the defeat,) near Shepard's mills; and never saw him again till one of the refugees directed me to his home in this city, a week ago. I saw that he faithfully performed his duty behind Toronto, and if some who do not know have blamed him in the United States, I am sure that those who were his companions cannot have done so. . . .

In concluding, I would again entreat every friend of humanity to endeavor to get the United States government to interest itself in the matter of my unfortunate comrades. It is visionary to assert that the exertions of a few dozens of men, uninfluential, unconnected with politics, and worn down by pain and privation, could have the least effect in changing the destiny of Canada. And if not, why continue thus to torture them? But let us avoid all frontier movements—the best weapon in the hands of this great republic, with which to revolutionize the world, is surely a strict adherence to that wise, just, and honest policy, which carries in its train prosperity and peace. That is the true way to create admiration for institutions theoretically liberal and free. Had we succeeded in Canada in 1837, independence would have followed, but no war with America. War would only insure the oppression and captivity of tens of thousands who are happy in the bosoms of their families, would inflame the bad passions of two great nations, speaking one language, and capable, under such forms of government as they may respectively choose to uphold, of enlightening, benefitting and blessing mankind; but it would not soothe the griefs of the orphans and widows, the fathers and brothers, of those manly hearts which now beat on a far distant shore with fond and anxious confidence and hope that they will yet find opportune friends and deliverers in the land of Washington.

James Gemmel

19

Ann Parlin, Great Meeting in Relation to Rhode Island (Speech at the New York Shakespeare Hotel)

From August 4, 1842 to September 6, 1844, tens of thousands of radical "Locofocos" and "Dorrites" from throughout New England gathered intermittently—but persistently—at some of the grandest and most interesting popular expressions of political ideas and activism in the entire Jacksonian period. These "Great Clam Bakes" joined the traditional, ancient Narragansett feast with rabid, radical locofocoism and the rhetorical stirrings of republican revolution. The "clambakarians," as one hostile press dubbed them, drew their inspiration from the ongoing constitutional crisis in Rhode Island, what historians have called the "Dorr War," after the reformist leader Thomas Wilson Dorr. Rhode Island possessed, as of August 1842, the oldest existing written constitution in the world. King Charles II had issued the famous "Charter" in 1663 and it was hallowed by virtually all Americans as one of the country's truly great founding documents. By the late 1830s, however, the Charter positively disenfranchised a majority of the state's white male population and critics charged that the state no longer qualified as a republic. Accordingly, "Suffragists" gradually built a grassroots reform movement culminating in a new constitution approved by popular vote ("The People's Constitution") and a new governor (Thomas W. Dorr) in the Spring of 1842. The Charter government, however, refused to yield power to the irregularly formed People's Government, successfully resisting Dorr's hapless efforts at military confrontation at the Providence (May 1842) and Chepachet (June 1842) arsenals.[31]

Though the military struggle for a new constitution ended as a farcical failure and most members of the Dorr government were either exiled or in prison, the suffragist women of Rhode Island refused to relinquish the revolutionary principles involved. Ann Parlin was one such woman, and as her speech before New York locofocos at the Shakespeare Hotel indicates, Parlin devised and implemented the Great Clam Bakes, marking her as the key activist figure in the Suffragist movement while Dorr languished in exile. Parlin made her speech on November 5, 1842, at the end of the clam-baking season, which no doubt left her in a reflective mood. Fully aware that hers would be the first speech by a woman ever delivered at that venue, Parlin spent the majority of her time reminding her audience that women had shaped history in places and times far removed from Jacksonian Rhode Island. Parlin argued that right-thinking radical men and women alike shared responsibility for the future. Most importantly, women's capacity to produce new generations and etch upon them the past's wisdom all but destined the historical victory of republican principles. People do, in fact, govern themselves, and so long as warriors in the present kept alive this great republican idea, the young would inexorably embrace its truth.

"Great Meeting in Relation to Rhode Island"[32]

A speech by Ann Parlin

The large ball room of the Shakespeare Hotel was last night filled with the most respectable audience we have ever known at a meeting the object of which was directly associated with politics. The announcement that Mrs. Dr. Parlin would address the citizens of New York, had attracted a large number of the fair sex, who testified by their enthusiasm their deep interest in the cause for the support of which the meeting had been called. On entering the room, Mrs. Parlin was received with every demonstration of favor. Mr. Edward J. Webb was called to the chair, and opened the proceedings.

He introduced Mrs. Parlin by some neat complimentary remarks.

Mrs. Parlin then rose and addressed the meeting. She was aware, that in appearing before them, she might be accused of departing from the social forms and usages, which, from the earliest times, have restricted the action of the sex to which she belonged within the narrow circle of domestic occupations. Nor could they be more surprised to see her there than she herself was, to be on a stand hitherto occupied by men only. But, like the dumb son of Cresus, on whose tongue words distinct and clear were forced by his fear for a father's life, when the assassin's dagger was lifted over his head, accents of unwonted force and import came on her lips in defence of her husband, his freedom, reputation and life. She deemed it unnecessary, in a country where a virile education was given to so many women, to apologise for having acted a manly part during their civil discords—for presenting herself then, before them, on behalf of the unfortunate victims of aristocratic tyranny.

She was not learned either in ancient or in modern annals, but she had read in elementary books of history, that the wrongs of a Roman matron changed the Roman government from a monarchy into a republic—that the indignant aspirations of a plebeian wife was the cause of elevating to the consulate Roman citizens of plebeian birth—that the high daring of a virgin shepherdess turned in favor of France the tide of war, which for half a century had rolled adverse to her arms—that in Greece, when she awakened from the deathlike sleep of centuries of bondage, fierce Amazons led her fleet to glorious battles, once more presenting to an astonished world the spectacle of women fighting like men, and men flying from the contest like women. In Spain, young, (and before the voice of patriotism had called them to act,) retiring and timid maids were seen standing undaunted on the gory beach, inspiring the enthusiasm of their own heroic valor in the warriors of Arragon and Castile.

It had not yet been her fortune to emulate those heroines whose names will forever live in the annals of fame—but she felt here a spirit which convinced her that it required no greater exertion of physical courage to meet the swords of soldiers than she had exercised to assume enough of moral courage to sustain her in asserting the cause of popular freedom, retiring as she had ever been before. [Cheers.]

For she could not foresee the kindness of their reception, and the encouragement of their looks, which so eloquently told her that they understood her position, communed with her feelings, shared in all her patriotic sympathies, and did full justice to the purity and singleness of her motives. Allow her to state to them very briefly the circumstances which had led her to endeavor to awaken the patriots of Rhode Island from the torpor of discouragement, to inspire in the women there her own sentiments, and which had at last brought her from a home where she had always before kept strictly within the bounds of female avocations, to this great emporium of salutary political agitations, this fountain city from which has so often emanated the pure streams of Democratic principles.

After untoward events, too recent to require a recital, had destroyed their hopes of immediate emancipation from aristocratic thralldom, the patriots who had not fled were thrown into prison, and there dealt with as felons. A band of ruthless aristocrats strode over their State, spreading terror throughout the land. Informers, spies, denunciators crowded the cities, the hamlets, and the isolated abodes of husbandmen, violating everywhere the sanctities of private life—vengeance, and all the resentments of individual hatred mingling all the while their vile worship to the despotic measures of the victorious party. The press, too, faithless to its high mission of enlightenment and freedom, had passed to the side of fortune, and to add to their calamities, the President of the United States, yielding to the perfidious arts of some of his advisers, had given to their adversaries the sanction of his name.

No one dared to act, but few ventured to speak. In that period of gloom she looked round her for a leader to step forward to the rescue of American freedom! None appeared. . . .

In conversing with her female friends, she ascertained that they were animated with sentiments kindred with those feelings that made her heart to pant with emotions of alternate grief and indignation. She took in her own name, and careless of the consequences, spurning the abuse of the Algerine press, the initiative of calling these great gatherings, in which the spirit of resistance to oppression suddenly revived in every breast. These meetings had reanimated the desponding, infused life and daring into hearts before infirm of purpose. Their tyrants had marked these symptoms of returning energy. They were aware that there still rankled in every soul a deep undying hatred of their acts, in every generous mind, an inflexible resolution to throw off their ignoble sway. That she had been (citizens of New York) one of the humble instruments in the hands of God to rekindle from under the ashes where they slumbered, the noble passions in the hearts of their patriots might well make her proud, did she not recollect that between these symptoms of future success, and a full accomplishment of their designs, a wide field still spread before them. . . .

She asked them to listen to the testimony of one who daily visited the captives in their dungeons. The horrors of the British prison-ships, of which she heard, in the history of their first war, could bear no comparison with what she witnessed in the jails of Rhode Island, aggravated, too, as they were by the reflection that the executors of cruelties which no nation save England was supposed capable of inflicting on prisoners of war, were Americans. [Applause.]

It was the indignation inspired within her by scenes like those, which drove her from her quiet home, and urged her before the public, to breathe into the hearts of matrons and maidens the energy of her own feelings. She believed, when she began this pilgrimage in behalf of human rights and she still believed, that the cause which enlisted the sympathies of woman, would triumph at last by the action of men. Let such as might be tempted to censure her for appearing before the people in her own state, and presenting herself to that auspicious gathering of democracy—let them, she said, remember the patriotism of American women during the revolutionary war—their urging their husbands, brothers and sons, like Spartan matrons, to enlist under the banners of freedom; their memorable resolution to forego, as long as the war continued, the use of all those luxuries imported in British ships or manufactured in England, which she lavishly spread over the land, to enervate men and corrupt women.

It was (Mrs. P. continued) only the adolescence of the coming generation which was confided to the tuition of men; their earlier childhood was entrusted to them. It was from woman they received the precepts which their tender minds, then more easily impressed, imbibed as principles, opinions and rules of action never after to be effaced. So far it might truly be asserted, that the future of a nation was always prepared and moulded by women.

The present, which in Rhode Island belonged to the oligarchy, was like the leaves of this protracted autumn still, hanging on the trees, but sere, withered and ready to fall before the first blast, never again to resume life and verdure. The aristocracy had lived one season; but they had no harvest to expect from coming years. Every spring, together with the renovated life it breathes into matter, sends forth on the stage of political action, thousands of Suffrage youths. It was out of their hands they should receive, from the grave where it now rested, embalmed in a Nation's tears, the true, the real, the only constitution Rhode Island ever had or ever would accept. [Cheering.] . . .

When the majority of the present Congress, already morally dead, shall have come to its dissolution; when the Senate should have received, as new blood infused into their bodies, another and a better life, in the accession of new members fresh from the people, instinct with their opinions and obeying their dictates; when John Tyler (the glorious affixer of five vetoes on five unconstitutional bills,) [Cheers] restored by the cheerings of a grateful nation to the full vigor of his native energies, shall have brushed away both the spiders and the webs which those obscene insects had spun in his cabinet, then would come the auspicious time for a mightier effort to enfranchise Rhode Island! Then the voice of the first Magistrate will not be heard as it was before, condemning her right to obtain equal justice. Then she will have a fair field; reason and right her only weapons—public opinion the umpire between her and her oppressors—and the prayers of the good and the enlightened for the success of her holy cause. [Cheers.]

But while those events foretold by all the signs that ever mark the coming triumph of the people, are yet unaccomplished—the victims of their love of freedom—of their faith in the principles proclaimed by the venerable fathers of Democracy, languish in fetid dungeons—they are fed with loathsome aliments, which the famished serfs of English aristocracy would spurn! They were even deprived of sleep, that balmy solace of the wretched sufferer, is driven from their very lids by vermin which prey on their living bodies, as if they were already given up, to the noxious insects of the tomb.

It is in order to alleviate these sufferings of their fellow citizens that she now addressed them, not to ask for munificent contributions (those she well knew were obtained from the opulent, and they never tax themselves except to reward such as they use as instruments for their purpose,) but from every one here to solicit a small portion of one day's earnings, the numbers will make up for the smallness of the offering. Bread, and the coarsest garments, to the purchase of those only would their alimonies be applied. [Cheers.]

Mrs. Parlin then concluded. She would now close her remarks (for she had said enough for such as could feel). To them she offered in acknowledgment the grateful thanks of the victims. To such as would give, if they had it to give, she offered the same thanks for their kind sympathies. Allow her to say, that it was only after she had exhausted her own means that she applied to others to relieve her unfortunate fellow citizens. And now she bade them farewell. Defend me when I am gone against the slanders of those who would say that vanity, a desire of notoriety, brought me here.

She could read in the kindness of their looks a better appreciation, a more righteous judgment on her motives and purpose. It was their good opinion she wished to have and to preserve. As regarded the Algerines, what had she to hope from them—from men who brutally assailed and bruised a woman in the street, and as an apology for the brutal act, declared that they had mistaken her for her [Mrs. P.]. And this, too, because she maintained the heaven-born sentiment that government should be a shield and buckler for the protection, not a chain and manacle for the enslavement of the people. Mrs. P. sat down amid tremendous and enthusiastic cheering.

Levi Slamm, Battling the Empire

In the early 1840s, the British Empire steadily crept its way around the globe, increasing its reach in virtually all corners of the earth. Though the British lost many American colonies in 1783, they endured a generation of cataclysmic battle with the French Revolutionary and Napoleonic regimes, emerging in 1815 as the foremost global power. Britain was the world's first military, industrial, and cultural power, rivaled only by defeated and declining France and the young but promising United States. The Empire felt the Americans' troublesome influence most keenly during the Napoleonic Wars and the Jacksonian era, when American power entrenched itself across the western continent. From 1837–1839, American filibusters and Canadian republican revolutionaries unsuccessfully contested imperial rule in Canada, pushing the British to reconsider governance in the settler colonies. The 1839 Durham Report on the Canadian rebellions recommended internal self-government in areas directly settled by Englishmen, providing the basis for the later Dominion and Commonwealth systems.

This slow pace toward a version of republicanism hardly appeared benevolent to American contemporaries. Radical Democrats like New York's Levi Slamm looked on in horror as Queen Victoria added jewels to her crown. To Slamm and his fellow "Young American" radicals, the British Empire constituted a corporate-aristocratic elite ruling over an absolutely titanic portion of the planet and the population. It was medieval feudalism writ large: the all-powerful State farming out titles, commissions, and corporate charters without regard to any natural laws or preexisting socio-political orders. In the following articles, Slamm's New York *Daily Plebeian* attacks the British Empire as the greatest force of piratical destroyers that has ever existed and an institution too powerful for individuals around the world to ignore. In the first piece, Slamm identifies the Empire as a violent, destructive evil, as evidenced in the Opium Wars with China. The second article (a letter-to-the-editor) turns to examine the effects of imperial land and trade regulations in Ireland, including the mass starvation steadily driving the Irish diaspora. Slamm then considers the recent proceedings of an Ohio "Oregon Committee" meeting, and the Anglophobic sentiments proliferating throughout the American West.

According to the most extreme anti-British voices, only the unceasing spread of American republicanism could counter the unceasing spread of British imperialism. The great tragedy for this chapter of liberal history, of course, remains that the most radical of liberals were so often scared from their most significant first principles. In fearful and prideful response to Victoria's empire, Americans haphazardly and incrementally organized and justified their own.

Slamm's attacks continue, and we travel from Afghanistan to China and India, then across the Pacific Ocean to the Hawaiian Islands. At every turn, in virtually every section of the planet, British imperialism asserted its position and power, accumulated authority and legitimacy, and even assumed the position of moral supremacy in the fight against the slave trade. "Young Americans" like Slamm perceived that republicanism and democracy were thus surrounded by the world's foremost corporate aristocratic institution. American coasts were under constant threat from the Imperial Navy (no less so than the Chinese); the northern border stretched for thousands of miles and presented the constant threat of land invasion from British regulars, Canadian militia, and Native Americans alike; while across the South and West, Britain sought to acquire Texas, Oregon, and Pacific territories like the "Sandwich Islands." Victoria's tentacles threatened to choke the life out of American democratic republicanism, making the Revolution a momentary historical blip in the proliferation of a veritably British global socio-political order. Modern readers will likely notice that Slamm was painfully uncritical of curiously American socio-political orders, including southern slavery and the political coalitions (like his own) that protected and expanded slavery's reach.

Slamm addresses the ethics of imperial activity, focusing on British duplicity in Afghanistan, violence in China, untrustworthiness in Hawaii, and heartless pragmatism in India. Slamm's opposition to British imperialism was far from the Cold Warrior's feverish fears of global communism. He did not propose an

American Empire of his own to battle Victoria in a fresh round of global warfare; rather, he hoped to rouse people everywhere to several facts the "Young Americans" considered both manifest and unavoidable. First, Slamm believed that people did indeed rule themselves, and though most humans failed to assert their right to self-government they could not be dispossessed of this right. Second, he argued that once a population had resolved to live free, no institutions were powerful enough to deny them their rights. Should "Young India," "Young China," "Young Ireland," and even "Young Hawaii" take their places alongside "Young America," imperialism simply could not withstand the republican assault. Though he never expected as much, Slamm's contributions to the concepts of "Manifest Destiny" and "American exceptionalism" provided early and necessary political support to the rapidly developing American empire.

"Oppression vs. Freedom"[33]

By Levi D. Slamm

The news from Great Britain, received by the Great Western, has somewhat astonished us, inasmuch as we expected to learn that the famishing multitude who were a short time ago struggling to better their condition, had made some progress in the cause; but it would appear that "agitation" is not the means whereby the suffering population of the British empire hope to obtain the enjoyment of their rights. It is very strange that a people on the verge of starvation, "with every thing to gain and nothing to lose" except their lives, the which they would cheerfully risk in defence of their country, will not make an effort for their own freedom; and it is a great pity that while they call themselves men, they will allow the rest of the world to consider them as no better than creatures well trained to bear their masters burdens. Yet so it is; and it would seem that they have yet to learn that,

"Who would be free himself must strike the blow."

There are many men in this country who desire that the condition of the people of Great Britain should be represented, and their voice regarded by the government; and there is no doubt that such persons would be glad to hear that those people had obtained their liberty, though it might be by means of sword and gun, "e'en at the cannon's mouth!" But at the same time, if they were to hear, beforehand, that such means were to be used for the attainment of their object, no doubt they would express their dissent to such a measure, on the ground that a vast loss of life and destruction of property must inevitably ensue. Such people seem to look at things as they are, and not as they should be; and while they would shudder to hear of the destruction of the royal palace, the retreat of Queen Victoria, and her darling Albert to Hanover, the abolition of titles and hereditary pensions, together with all singular the clap-traps, and other machinery of the present government of Great Britain, they could read with the utmost complacency the news by the last steamship, wherein it might be stated that the British troops made a glorious descent on Quang Whang, in China, which resulted in the complete destruction of the town, and the retreat of some thousands of helpless women and children into the water, or the wilderness, or elsewhere, "to escape the just indignation of her Majesty's forces."

Thus the world wags. Far-off calamities are read of, and wondered at for a moment, and then forgotten; her majesty's troops may travel hither and thither, bearing destruction and desolation in their path, and it is all right; nothing is said against it, though they may proceed, as in the China war, against people who never injured them, and who so far from being aggressors, are too weak and timid to defend themselves against the attack of one-tenth their numbers; but let a people rise up against oppression, declare their hostility to monarchical government, and maintain their declaration by force of arms, and straightway a cry is raised against them, and they are denounced as thieves and robbers, state-prison convicts and *sans culottes* whose chief object is plunder, and whose desert is death, summarily without jury or benefit of clergy. Much would be said about the loss of human life, and the great destruction of property which must ensue, if such "wicked and wayward men," were suffered to go on in their mad career, the sympathies of men in the same condition of life, would be enlisted in behalf of their oppressors, the standing army would be arrayed against the "sons of liberty," and even ministers of the gospel, whose great Head and Leader, taught His hearers, the people, to "call no man master," would be hired to preach against them and persuade them that "whosoever resisteth the powers that be receiveth unto himself damnation." In short, all the power that men can exert, fairly or unfairly, justly or unjustly, is brought to bear against a people struggling for their rights. Under such disadvantages do the people of Great Britain labor, and all men of feeling pity them. Under such disadvantages do the people of RHODE ISLAND labor, but who pities them? Will the Federalists answer?

"Ireland and Her Wrongs"[34]

By "Emmett"

"Never was a people on the face of the globe so cruelly treated as the Irish."—O'Connell.

Let us look a moment at the clamor raised by some of the New York press, at the course pursued by the Plebeian, in reference to the subject of Repeal, and the foundation upon which it is based.

I lay it down in the first place as an admitted principle in modern civilized government, that when the grievances of a people become intolerable, and their natural inalienable rights are trampled upon by their rulers, they are justified in rising to abate those wrongs; has this been the case with Ireland? I appeal to the history of that country, from the commencement of the English dominion over her, in 1172 to the present time, in answer. It commenced in blood, was continued in blood and rapine, up to 1800, when the last spark of independence and separate government was extinguished by the fraudulent abolition of her national legislature, the Irish Parliament. . . . Let all who doubt read Irish history. . . . Irish citizens, who may happen to be resident in this country, are equally justified in aiding their brethren at home; for the British law itself, holds that a native born Englishman, Scotchman or Irishman, cannot by any act of his expatriate himself and cease to be a Briton, by attaching himself to any other government or country. Now as to the question whether natives of the United States have the same right to help a suffering people as they themselves have: In the aid extended to the Greeks and Poles, in their last struggle, England herself offers a striking authority in point. France also in the assistance furnished us during the Revolution; although one government has not the right to interfere with the mere municipal or civil policy of another, yet when a people are oppressed and deprived of their natural rights, and that people belong to a nation who were basely and cruelly conquered, whose consent to a union was never fairly obtained; but who were beaten down by overwhelming force, crushed and kept in subjection by sheer physical power, until they were exhausted; to say that the people of another government, nay the government itself, has not the right to sympathize, to assist them, is contrary to all humanity—to all history—for history is replete with instances of governments interfering to prevent one and another from perpetrating a wrong upon a weaker. The British government has recently taken violent possession of the Sandwich Islands, and these same papers are loud in their calls upon the government of the United States to interfere.

But the New York American gravely says—As well might the British government have interfered in the disputes between our separate States as the people of this country with the Irish question. By no means—there is no State in the Union but that came in voluntarily; nor is there a State in this Union where the natural and fair rights of the people are wrongfully infringed so as to afford such States any grounds to cast off the authority of the general government. This subject of government is a great bugbear; what is government? It is composed of a few men, or one woman, if you please, who is placed over the destiny of millions for their welfare. To say that we must pay a blind reverence to that accidental power and disregard the cries of the many, our own flesh and blood, for whose happiness that government was alone instituted, in contrary to the dignity of human nature, and the precepts of the Christian religion. The Irish people do not ask (although we think they might) an actual dismemberment of the kingdom, but the restitution of their native parliament; this we enjoyed when we were colonies, and this the provinces of Upper and Lower Canada now enjoy under the British government.

"Opposition to the British Empire"[35]

By Levi D. Slamm

In the address of the Oregon Committee of Ohio to the Eastern States . . . [it] says "if anything distinguishes the Western pioneer, it is a lively jealousy of the growing power, and a deep, instinctive, unalterable, and unmitigated hatred of Great Britain." What is remarkable, this sentiment was promulged at a popular convention, attended by at least 20,000 citizens of New York, at about the same time the address of the people of the Far West was published upon a question which seems to occupy the attention of our whole Western population, and yet we are told by the Federal press that it is a misrepresentation of the popular feeling. He must be blind who does not know that opposition to the British empire is not alone the prevalent idea of our people, but that it is the prevalent idea of the world. The system of ethics which prevails and which has for years marked the conduct of the British government in all its foreign relations has created this universal feeling of hatred and contempt. England, in her domestic policy, it is said, is governed by her Constitution. And where can that Constitution be found? What Englishman has ever read it? It may be collected from Blackstone's Commentaries on English laws, and from innumerable books, report and decisions. The principles collected from them, and they are varied in hue and antagonist in doctrine, form its fences of legislation! Thus are principles or doctrines applied, which for the time being, accord with or promote the views of the dominant party with no regard to any rule of truth, justice or right. Internationally the British government has pursued the same line of conduct. Its grand object has been to increase its POWER. The restraints of moral honesty are never permitted to operate on British policy, when they will impede the accomplishment of this primary and momentous purpose. Professions of peace and good will are indeed, on some occasions used, but their hollowness is now so easily distinguished, that they only contribute, among thinking men, to increase the detestation which they were intended to extenuate.

Opposition to British empire, we repeat, is the sentiment of the whole world. That government has earned the reputation of the Great Universal Robber, and what other feeling can pervade? Her history has been one of fraud and treachery. Neutralities have been instituted to prevent the interruption of neutral commerce with her consent, and she has been the first and most violent in destroying them. She has time and again broken the law of nations by insulting their ambassadors. She has, while professing herself the friend of liberty, entered into alliances with and subsidized the plunderers and oppressors of unhappy but glorious Poland. She has, while pluming herself on her love of order and religion, and while rolling her eyes in holy horror at the cruelty of the nation with whom she was at war, suffered the Indies to be pillaged, and its inoffensive inhabitants slaughtered by her subjects. She has, while professing a religious abhorrence of the enslavement of the Africans, enslaved with iron shackles, millions of Asiatics. In our own revolution, she did encourage the Indians to tomahawk our own people, and she did hire mercenaries of European princes to do the work of death in a contest in which they had no immediate concern. She turned counterfeiter by forging assignats, during the French revolution, and by her wily machinations and intrigues, overclouded the morning which rose so beautifully in the political horizon of France. The budding hopes of those who meditated in that most popular contest, the establishment of Republican and the demolition of absolute rule, were blasted by the murderous policy of Britain, and a movement, originating in the purest and most elevated designs, brought to a sanguinary and most untoward conclusion. Look too, at the means she used to consummate the Union of Ireland—bold and forced bribery, open and profligate corruption, the intimidating influence of ninety thousand armed mercenaries. These were the means resorted to, and which induced the Irish Parliament, by a meagre majority, to vote itself out of being, and to merge itself into that of Great Britain. We need say nothing of her recent acts of bloodshed and treachery—the slaughter and pillage of the Chinese and Hindoos, and her theft of the Sandwich Islands. These incidents in her history, are fresh in the public mind. The British government would unparadise the world to perpetuate its power, and the feeling of universal opposition which is developed, is but the consequence of its treacherous conduct.

"British Honor at Cabul"[36]

By Levi D. Slamm

The London *Athaenaeum* for January 7th . . . contains a frank confession of the duplicity and treachery of the British authorities towards the Afghans, which led to the destruction of the Envoy of Queen Victoria, Sir Wm. Macnaghten. It is in the form of a narrative of the military operations in Cabul, by Lieut. Eyre, now in India. . . .

Through the pressing representation of the military commanders, made after the first disasters in Upper India, negotiations were opened with the invaded and injured Afghans, and a treaty concluded and solemnly ratified, by which the British forces solemnly pledged themselves to evacuate Cabul, surrender its fortresses to their owners, and retire under Afghan protection, which they would have faithfully obtained.

But the Afghans doubted British honor. Mahomed Akber Khan, to test the sincerity of the English army, pretended to propose to the British Envoy a secret scheme by which Sha Soojah, the puppet of the foreigners, was to continue to act the mock king, and themselves remain in possession of Cabul, and break their treaty.

"It is with deep humiliation," says the *Atheneaum*, "that we recorded here, that the British Envoy was a consenting party to these disgraceful proceedings, and gave a written sanction to the arrangement. From that moment the British forces were doomed to destruction." Sir William soon set forward to meet the parties who were thus testing his honors and proving the hollowness of his most sacred engagements, and his base treachery towards their country. Who can wonder that they seized and slew the principle traitor? Who can regret the fearful retribution which was inflicted on the abettors? One thing is to be deplored—the greediness of gain, the lust of power, that can induce men, pretending to be Christians, and full of truth and integrity, to degrade themselves and assume the character of knaves and cheats.

"Correspondence of the Plebeian"[37]

Mr. Editor—The affairs in China may have ceased to interest the good people of the United States, and even the East India squadron may have been forgotten amidst the more weighty matters which press upon the mind of the public. We wish, therefore, to awaken your slumbers, and to represent that the war is not ended in China, or has the East India squadron quite all left its shores.

The Boston sailed on the 28th of September with the news of a treaty, and is now looking out for our fishing and other interests about New Zealand and the Islands of the Pacific. This old ship is still at her post, watching the result of a war, the history of which no historian will have the hardihood to undertake to defend.

The "Canton Press" herewith transmitted, will inform you of a riot in Canton. This riot, as it is called, is but a lingering flash from the popular feeling which exists in China. It may be called a mob affair, but while every body knows how the war began, and how hostilities have ceased, it were idle to believe a people so injured could rest in peace.

It would be vain and useless to expect profound peace under the circumstances; and this outbreak at Canton will be but a prelude of what is to take place at the Five Ports, and will again be enacted in Canton.

The Chinese people and the Chinese government, alike, are most deadly hostile to every thing English. They feel their power, and bend to the necessity, hence they will sign any sort of a treaty—willing on any terms to get their great ships of war and steamers out of their waters. The force of might ably prevails, and whatever you may think we know not—but have made up our minds upon one point, which is, that England has only begun the game in this Empire, and before long all the rascals and gamblers in the world, who have no business in smuggling, or the slave trade, or piracy, will be coming this way to assist her in conquering one of the greatest, and we believe, the happiest nation on earth, this same China; for it is certain that no present treaty will bind a people whose altars have been torn down—whose cemeteries have been torn up—and whose females have been ravished, or who, to prevent it, have destroyed themselves by poison, or throwing themselves with their young ones into cisterns.

Besides the inalienable right of soil, what is to be considered safe so long as a flag of the despoiler flies on the Chinese island of Hong Kong?—Why may not the same some day be seen on Nantucket, or upon the top of our own Hempstead Hill? And then Nantucket or Long Island is British ground. But to return from the heroics.—John Bull has an awful day of retribution to look to when the world wakes up.

We have seen the Chinese people. They are a great people. They have been under the best government that nature could provide for them under the circumstances. We are sure the worst of them are as well off as the worst of other people, and we think the best are a great deal better off than any other people. No one has been seen idle, no one has been seen drunk; and this, in ten month's experience, is saying something. Why, then, shall it be considered just that a war is waged against a nation to make them eat opium, and drink and buy rum, and foreign goods, leaving their own simple way of living to cause the employment of people in India in the poppy fields? We ask this?

For shame, old England! Thou setter up of morals! Thou emancipator of blacks, and enslaver of yellow skins, and of the fair bright Irish! Who, at this day, are greater slaves than the most bow-legged negroes south of "Mason & Dixon's line."

With regard to the citizens of the United States in China, they, who are not connected with British houses, are concerned in the opium trade, there is nothing to fear . . . from a popular outbreak. . . .

Macao Roads, Jan. 1st, 1843.

"British Usurpation of the Sandwich Islands"[38]

By Levi D. Slamm

The policy of our government, avowed at a time when we were comparatively weak, as compared to other States, was to hold all nations "enemies in war, in peace friends." Since the announcement of this rule of national conduct, two generations have passed away, and with the strength which time has brought to us, we are no longer required to bend principle to policy, but dare speak out as we should whenever events which European and monarchical aggression upon the rights of the people and the interests of the civilized world require remonstrance. Our Congress at its last session provided for the support of a Commissioner to the Sandwich Islands, and in pursuance of the authority thus vested in him, the President appointed an individual to discharge the trust. Before that minister can reach his destination, news arrives that his mission will be fruitless, and that the British have usurped authority over 200,000 free islanders of the Pacific seas. What . . . is now required of our government? She has within the last ten years seen the British nation possess itself of all the avenues to the commerce of the entire world, that it had not mastered during the thirty years' struggle—Asia, Africa and Australia under her perfect control, and her restrictive system at home, and for her wide spread colonies, effectually excludes all commercial and mechanical competition on the part of other countries, that rely upon their own resources solely. Her late acquisition of the Sandwich Islands, viewed in connection with her claim to the mouth of the Columbia river, especially affects the United States. Owning these two stations, she can, if she be so disposed, put an end to our whale fisheries, and deprive us of the 20,000 able seamen that they support. This small group of islands can be of no . . . intrinsic value, for she owns already thousands of unsettled square miles; her aim is to destroy the American preponderance in these seas, and to lop off one fourth of the means which support our formidable commercial marine. What our government may feel disposed to do in the premises, we can hardly venture to guess, but we would think that the same policy which forced us to announce many years ago, in our feeble state, that we would endure no European interference in the affairs of the western hemisphere, would justify us in abating the evil of which we now complain. English artifices are constantly astir all around us. They have been noted in regions closely connected with us—they may be pushed too far in other quarters for the tolerance of even our peaceful people.

"From the Cincinnati Gazette: India" (19 July 1843)[39]

This is a fated land. From its first possession by European power, it has been the theatre of fraud, rapine, and blood. There is no crime in the record of history so black that we shall not there find its parallel; no scene of human butchery so desolating that we shall not there witness its counterpart. India has been visited by every evil which villany breeds; she stands a living monument of the blackest oppression.

Avarice planted the European on her soil. He went there to get money; to get it fairly if he could; but to get it; by persuasion, by dexterity, or by plunder. He succeeded. But there mingled in afterwards the desire for possessions—for an extension of empire; and then the governments of Europe made it the theatre for their political movements. Chief was arrayed against chief; nation against nation; until weakened by divisions, and limited in resources, India fell an easy prey to European authority. Yet what a sacrifice of life was occasioned by this subjugation! Myriads fell ignorant of the harm they had done. Nor was the condition of India bettered, in any way, under this European sway. The country was too extensive—the people too numerous—to be governed by military force. The same policy by which it was subdued was adopted to render that subjugation complete. One chief was made to check another; one nation was set to war with another; and thus, by hostility set on foot, or a jealousy fermented among them, by the Europeans, was India made, and kept, a tributary.

And how revolting are the scenes which its history presents! Sometimes, whole sections of the country were reduced to beggary. For months together, said one familiar with its condition in the last century, these creatures of sufferance (the East Indians) whose very excess and luxury in their most plenteous days had fallen short of the allowance of our (English) austerest fasts, silent, patient, resigned, without sedition or disturbance, almost without complaint, perished by an hundred a day in the streets of Madras; every day seventy at least laid their bodies in the streets, or on the glacis on Tanjore, and expired in the granary of India. And then again, when some chief bolder in heart, and wider in view, saw that "he had to do with men who either would sign no convention, or whom no treaty and no signature could bind, and who were the determined enemies of human intercourse, itself," and thereupon resolved "to put perpetual desolation as a barrier between him and those against whom the faith which holds the mortal elements of the world together, was no protection," with what terrible vengeance did he execute his purpose? Who does not recollect this determination of Hyder Ali, and the memorable burst of eloquence with which Mr. Burke described his resolution, and its execution:

"Having terminated his disputes with every enemy, and every rival, he drew from every quarter whatever rudiments in the arts of destruction; and compounding all the materials of fury, havoc, and desolation, into one black cloud, he hung for a while on the declivities of the mountains. Whilst the authors of these evils were idly and stupidly gazing upon this menacing meteor, which blackened all their horizon, it suddenly burst, and poured down the whole of its contents upon the plains of the Carnatic. Then ensued a scene of woe the like of which no eye had seen, no heart conceived, and which no tongue can tell. All the horrors of war before known or heard of, were mercy to that new havoc. A storm of universal fire blasted every field, consumed every house, destroyed every temple. The miserable inhabitants flying from their flaming villages, in part were slaughtered; others without regard to sex, to age, or the respect to rank, or sacredness of function, fathers torn from children, husbands from wives, enveloped in a whirlwind of cavalry, and amidst the goading shears of the drivers, and the trampling of pursuing horses, were swept into captivity in an unknown and hostile land. Those who were able to escape the tempest, fled to the walled cities. But escaping from fire, sword, and exile, they fell into the pains of famine."

These were the evils which Plunder—"a heroic avarice"—as it was called, brought upon that land in the last century, under British rule. Nor have they been lessened since. Modified, they may be; there is now, no doubt, less of extortion, less of rapine, but not a whit less of injustice and wrong: for the natives are slaves; are treated as such; and if they resist their iron vassalage, they are butchered by thousands! It is the same cause which produced the devastation of the Carnatic, and which led to the late battle on the Scind. It was wrongs of this kind which caused Mr. Burke to speak as he did in behalf of India, and if a kindred spirit existed, at this time, in the House of Commons, if any thing but a thirst for dominion blinded the English people, no shouts of exultation would be heard for battles won over this abused, and oppressed race! But it is not so. The plains of India are conquered; not satisfied, British ambition grasps at the mountain barriers; and these gained, she will claim to sway even the Barbarian powers that live beyond them!

And all this, be it remembered, is the work of a power which calls itself Christian; which talks of its philanthropy; which boasts that there is no slavery on British soil!

21

Abram D. Smith,
In Re Booth

Virtually no one is aware that Abram D. Smith ever existed. His life has gone almost unnoticed by historians, yet Abram D. Smith was not only floated by some for vice president on the Republican ticket in 1860, but he briefly served as president of the Republic of Canada more than two decades earlier. Smith was born in 1811, in one of the many upstate New York small towns dotting the Adirondacks, likely an antinomian Congregationalist. As a young man and law student, Smith encountered the radical classical liberal philosophy of the New York "Locofocos," imbibed deeply in their brand of romantic, revolutionary republicanism, and moved west with his family. The Smiths settled in Ohio and Abram threw himself into Democratic politics. As a city councilman in Cleveland, he delivered speeches of the "ultra Locofoco kind," in the words of a local paper. In his spare time, he conspired with fellow "Brother Hunters" and "Patriots," as they called themselves, to violently overthrow British rule in Canada (but we will have to wait to explore this particular exciting chapter in Smith's life). When the attempt at Canadian rebellion promptly dissolved, Smith returned to a relatively obscure life of quiet reformism. He joined the County Anti-Slavery Society and became a trustee for the Cleveland Female Seminary, "a private school for young ladies."

The Smiths moved to Milwaukee, Wisconsin, in 1842, where Abram, styled "Governor of the People," gave expansionist speeches laced with radical liberal visions of American Manifest Destiny. He practiced law and delivered inspiring speeches, winning him election to the state Supreme Court. In 1852, a Missouri slave named Joshua Glover escaped his master and resettled in Racine, Wisconsin. When federal marshals tracked, captured, and beat Glover on March 10, 1854, locals alerted famous abolitionist and publisher of the *Milwaukee Daily Free Democrat*, Sherman Booth. Booth led a crowd of 5,000 in an assault on the city jail on March 13, 1854. The crowd broke into the jail, freed Glover, and made public demonstrations of their victory. Officials soon charged Booth with aiding and abetting a fugitive slave.

Booth's attorney, Byron Paine, appealed to the court to release his client, claiming that the Fugitive Slave Act violated the rights of Wisconsin by denying citizens due process of law. Smith's decision of June 7, 1854, nullified the Fugitive Slave Act in the state of Wisconsin. In this first of two selections from Smith's arguments, he outlines the nature of the case before him, weighs the various claims involved, and explains his reasoning that the Fugitive Slave Act was indeed an unconstitutional breach of authority, incommensurate with the national government's strictly delegated powers.

In the second selection, Justice Smith verbally elaborates before the court his earlier written decision. Smith argues that state judges have obligations and duties to protect the rights of citizens regardless of the unconstitutional pronouncements of the U.S. Supreme Court and the Congress of the United States. He maintains that the parties to the Constitution—the states, the people, and the United States—have equal rights and duties to interpret the document and protect the parties' rights as need be. Though Missouri pronounced Joshua Glover a slave and the national government unconstitutionally employed slave-catching marshals, Smith declares it his duty and right as a representative of both Wisconsin and the people of Wisconsin to resist any and all actions and legislations that violate the terms of the Compact. *In re Booth* rocketed Smith to superstardom in the emerging anti-slavery community and steadily progressed to the U.S. Supreme Court. In *Ableman v. Booth* (1859), Chief Justice Taney and a unanimous court overruled Smith. Meanwhile, a land scandal rocked Wisconsin state politics and upset the careers of many, including Smith, who stood "accused of accepting $10,000 in railway bonds" as a bribe. While he admitted to taking the bonds, he claimed it never influenced his opinion regarding land grants to the railroad. While Smith retained much of his anti-slavery fame, his credibility never recovered and the Democratic Party nominated a new candidate to Smith's position on the court.

He was thus rendered "a man without a party," and though 40 Republican editors throughout the state endorsed his nomination on their own 1859 ticket, he received only 15 of 61 votes in caucus. From December 1860 to early 1862, Smith published the Milwaukee *Free Democrat* and coauthored the Direct Tax Act while visiting Washington in late 1861. The act levied land taxes in rebellious states. If landowners failed to pay, the national government assumed control of the property. The following year, Smith joined the Direct Tax Commission in the South Carolina Sea Islands. He arrived at his post in the conquered islands to a gaggle of northern missionaries and a progressive atmosphere of managed freedmen's education, development, and training projects. Smith adjudicated disputes relating to the divisions of property and delinquent taxes, advocated full citizenship for freedmen, and delighted in General Sherman's Special Field Order No. 15 in early 1865, which granted huge tracts of land to freed slaves throughout the South, believing that "the betterment of the freedmen was inherently tied to their ability to own land in the area where they had been born and raised." He struggled with severe alcoholism and probably harder drug use that continually hampered his job performance. The man without a party, the former president of Canada, and the one-time anti-slavery hero of States' Rights, died in 1865 en route to New York after being relieved of his commission in disgrace.[40]

In re Booth, Abram D. Smith, Justice of the Wisconsin State Supreme Court[41]

On the 27th ult, application was made to me by Sherman M. Booth, the petitioner, for a writ of habeas corpus, to be directed to Stephen V. R. Ableman, who, it was alleged restrained the prisoner of his liberty. Accompanying the petition was a copy of the process, by virtue of which, it was alleged, the petitioner was held in custody. This warrant charged Booth "with having, on the 11th day of March, 1854, at the city of Milwaukee, in said county and district, unlawfully aided, assisted, and abetted a person named Joshua Glover, held to service or labor in the state of Missouri, under the laws thereof, and being the property of one Benammi S. Garland, and having escaped therefrom into the state of Wisconsin, to escape from the lawful custody of Charles O. Cotton, a deputy of the marshal of the United States for said district, pursuant to the provisions of the act of congress in that case made and provided, approved September 18, 1850."

In his application or petition, the petitioner alleges the illegality of his imprisonment to consist in the following, that the act of congress referred to in the said warrant, is unconstitutional and void; also that congress has no constitutional power or authority to punish the offense with which said Booth is charged and for which he is detained; that the act of congress of 1850 is in violation of the provisions of compact, unalterable, except by common consent, contained in the ordinance of 1787, for the government of the territory northwest of the Ohio river, and that therefore said act is not in force in said state."

Upon this application, I could not hesitate to issue the writ according to the prayer of the petition. I cannot but feel the immense responsibility throw upon me alone, and may be pardoned for expressing my regret that I am deprived of the aid and counsel of my associates, so much better able to cope with the grave and intricate questions involved than I am myself. Whether by design, or from necessity, this application has been made to me, I meet the emergency with all the anxiety and concern which it cannot fail to excite, and, I hope, with some share of the firmness which the occasion and the nature of the questions involved imperatively demand.

The warrant, by virtue of which the petitioner was held, was not issued by a federal judge or court, but by a commissioner of the United States. No exclusive or ultimate jurisdiction can be claimed for an officer of this kind. As one of the justices of the highest judicial tribunal of this state, which tribunal represents in that behalf the sovereignty of the state, I could not deny to any citizen or person entitled to the protection of the state, the proper process by which the validity of a warrant issued by such authority, could be examined. . . Indeed, we may go farther, and say, that as every citizen has a right to call upon the state authority for protection, and as the judicial power in that only to which application can usually be made by the citizen, it is the duty of the judicial officer, when applied to, to see that no citizen is imprisoned within the limits of the state, nor taken beyond its limits, except by proper legal and constitutional authority. It is not in the power of anybody to divest the state judiciary of such authority, nor can anybody, but the people themselves, absolve the judicial officers of the state from the performance of their duty in this behalf.

The States will never submit to the assumption that United States commissioners have the power to hear and determine upon the rights and liberties of their citizens and issue process to enforce their adjudications, which is beyond the examination or review of the state judiciary. They will cheerfully submit to the exercise of all power and authority by the federal judiciary, which is delegated to that department by the federal constitution; but they have a right to insist, and they will insist, that the state judiciary shall be and remain supreme in all else, and that the functions of the federal judiciary within the territory of the states shall be exercised by the officers designated or provided for by the constitution of the United States, and that they shall not be transferred to subordinate and irresponsible functionaries, holding their office at the will of the federal courts, doing their duty and obeying their mandates, for which neither the one nor the other is responsible.

Every jot and tittle of power delegated to the federal government will be acquiesced in, but every jot and tittle of power reserved to the states will be rigidly asserted, and as rigidly sustained.

It is only by exacting of the federal government a rigid conformity to the prescribed limitation of its powers, and by the assertion and exercise on the part of the states of all the powers reserved to them, and a due regard by both of their just and legitimate sphere, that obedience can be rightfully exacted of the citizen, to the authority of either.

The constitution of the United States is the fundamental law of the land. It emanated from the very source of sovereignty as the same is recognized in this country. It is the work of our fathers, but adopted and perpetuated by all the people, through their respective state organizations, and thus become our own The citizen has, by his vote, mediate or immediate, established it as the great charter of his rights, and by which all his agents or representatives in the conduct of the government are required to square their actions.

I recognize most fully the right of every citizen to try every enactment of the legislature, every decree or judgment of a court, and every proceeding of the executive or ministerial department, by the written, fundamental law of the land. No law is sacred, no officer so high, no power so vast, that the line and the rule of the constitution may not be applied to them. It is the source of all law, the limit of all authority, the primary rule of all conduct, private as well as official, and the citadel of personal security and liberty. Every one has a right to resist an unconstitutional enactment of the legislature; but he does so upon his peril, until the conformity or nonconformity of the act with the constitution is judicially determined. Passive obedience cannot be exacted, nor can private judgment in this behalf become the rule of action.

To yield a cheerful acquiescence in, and support to every power constitutionally exercised by the federal government, is the sworn duty of every state officer; but it is equally his duty to interpose a resistance, to the extent of his power, to every assumption of power on the part of the general government, which is not expressly granted or necessarily implied in the federal constitution.

Nor can I yield to the doctrine early broached, but as early repudiated, that any one department of the government is constituted the final and exclusive judge of its own delegated powers. No such tribunal has been erected by the fundamental law. To admit that the federal judiciary is the sole and exclusive judge of its own powers, and the extent of the authority delegated, is virtually to admit the same unlimited power may be exercised by every other department of the general government, both legislative and executive, because each is independent of and coordinate with the other. Neither has any power but such as the states and their respective people have delegated, and all power not delegated remains with the states and the people thereof. In view of the vastly increasing power of the federal government, and the relatively diminishing importance of the state sovereignties respectively, the duty of the latter to watch closely and resist firmly every encroachment of the former becomes every day more and more imperative, and the official oath of the functionaries of the states becomes more and more significant. Increase of influence and patronage on the part of the federal government naturally leads to consolidation, consolidation to despotism and ultimate anarchy, dissolution, and all its attendant evils.

If the sovereignty of the states is destined to be swallowed up by the federal government; if consolidation is to supplant federation, and the general government to become the sole judge of its own powers, regardless of the solemn compact by which it was brought into existence, and of the source of its own vitality, as a humble officer of one of the states, bound to regard the just rights and powers both of the union and the states, I want my skirts to be clear, and that posterity may not lay the catastrophe to my charge. I am truly thankful for the same feeling of conscientious firmness on entering upon the discharge of the duty before me, as would be required in case of direct invasion, open rebellion, or palpable treason, against our common country.

Without the states there can be no union; the abrogation of state sovereignty is not a dissolution of the union but an absorption of its elements. He is the true man, the faithful officer, who is ready to assert and guard every jot of power rightfully belonging to each, and to resist the slightest encroachment or assumption of power on the part of either.

Suppose, in a time of profound peace and quiet, the federal government should pass a law suspending habeas corpus [the privileges], would the state governments have the power to call to account the federal officers who had violated the compact in this behalf? the congress who had passed, and the executive who approved it? Would the state courts be bound by it? Not at all. Such an act of congress would simply be void, and it would be the duty of every state and federal court so to pronounce it, and it would afford no protection to any officer, state or federal, for refusing to obey such writ. I mention these illustrations to show that a great portion of our federal constitution rests in compact, while still another rests in grant. Where powers are granted, they are to be exercised; where rights rest in compact, they have still the force of law; but the federal government has no power to legislate upon them; they are to be obeyed and enforced by the parties to the compact, the states themselves.

Can it be supposed for a moment, that had the framers of the constitution imagined, that under this provision the federal government would assume to override the state authorities, appoint subordinate tribunals in every county in every state, invested with jurisdiction beyond the reach or inquiry of the state judiciary, to multiply executive and judicial officers ad infinitum, wholly independent of and irresponsible to the police regulations of the state, and that the whole army and navy of the union could be sent into a state, without the request, and against the remonstrance of the legislature thereof? If the members of the convention had dreamed that they were incorporating such a power into the constitution, does any one believe that it would have been adopted without opposition and without debate? And if these results had suggested themselves to the states on its adoption, would it have been passed by them, jealous as they were of state rights and state sovereignty? The idea is preposterous. The union would never have been formed upon such a basis. It is an impeachment of historic truth to assert it.

Congress has the power to legislate in regard to fugitives from justice or labor. But it may be asked, how are the rights, here stipulated and guaranteed, to be enforced? I answer that every state officer—executive, legislative, and judicial—who takes an oath to support the constitution of the United States is bound to provide for and aid in their enforcement, according to the true intent and meaning of the constitution. But what if one or more states should refuse to perform their duty, and its officers violate their oaths and repudiate the compact? The simple answer is, that when the state and federal officers become so regardless of their oaths and obligations as the question implies, anarchy or revolution, or both, must supervene, for the government would be a willful departure from the fundamental law of its organization, and the people would be absolved from their allegiance to it.

The Fugitive Slave clause as finally adopted reads, "but shall be delivered up on claim of the party to whom such service or labor is DUE." Here is a fact to be ascertained, before the fugitive can be legally delivered up, that his service or labor is really due to the party who claims him. How is the fact to be ascertained?

What authority shall determine it? Clearly the authority of the state whose duty it is to deliver up the fugitive when that fact is determined. Until the issue which the constitution itself creates is decided, the person is entitled to the protection of the laws of the state. When the issue is determined against the fugitive, then the constitutional compact rises above the laws and regulations of the state, and to the former the latter must yield.

To my mind, this seems very clear and simple. The whole proceeding is clearly a judicial one. The law of 1850, by providing for a trial of the constitutional issue, between the parties designated thereby, by officers not recognized by any constitution, state or national, is unconstitutional and void.

It has been already said that until the claim of the owner be interpreted, the fugitive in this state is, to all intents and purposes, a free man.

The passing of judgment upon any person without his "day in court," without due process, or its equivalent, is contrary to the law of nature and of the civilized world, and without the express guaranty of the constitution, it would be implied as a fundamental condition of all civil governments. But the tenth section of the act of 1850 expressly nullifies this provision of the constitution.

What, then, is to be done? Let the free states return to their duty, if they have departed from it, and be faithful to the compact, in the true spirit in which it was conceived and adopted. Let the slave states be content with such an execution of the compact as the framers of it contemplated. Let the federal government return to the exercise of the just powers conferred by the constitution, and few, very few, will be found to disturb the tranquility of the nation or to oppose, by word or deed, the due execution of the laws. But until this is done, I solemnly believe that there will be no peace for the state or the nation, but that agitation, acrimony, and hostility will mark our progress, even if we escape a more dread calamity, which I will not even mention.

However this may be, well knowing the cost, I feel a grateful consciousness in having discharged my duty, and full duty; of having been true to the sovereign rights of my state, which has honored me with its confidence, and to the constitution of my country, which has blessed me with its protection; and though I may stand alone, I hope I may stand approved of my God, as I know I do of my conscience.

Smith's Oral Remarks[42]

One great aim of the founders of our government (among others) was to secure beyond contingency personal liberty, and to protect and preserve, as far as practicable, the independence and sovereignty of the respective states (without whose agency such personal liberty could not be protected and secured), as far as was consistent with the practical efficiency of the federal government about to be organized.

It should be remembered that "error does not become truth by being often repeated, nor does truth lose any of its force or beauty by being seldom promulgated." Nor does vice become virtue by persistence in its practice; nor bad government grow better by acquiescence in its evils; nor, where a people have adopted a written fundamental law for the government alike of themselves and their rulers, does the infraction of that law become healed by a denial of its occurrence.

I am willing that the decision of the supreme court of the United States, in every case determined by them, within the scope of their jurisdiction, should be regarded as full and binding authority, as the law of the particular case so determined. But when it is strenuously contended that I am compelled to adopt their interpretation of the constitution and laws of the United States, and of their own powers, and the powers of congress, without thought or inquiry—to take "what is written is written" as the end of the law, simply because it is written—that my own conscience and oath must be tamely subjected to the prescriptions of another tribunal, governed by the same laws and bound by the same oath, notwithstanding the high respect, approaching even to veneration, which I have for that high tribunal, I must be permitted to say, that no man or body of men is made by the constitution the keeper of my conscience, nor does it impose upon any man or body of men the fulfillment of my official oath and obligations, or the power of releasing me therefrom. When duty and obligation require a steady and undeviating adherence to authority and precedent, no one will be more firm and anxious in insisting upon such adherence. But when the like duty and obligation require a departure from such precedent and authority, in obedience to a paramount law, the fundamental law, to which each and all are equally bound, I hope to be found just as firm in my adherence to the latter.

The constitution of the United States is, in its more essential and fundamental character, a tripartite instrument. The parties to it are THE STATES, THE PEOPLE, and THE UNITED STATES. The latter is, indeed, a resulting party, brought into existence by it, but when thus created, bound in all respects by its provisions. It is practically represented by its several departments, deriving their power directly and severally through its respective grants. It is derivative, not original. Previous to the operative vitality of the constitution, this third party to the instrument was nonexistent, and of course, powerless. The other two parties, the states and the people, were preexistent, endowed with all the essential elements of sovereignty.

One great and fundamental mistake has been made in respect to the second party to the constitution, namely, the people. This party here spoken of cannot be considered as the people inhabiting the whole territory embraced within the boundaries of the original thirteen states, as operating in mass, as one undivided and indivisible community. Previous to the formation of the government of the United States, there was no such political existence. The "people" mentioned in the preamble to the constitution, and often referred to in judicial discussions, must, it seems to me, necessarily mean the people of the United States—that is, the people of the several states united, so many uniting as were deemed a sufficient number to warrant the institution of the new government and render safe the delegation of certain powers before possessed by the respective states. The state governments preexisted. As the people of the respective states, did they adopt the constitution. By the authority of the states were the people called upon to adopt or reject the constitution. By the people of the respective states was it adopted, and, when ratified by nine states (not a majority of the people of the Union to be formed), was it to become operative. The states, as such, were distinctly recognized through every stage of progress, from the inception of the consummation of the plan of Union, and through the state organizations only could the first step be taken, and through those organizations only can the people of the Union now impress their will upon the measures or action of the government. Indeed, the federal constitution provides no mode by which, in any case, can the people of the Union affect the federal government, but through the state organizations, and by the instrumentalities furnished by the governments of the respective states.

The states derive not one single attribute of power or sovereignty from the constitution of the United States. On their separation from Great Britain, they were each sovereign and independent; as completely so as the government from which they had revolted. They retain all the attributes of sovereignty which they have not delegated or relinquished. Nor does the constitution address itself, in a single instance, to the people of the whole Union as one indivisible community, but always to the people or to the constituted authorities of the respective states. But the new entity brought into existence by the constitution does derive every jot and tittle of its power from that instrument. Without it, the state existed and performed all the functions of government. Without it, the federal government had not a shadow of existence. If that instrument ceased to operate, the states would move on, performing their present functions, and probably resuming the powers before delegated; but the government of the Union would cease altogether.

I make these remarks, because persons in their zeal for federal supremacy seem to have lost sight of the true relations subsisting between the confederacy and its members. The rights and sovereignty of the latter would seem to be sacrificed to the exaltation and glory of the former. But returning to elementary principles, it will not be difficult to determine the just rights and limitations of both.

Test the third clause of the second section of the fourth article of the constitution by this rule: "No person held to service or labor in one state under the laws thereof, escaping into another, shall, in consequence of any law or regulation therein, be discharged from such service or labor; but shall be delivered upon claim of the party to whom such service or labor may be due." What power or authority did the states relinquish by this clause? At most, the right, and power, if you will, to enact any law or regulation by which such escaping fugitive shall be discharged from such service or labor. They also covenanted that the fugitive should be delivered up. But did they delegate to the federal government the right to enter their territory and seize him? Did they authorize that government to organize a police establishment, either permanently or temporarily, armed or unarmed, to invade their territory at will, in search of fugitives from labor, ranging throughout their whole extent, subject to no state law, but enjoying a defiant immunity from all state authority or process while executing their mission? Did the states relinquish the right or power to prescribe the mode by which they would execute their own solemn compact in delivering up the fugitive? Every just regard to dignity and self respect on the part of the states forbids it. Every sentiment of delicacy, not to say justice, on the part of the national functionaries should revolt at it.

In Virginia, he may be, indeed, a chattel; but in Wisconsin he is a MAN. The laws of Virginia make him a chattel there; but the constitution of the United States and the laws of Wisconsin regard him as a person here. Under the constitution, the fugitive leaves the attribute of the chattel behind him in the state from which he flees, and goes forth as a PERSON. The law which makes him property in Virginia does not go with him beyond the limits of that state. On his escape from such limits, he ceases to be property, but is a person liable to be reclaimed. The person may escape but the property cannot. The states are no more bound to recognize the fugitive slave as property than a fugitive apprentice as property. The relation of master and servant is recognized so far, and so far only, as the obligation of service is implied from such relation. Even such obligation is not recognized as full, complete, present, and operative, but as attaching to that relation in another state. So much of the law of the state from which he fled, as required of him service to his master there, is to be regarded, and from that obligation of service, imposed by that law, the state may not discharge him. The law of Virginia, which requires of the slave service to his master, is recognized as the law there, not here. We may not discharge a fugitive from the service which, by law, he owes in Virginia. But by that law, he owes no service here. The master may capture him in Wisconsin. We must deliver him up to his master, on the establishment of his claim; but his master has no right to command his service in Wisconsin. He must not beat him. He may take him back to Virginia, but he cannot command his service here. When he gets to Virginia, he will owe service by the law of that state, but not till then. By the law of that state, he owes the service, and by that law only. That is the law of Virginia, but not the law of Wisconsin. If the master demand service here of his fugitive, and beat him for disobedience, he is punishable by our laws. Nor could the master, having captured the fugitive in this state, sell or hire him to another. He has just the control over him requisite to his extradition, and no more.

If the free states are bound by the Fugitive Slave clause of the constitution to recognize the full and complete rights in the owner of the fugitive slave, as property, to the "same extent" as they were recognized in the state from which he escaped, then it will soon be claimed that the free states may be made a highway for slaveholders traveling with their slaves; a thoroughfare for internal slave traders, over which to transport their living chattels from state to state; and state sovereignty itself must succumb to the slaveholders' authority. . . .

The simple answer to this is that the constitution does not guarantee the right. It guarantees no right. No power is granted in the constitution to the federal government to enforce or guaranty any right in regard to fugitive slaves, or any other slaves. . . .

Every day's experience ought to satisfy all, that the states will never quietly submit to be disrobed of their sovereignty; submit to the humiliation of having the execution of this compact forced upon them, or rather taken out of their hands, by national functionaries; and that, too, on the avowed ground that they are so utterly wanting in integrity and good faith that it can be executed in no other way. On the contrary, if the federal government would abstain from interference, the states would adequately fulfill all their duties in the premises, and peace and order would be restored.

But they will never consent that a slave owner, his agent, or an officer of the United States, armed with process to arrest a fugitive from service, is clothed with entire immunity from state authority; to commit whatever crime or outrage against the laws of the state, that their own high prerogative writ of habeas corpus shall be annulled, their authority defied, their officers resisted, the process of their own courts treated with contempt, their territory invaded by federal force, the houses of their citizens searched, the sanctuary of their homes invaded, their streets and public places made the scene of tumultuous and armed violence, and state sovereignty succumb, paralyzed and aghast, before the process of an officer unknown to the constitution and irresponsible to its sanctions. At least, such shall not become the degradation of Wisconsin, without meeting as stern remonstrance and resistance as I may be able to interpose so long as her people impose upon me the duty of guarding their rights and liberties, and of maintaining the dignity and sovereignty of their state.

Spooner, Abolition Plan/ To the Non-Slaveholders of the South

Lysander Spooner (1808–1887) lived during a period of world history in which daily life for hundreds of millions around the globe changed in profound and dramatic ways. In the United States, perhaps the most significant and transformative single change during the whole of the century was the abolition of (private) slaveholding. As a penetrating and challenging legal thinker, Spooner left important marks on the anti-slavery debate and the long history of abolitionist activism before the Civil War. Most significantly, he argued in "The Unconstitutionality of Slavery" that the Constitution should and must be interpreted as an anti-slavery document, most especially because slavery contradicted natural law, and even the Constitution was bounded by natural law. The "supreme Law of the Land," therefore, is not permitted to contradict the natural rights of individuals, including those condemned to slavery by unjust, unnatural legislation. In response to the Dred Scott decision of 1857, Spooner released the self-published broadside that follows. Addressed "To the Non-Slaveholders of the South," Spooner's "Abolition Plan" called for what can only properly be described as abolitionist filibustering into and throughout the South to free the slaves and rouse rebellions. Spooner argues that it is the moral duty of Americans everywhere, but particularly nonslaveholders in the South, to assist the slave in seizing his person and property from the slaveholders great and small. Perhaps most significantly for the history of liberal thought, Spooner accepts the time-honored Lockean premise that slavery indeed represented a state of war between slave and slavemaster. Justifiably, then, any individuals who would be combatants in such a war between individuals (or institutional groups of individuals) are entirely justified in killing their enemies if necessary. Rather than endorse the wholesale slaughter of slaveholders, however, Spooner advises anti-slavery filibusters to assist the slaves in turning masters' whips against themselves until sufficient "chastisement" shall have taken place to ensure compliance with respect for former slaves' rights.

"Abolition Plan, To the Non-Slaveholders of the South"[43]

By Lysander Spooner

We present to you herewith "A Plan for the Abolition of Slavery," and solicit your aid to carry it into execution.

Your numbers, combined with those of the Slaves, will give you all power. You have but to use it, and the work is done.

The following self-evident principles of justice and humanity will serve as guides to the measures proper to be adopted. These principles are—

1. That the Slaves have a natural right to their liberty.

2. That they have a natural right to compensation (so far as the property of the Slaveholders and their abettors can compensate them) for the wrongs they have suffered.

3. That so long as the governments, under which they live, refuse to give them liberty or compensation, they have the right to take it by stratagem or force.

4. That it is the duty of all, who can, to assist them in such an enterprise.

In rendering this assistance, you will naturally adopt these measures.

1. To ignore and spurn the authority of all the corrupt and tyrannical political institutions, which the Slaveholders have established for the security of their crimes.

2. Soon as may be, to take the political power of your States into your own hands, and establish governments that shall punish slaveholding as a crime, and also give to the Slaves civil actions for damages for the wrongs that have already been committed against them.

3. Until such new governments shall be instituted, to recognize the Slaves as free men, and as being the rightful owners of the property, which is now held by their masters, but which

337

would pass to them, if justice were done; to justify and assist them in every effort to acquire their liberty, and obtain possession of such property, by stratagem or force; to hire them as laborers, pay them their wages, and defend them meanwhile against their tyrants; to sell them fire-arms, and teach them the use of them; to trade with them, buying the property they may have taken from their oppressors, and paying them for it; to encourage and assist them to take possession of the lands they cultivate, and the crops they produce, and appropriate them to their own use; and in every way possible to recognize them as being now the rightful owners of the property, which justice, if administered, would give them, in compensation for the injuries they have received.

4. To form Vigilance Committees, or Leagues of Freedom, in every neighborhood or township, whose duty it shall be to stand in the stead of the government, and do that justice for the slaves, which government refuses to do; and especially to arrest, try, and chastise (with their own whips) all Slaveholders who shall beat their slaves, or restrain them of their liberty; and compel them to give deeds of emancipation, and conveyances of their property, to their slaves.

5. To treat, and teach the negroes to treat, all active abettors of the Slaveholders, as you and they treat the Slaveholders themselves, both in person and property.

Perhaps some may say that this taking of property, by the Slaves, would be stealing, and should not be encouraged. The answer is, that it would not be stealing; it would be simply taking justice into their own hands, and redressing their own wrongs. The state of Slavery is a state of war. In this case it is a just war, on the part of the negroes—a war for liberty, and the recompense of injuries; and necessity justifies them in carrying it on by the only means their oppressors have left to them. In war, the plunder of enemies is as legitimate as the killing of them; and stratagem is as legitimate as open force. The right of the Slaves, therefore, in this war, to take property, is as clear as their right to take life; and their right to do it secretly, is as clear as their right to do it openly. And as this will probably be their most effective mode of operation for the present, they ought to be taught, encouraged, and assisted to do it to the utmost, so long as they are unable to meet their enemies in the open field. And to call this taking of property stealing, is as false and unjust as it would be to call the taking of life, in just war, murder.

It is only those who have a false and superstitious reverence for the authority of governments, and have contracted the habit of thinking that the most tyrannical and iniquitous laws have the power to make that right which is naturally wrong, or that wrong which is naturally right, who will have any doubt as to the right of the Slaves (and those who would assist them) to make war, to all possible extent, upon the property of the Slaveholders and their abettors.

We are unwilling to take the responsibility of advising any general insurrection, or any taking of life, until we of the North go down to take part in it, in such numbers as to insure a certain and easy victory. We therefore advise that, for the present, operations be confined to the seizure of property, and the chastisement of individual Slaveholders, and their accomplices; and that these things be done only so far as they can be done, without too great danger to the actors.

We specially advise the flogging of individual Slaveholders. This is a case where the medical principle, that like cures like, will certainly succeed. Give the Slaveholders, then, a taste of their own whips. Spare their lives, but not their backs. The arrogance they have acquired by the use of the lash upon others, will be soon taken out of them, when the same scourge shall be applied to themselves. A band of ten or twenty determined negroes, well armed, having their rendezvous in the forests, coming out upon the plantations by day or night, seizing individual Slaveholders, stripping them, and flogging them soundly, in the presence of their own Slaves, would soon abolish Slavery over a large district.

These bands could also do a good work by kidnapping individual Slaveholders, taking them into the forest, and holding them as hostages for the good behavior of the whites remaining on the plantations, compelling them also to execute deeds of emancipation, and conveyances of their property, to their slaves. These contracts could probably never afterward be successfully disallowed on the ground of duress (especially after new governments, favorable to liberty, should be established) inasmuch as such contracts would be nothing more than justice; and men may rightfully be coerced to do justice. Such contracts would be intrinsically as valid as the treaties by which conquered nations make satisfaction for the injustice which caused the war.

The more bold and resolute Slaves should be encouraged to form themselves into bands, build forts in the forests, and there collect arms, stores, horses, every thing that will enable them to sustain themselves, and carry on their warfare upon the Slaveholders.

Another important measure, on the part of the Slaves, will be to disarm their masters, so far as that is practicable, by seizing and concealing their weapons whenever opportunity offers. They should also kill all slave-hunting dogs, and the owners too, if that should prove necessary.

Whenever the Slaves on a plantation are not powerful or courageous enough to resist, they should be encouraged to desert, in a body, temporarily, especially at harvest time, so as to cause the crops to perish for want of hands to gather them.

Many other ways will suggest themselves to you, and to the Slaves, by which the Slaveholders can be annoyed and injured, without causing any general outbreak, or shedding of blood.

Our plan then is—

1. To make war (openly or secretly as circumstances may dictate) upon the property of the Slaveholders and their abettors— not for its destruction, if that can easily be avoided, but to convert it to the use of the Slaves. If it cannot be thus converted, then we advise its destruction. Teach the Slaves to burn their masters' buildings, to kill their cattle and horses, to conceal or destroy farming utensils, to abandon labor in seed time and harvest, and let crops perish. Make Slavery unprofitable, in this way, if it can be done in no other.

2. To make Slaveholders objects of derision and contempt, by flogging them, whenever they shall be guilty of flogging their slaves.

3. To risk no general insurrection, until we of the North go to your assistance, or you are sure of success without our aid.

4. To cultivate the friendship and confidence of the Slaves; to consult with them as to their rights and interests, and the means of promoting them; to show your interest in their welfare, and your readiness to assist them. Let them know that they have your sympathy, and it will give them courage, self-respect, and ambition, and make men of them; infinitely better men to live by, as neighbors and friends, than the indolent, arrogant, selfish, heartless, domineering robbers and tyrants, who now keep both yourselves and the Slaves in subjection, and look with contempt upon all who live by honest labor.

5. To change your political institutions soon as possible. And in the meantime give never a vote to a Slaveholder; pay no taxes to their government, if you can either resist or evade them; as witnesses and jurors, give no testimony, and no verdicts, in support of any Slaveholding claims; perform no military, patrol, or police service; mob Slaveholding courts, gaols, and sheriffs; do nothing, in short, for sustaining Slavery, but every thing you safely and rightfully can, publicly and privately, for its overthrow.

White rascals of the South! Willing tools of the Slaveholders! You, who drive Slaves to their labor, hunt them with dogs, and flog them for pay, without asking any questions! We have a word specially for you. You are one of the main pillars of the Slave system. You stand ready to do all that vile and inhuman work, which must be done by somebody, but which the more decent Slaveholders themselves will not do. Yet we have heard one good report even of you. It is, that you have no such prejudices against color, nor against liberty, as that you would not as willingly earn money by helping a Slave to Canada, as by catching a fugitive and returning him to his master. If you are thus indifferent as to whom you serve, we advise you henceforth to serve the Slaves, instead of their masters. Turn about, and help the robbed to rob their robbers. The former can afford to pay you better than the latter. Help them to get possession of the property which is rightfully their due, and they can afford to give you liberal commissions. Help them flog individual Slaveholders, and they can afford to pay you ten times as much as you ever received for flogging Slaves. Help them to kidnap the Slaveholders, and they can afford to pay you more than you now get for catching fugitive Slaves. Be true to the Slaves, and we hope they will pay you well for your services. Be false to them, and we hope they will kill you.

Lawyers of the South! You can, if you will, exert a potent influence for good, in this matter. If, in the true spirit of law as a science, you shall see a man in the most crushed of human beings; and, recognizing his right to obtain justice by such means as may be in his power, you shall take the side of the oppressed, in this controversy, and teach them to trample on their tyrants, and vindicate their manhood—if you do this, and then aid in establishing new institutions, based upon liberty, equality, and right, you will have the satisfaction of doing your part towards bringing into life a great, free, and happy people, where now all is crime, tyranny, degradation, and death. If, on the contrary, you shall take the side of the Slaveholders, and continue to be—as, professionally, under Slave institutions, you must forever be—the degraded, pettifogging pimps, hirelings, and tools of a few soulless robbers of their species—denying continually the authority of justice, and the rights of humanity—if you shall do this, we need not attempt to tell you what your true rank will be in the scale of lawyers, statesmen, patriots, or men.

Merchants of the South! We hope you will deliberately consider this matter, and make up your minds whether the Slaves have the right to take the property of their masters in compensation for the injuries they have suffered. If you decide that they have that right, we hope you will act accordingly, and will not hesitate to buy of them cotton, or any other property which they may have taken from their masters; and give them, in exchange, weapons, or any other articles they may need. If you will but do this, you will soon put an end to Slavery.

Non-Slaveholders generally of the South! If it is right for the Slaves to take the property of their masters, to compensate their wrongs, it is right for you to help them. Your numbers, compared with those of the Slaveholders, are as five or six to one. It will be perfectly easy for you, by combining with the Slaves, to put them in possession of the plantations on which they labor, and of all the property upon them. They could afford to pay you well for doing them such a service. They could afford to let you share with them in the division of the property taken. We hope you will adopt this measure. It will not only be right in itself, it will be the noblest act of your lives, provided you do not take too large a share to yourselves; and provided also that you afterwards faithfully protect the Slaves in their liberty, and the property assigned to them.

Finally, we say to all, correspond with us of the North. Let each person who receives or sees one of these sheets, send his letters to the one who sent it—with liberty to publish them in the northern papers. This correspondence, we are confident, will be a more interesting literature than the South has ever furnished; and will enlist the feelings of northern people to such a degree, that we shall be induced to go, in large numbers, to your assistance, whenever you shall need us.

For Further Reading

C. Bradley Thompson, ed., *Antislavery Political Writings, 1833–1860: A Reader* (Armonk, NY: M. E. Sharpe, 2004).

Part Three:

The Century of Statism and Beyond

23

American Reactions to Italian Fascism, 1922

In late October 1922, Benito Mussolini followed a column of 30,000 "Black Shirts" into Rome, where he was greeted with an automobile furnished by the King of Italy himself, Victor Emmanuel III. The king refused a petition to declare martial law tendered by the existing government led by Prime Minister Luigi Facta, tacitly recognizing "Fascisti" rule in the personage of the new movement's leader. In the following months, Mussolini and the Fascists terrorized their enemies throughout Italy and consolidated political power; the movement birthed in Mussolini's private circles of veterans only a few years earlier bloomed into an international curiosity, "Fascism." In the United States, American opinion makers exhibited reactions ranging from shocked disbelief to impartial curiosity and what can properly be described as jubilant and mystical support for a "nation" of people reclaiming their government from leftist radicals and feckless politicians alike. The Kansas City *Star* identified Mussolini's fascism with the by-then familiar concept of "100 percent Americanism," while joining a host of other observers in praising the Fascist's unmatched anti-communism and supposed returns to individualism, the rule of law, and respect for private control of property. Papers like the Fort Worth *Star-Telegram* reacted to Mussolini's rise to power with measured unease rooted in fears of another general European war sparked by Italian conquests along the Adriatic. Even many of those who supported his anti-communism feared Mussolini's militaristic rhetoric. Common to these accounts is the certainty that fascist success depended upon appeals to the Italian middle class and veterans of the First World War. As such, many American citizens positively identified with the fascist movement and found the events in Italy useful for interpreting their own more immediate, local world. In the years of its infancy, fascism provided Americans with either an image of what they could achieve as a united, 100 percent American whole, or a portent of disruption, war, and desolation to come.

"Fascisti Idea to Spread—Exiled Russians Would Adopt Plan in Own Country—One Million Men in Italy are Banded Together to Advance Nationalism and War on Socialists and Communists"[44]

Rome. Aug. 9.—

Founded by an Editor.

Fascism is not three and a half years old, having been founded in Milan by Sig. Mussolini, editor of Popolo d'Italia in April, 1919. The first action took place April 19, immediately after its organization, when only 350 members, all distinguished war veterans, attacked and destroyed the offices of *Avanti*, a Socialist newspaper. Since then with each attack on anti-national forces, thousands of youths have flocked to Mussolini's banner, just as sixty-two years ago they flocked to the army of Garibaldi, who started the war of redemption for Italy in Sicili with one thousand men and by the time he reached Naples had nearly one hundred thousand followers.

The Fascisti's ideals consist of 100 per cent nationalism. They believe in applying patriotism with force; they not only have no patience with 50 per cent Italianism, but they believe also in clubbing "50 per centers." They have no special theory of government, but want the best government that is obtainable. For the time being they are monarchial, but if tomorrow they should see that a republic would be better for Italy they would be republicans. What they want is the greatest well being and the maximum prosperity for the nation, not by class struggle, but by co-operation among the various classes.

Not a Secret Organization.

Fascism is not a secret organization like the Ku Klux Klan, for everybody knows its constitution, and its members wear uniforms which everybody can see. They use illegal means because the constitutional powers do not deal with the situation.

Sig. Mussolini is only 38 years old. Until the end of 1914 he was an ardent Socialist and director of *Avanti*. The world war converted him to nationalism. He founded the Popolo d'Italia, fought bravely in the war, was elected a deputy at the last elections and is now considered the most powerful man in Italy. One million men obey him without ever questioning his orders.

"Discipline—and Work' Aim of Italy's Man of Hour and Fascisti Head"[45]

By the United News

Rome. Aug. 20.—Benito Mussolini, Italy's Man of the hour, is planning for the future, when the Fascisti, which he leads, comes into political power, according to him.

The Fascisti, at a word from Mussolini, have laid down their arms and are organizing as a political party. They came into existence in 1919, since when their chief object has been to combat Socialism and Communism.

Mussolini, who shies from interviewers, answered questions briefly.

"What would be the first step you would take if in power?"

"Discipline."

"And then—"

"Discipline for all. That covers everything for a beginning."

"And your foreign policy?"

"Equilibrium and conciliation."

"What definite steps would you enforce to put Italy on a firm economic basis?"

"Work. Discipline and work. Fascism is great because it is a constructive, creative working force. Italy can be the same."

Italy's three political parties will be Mussolini's, the Popolari and the Socialists.

Of the last named, Mussolini said:

"They have become bourgeois. As soon as they are definitely removed from Bolshevism, need from extreme Fascism will be over."

Referring to the Popolari, or clericals, Mussolini said: "Priests should celebrate mass and not mix in politics."

"Fascisti Leader Backed by 1,000,000 Armed Men is Now Unchallenged Ruler of Italy"[46]

By Paul Scott Mowrer

Paris. Oct. 30.—Benito Mussolini, leader of the Fascisti, seems to be the unchallenged dictator of Italy.

Owing to the severe censorship that has been established in Italy the news from that country must be taken with some allowance but it appears that the black shirts and army helmets of Benito Mussolini's nationalist reactionaries are already supreme. The Fascisti, of whom there are said to be 1,000,000, are mobilized. Barracks and armories have been occupied and arms seized. . . . Already masters of Piedmont and Lombardy fascisti hold Florence, Siena and Pisa. In Rome they occupied the railway stations and public buildings until they were taken over by the army, which is honeycombed with fascism.

Made Feeble Protest.

Before disappearing the Facta government made a faint show of resistance and ordered up a poster accusing the Fascisti of sedition and promising to preserve order at all costs. It also desired to proclaim martial law but the King refused to sign the decree. It is therefore Benito Mussolini who has proclaimed and is executing martial law. All the bourses have been closed and Parliament, which was to have reconvened Nov. 7, will probably be dissolved.

Italian Free Masonry has issued a proclamation recognizing the Fascisti movement and the Pope, through the bishop, has appealed for peace and union. The Fascisti have proclaimed loyalty to the King, who is apparently well disposed toward the Fascisti.

The Fascisti program is frankly nationalist and perhaps even reactionary. The Fascisti proclamation announces that "military, political and administrative powers are transferred to a committee of action of four members with dictatorial positions."

The rights of workers of all categories will be respected, according to the proclamation, which adds that the new regime will be "generous toward nonmilitant adversaries but inexorable toward others." The aim of the movement is declared to be the "safety and grandeur of Italy."

The chief points of the interior program appear to be the exaltation of the army and a strong patriotic union of all Italy and especially of the north and south. Fascism originally sprang from the disgust of the moderate conservative elements at the government's failure to uphold the laws when the workmen seized the factories two years ago and at the apparent powerlessness of the government to repress the communist violence which followed.

Reds Were Fought.

Groups of Fascisti were first formed to combat the reds with their own weapons—assault and riot. They were so successful that communism seems to be effectively rowed in Italy. The army and navy are sympathetic; the organizations of war veterans are on their side and they also claim to have enrolled 800,000 workmen from the labor unions. Their professed desire is to put an end to the undignified feebleness and vaccilation which have marked the Italy policy, not only internal but especially external, ever since the armistice. They promise to insure respect for Italians and Italian interests all over the world. . . . They will insist on greater recognition of Italy's claims in the Mediterranean and especially in the Adriatic. They demand that Jugo Slavia [Yugoslavia] shall free Montenegro and they talk of annexing Dalmatia.

This program, unless modified, seems somewhat ominous for peace with Italy's neighbors.

"Men and Affairs"[47]

Washington, as well as the rest of the United States, has been struggling the past few days to get itself straight on Fascism, the Fascisti and the new Fascist government in Italy. It is not likely, however, that the Fascisti will ever have the vogue in this country that the Bolsheviki had. Americans soon got the idea that the Bolsheviki was somebody against the government, and against everything, so America adopted the word and it is now an indelible part of the English language. It is not so easy to classify or place the Fascisti and Fascist does not roll off the tongue like Bolshevik.

Mussolini, the Fascist premier of Italy, says that Fascism is a purely Italian question that as bolshevism is a purely Russian matter. It is possibly true that bolshevism is a purely Russian matter, but lots of American people have been officially classed by their friends or enemies as Bolsheviks and Bolsheviks they will be until they die.

Fascism seems a bit more intricate. It means, as far as can be judged from this distance, Italy for the Italians. The Fascisti in this country call it "America first." When it was said of Mr. Wilson that he kept us out of the war, it was a fascist sentiment that said it. When it is said of Mr. Harding that he kept us out of the League of Nations, it is again the fascist sentiment that speaks.

There are plenty of the Fascisti in the United States, it seems, but they have always gone under the proud boast of "100 percent Americans." The English language appears to grow more and more inelastic. It is pitiful to have to say such awkward compound words as pro-leaguer and anti-leaguer, when in most of the foreign languages an expressive single word would suffice. Of course we have had in this country a faction known as the Wilsonites, but even that is not a pretty word like Fascisti or Bolsheviki.

Some of Premier Mussolini's political opponents recently accused him of flirting with the Germans and possibly with Russians with the idea of forming an international Fascisti, or a sort of reactionary international movement. He denounces this as absurd, the Fascisti are for Italy first, last and all the time, and the rest of the world can go hang. The Democrats say it was the American Fascisti won the election in 1920.

"Revolt Against Socialism"[48]

Both the accession to power of the fascisti in Italy and the defeat of the labor party in the British municipal elections point the same way—revolt against socialism and return to individualism as the way to bring cost of government within revenue and to reduce it further in order to reduce taxes. . . .

National ownership of railroads, telegraphs and telephones, municipal ownership of public utilities and government monopolies of such commodities as tobacco are common in Europe . . . Fascism began in Italy as a revolt against socialism, and Mussolini evidently intends to go the whole way in restoring the public services and monopolies to private enterprise. That will relieve the government of enormous losses and will remove a horde of people from the public payroll. If the experience of France is an indication, all public services are greatly over-manned . . . He evidently sees that hard work and economy from the head of the government down to the humblest workman must be combined with that efficiency that is possible only for private enterprise in order that Italy may pay its way, reduce its debts and regain prosperity.

The deplorable fact about this return to economic sanity is that it is undertaken by a distinctly militarist party. If the fascisti should attempt to make good the claim to all the territory that was once Italian, they will embark their country in wars that will destroy all the fruits of their economic reforms.

"Middle Class Takes Fascism to Gain Rights—Revolt in Italy Projected by Underpaid 'White Collar' Folk, Says Writer"[49]

By J. W. T. Mason. (Written for the United Press)

The Fascisti success in Italy marks Europe's turning toward the middle classes. If the young and untried men Premier Mussolini has taken into his cabinet show an ability to handle the technical machinery of government, there will be a full recovery of the economic ground lost by the middle classes during the war.

As Bolshevism was an attack against all classes by the Russian workingmen, so the Fascisti movement is an attack against both the idle rich and overpaid laboring classes by the white collar men.

Alliance Formed.

Mussolini has formed an alliance with various workingmen groups. But, this is for the purpose of using them against the capitalists who crush the middle classes. Mussolini supports the policy of syndicalism. That is to say, he wants the workingmen to have a voice in the management of the factories. By setting workingmen and capitalists thus at odds, Mussolini expects the middle classes to hold the balance of power and acquire more for themselves.

The gravest problem Europe has had to face since the war has been the plight of the white collar classes. The workingmen of Europe have never before had such high wages, measured either by a money standard or by purchasing power. Similarly, the capitalists reaped enormous profits when war prices reigned.

Middle Class Loses.

But, the middle classes have lost ground. Their wages have not kept pace with the increased cost of living. The problem is especially acute in Italy, where middle class technical education has far outrun working class education. Italy in consequence has too many doctors, lawyers and other professional men for the number of inhabitants who have been educated to the point of using their services.

This is the fundamental reason why the middle class revolt against postwar conditions has started in Italy rather than in any other country. There is that additional burden for the middle class Italians to bear. If Mussolini can solve his own middle class problem, therefore, other countries will be incited to taking action themselves, since their own difficulties are not so complicated.

Only Hope of Recovery.

Without a recovery of the European middle classes, it is hopeless to expect the world ever to get to right. The cultural responsibilities of the middle classes will not be assumed by the other classes. The white collar men alone among the Europeans are willing to make sacrifices for social progress as distinct from economic progress.

But, under the financial burdens imposed on them by the war, they have been unable to do much more than keep alive. They are wearing the same old clothes, concealing their poverty as best they can.

They are now reaching the end of their patience. The Fascisti movement represents to them the possibility of successful self-assertion. For that reason, Italy has suddenly become the middle class leader for all Europe.

"The Cure for Bolshevism"[50]

Five years ago—and less—Europe meditated in anguished accents the need of a defensive front against the advance of bolshevism. Today, communism, through its third international, searches fanatically for means to combat the tide of fascism. This is as it should be. The pendulum swings.

So long as communism is only the goal of a fraction of the world's population it was inevitable that it should flow back to its mean limits. So long as fascism is only the goal of a part of the population, that, too, in time, must flow back to its boundaries. Fascism came into existence as a result of communism, the disease gave birth to the remedy.

Fascism is not far removed from normalcy; it is the existing order reduced to the terms of the small merchant and wage-earner who does not believe in millenniums but clings pathetically to the practical need of three meals a day. Bolshevism in Italy brought starvation and chaos, fascism drove out communism, which is in hiding, and reasserts popular authority. There is only one weapon bolshevism can use to repel advances against it and recapture its superficial influence, and that is to abandon communism. The majority, where not held in subjection as in Russia, inevitably asserts its desires.

Communism, on the face of the facts, is not one of them.

"Letter Tells of Conditions Now in Italy"[51]

An interesting letter has been received from Mrs. Gerda Hellberg Castelli of Rome . . . written of the conditions and especially the "Fascisti" in Italy, to Mrs. R. D. Campbell of this city. Mrs. Castelli and Captain Castelli will be remembered as residents here some years ago.

The letter follows:

Favor Organization.

"We, both my husband and I, are great 'Fascisti' and bless Mussolini who swept away the clique of rotten and selfish and incompetent politicians! I do not marvel if the countries abroad do not understand all what this means and have to judge 'Fascisti,' but one who has lived here for long and knows the Italians, feels that such a marvelous movement could not grow up so quick in any other country but Italy. It has been grand to witness, and I was sorry my husband was away at a congress in Bologna just the days of the 'revolution!' Because such it was, but one where not a workman went on strike, not a peasant left off work; it was done before they had time to think and move. Both peasant and workman of the saner type were glad for and desired the change, as it was felt everywhere Italy had no government at all! And chaos cannot last for long. And really it is quite a spiritual movement as well as patriotic, and idealistic, and we needed that badly after all these years of demagogism and party Socialism, and the world everywhere needs a bit of 'Fascism,' it seems to me.

"Mussolini is marvelous, so far at least; he speaks in a manner quite new (and more honest) to diplomacy and commands respect just for his fearless outspokenness. It is quite a pleasure to read the papers, now. And to see some sixty thousand young, fine and handsome men between eighteen and thirty years go in cortege in the Corso the 31st of October was a sight not to be forgotten. Half a million young men dead in the war, and yet so many fine ones left! Really, this country is inexhaustible!

Wants G. F. News.

"I am looking forward to seeing Ruth Carothers here and hear news about all in Grand Forks which we keep in such a good memory! I wonder if we ever shall come over to the United States again. I would like it very much, I assure you. . . .

"And here in Rome the sun shines always this autumn; such lovely weather we are having.

"Now I must stop, with best wishes for a happy Christmas and good New Year to Dr. Campbell and yourself from us both.

"Always yours sincerely,

—"Gerda Hellberg Castelli."

24

Smedley Butler and the "Business Plot" (1934)

Did a vast, powerful, and influential clique of businessmen and politicians briefly plan (and perhaps attempt to execute) a coup against President Roosevelt in 1934, which would have relegated the president to a figurehead in a new fascist, military government? Libertarian hero and icon of military history General Smedley D. Butler said as much under oath in front of the United States Congress. The centerpieces of the plot were Butler's popularity among the military and the policy of a return to sound money. Butler was approached by the conspirators as early as 1933 and he revealed the scheme publicly, though Congress did not begin investigating the claims until November 20, 1934. The McCormack-Dickstein Committee investigated the alleged plot for three months and published its findings, though newspapers began dismissing Butler's claims immediately after his testimony was given. John L. Spivak, a communist reporter for the magazine *New Masses*, observed and recorded the proceedings of the committee investigation, including key portions of testimony redacted from the Congress' official report (portions dismissed by the committee as hearsay). The redacted testimony transcribed by Spivak appears in **_bolded italics_** in the reproduction below.

In his testimony before Congress, Butler states that he was repeatedly visited by a somewhat shady cast of characters associated with the American Legion and a series of Wall Street and New York banking and bond trading firms. In July 1933, the first of these men suggested that Butler attend a Legion convention to deliver a prepared speech on the importance of returning to the gold standard and supporting a bonus for veterans of the Great War. Butler supported the soldiers' bonus, but he had no desire to attend the convention and become involved in backroom politicking. The clique repeatedly approached Butler before the convention and repeatedly attempted to bribe him with many thousands of dollars, and repeatedly Butler refused. Eventually, the men resolved to appeal to his sense of reason and revealed more of their plan. Butler was supposed to raise and lead a massive contingent of veterans and soldiers to practically force President Roosevelt to appoint him to the Cabinet as the newly minted "Secretary for General Affairs," leaving Butler to rule the country while the president remained a figurehead. The conspirators drew upon extensive travels from Germany and Italy to Stalin's Soviet Union and concluded that a bit of fascism was both necessary and proper in the United States as well. Should Butler continue to refuse, the plot's backers would move instead to other candidates, including General Douglas MacArthur. . . .

Horrified, Butler exposed the conspiracy and testified against the plotters before Congress. The McCormack-Dickstein Committee pursued Butler's claims, questioned several of the men implicated in the plot, and concluded that many key questions remained unanswered. It would appear that the plot never materialized and the conspirators either remained abroad and beyond the reach of the Committee, outright denied Butler's claims before the Committee, or simply claimed ignorance and the inability to account for large sums of money. Congress, much more concerned with chasing communists than fascists, dropped the issue and Butler's testimony remains the only significant evidence that such a conspiracy ever existed.[52]

Did the conspiracy really exist? Was it the passing pipe dream of a few crackpots and investment bankers, as contemporaries seemed to suspect? Was it an elaborate double-bluff, through which the Roosevelt administration tarred supporters of sound money as "gold-bugs" and cranks? Or was it all the fabrication of a Smedley Butler now past his prime and eager for fresh publicity?

Barring the appearance of fresh and creditable evidence, we should most certainly withhold final judgment—but, my! It is fun to speculate. And after all, so much of history is simply well-documented conspiracy.

Testimony of Maj. Gen. S. D. Butler (Retired), *Excerpts*[53]

CHAIRMAN. Without my asking you any further questions, will you just go ahead and tell in your own way all that you know about an attempted Fascist movement in this country?

BUTLER. May I preface my remarks by saying, sir, that I have one interest in all of this, and that is to try to do my best to see that a democracy is maintained in this country.

CHAIRMAN. Nobody who has either read about or known about General Butler would have anything but that understanding.

General BUTLER. It is nice of you to say that, sir.

But that is my only interest.

I think I had probably better go back and give you the background. This has been going on for a year and a half. Along—I think it must have been about the 1st of July 1933, two men came to see me.

One said his name was Bill Doyle, who was then the department commander of the Legion in Massachusetts. The other said his name was Jerry MacGuire . . . He had been State commander the year before of the department of Connecticut and was then living in Connecticut. Doyle was living in Massachusetts.

They were very desirous of unseating the royal family in control of the American Legion, at the convention to be held in Chicago, and very anxious to have me take part in it. They said that they were not in sympathy with the . . . present administration's treatment of the soldiers.

They presented to me rather a confused picture, and I could not make up my mind exactly what they wanted me to do or what their objective was, but it had something to do with weakening the influence of the administration with the soldiers.

They asked me to go to the convention, and I said I did not want to go—that I had not been invited and did not care anything about going.

Then MacGuire said that . . . the distinguished-guest committee of the American Legion . . . at MacGuire's suggestion, put
my name down to be invited . . ., *that Johnson had then taken this
list . . . to the White House for approval; that Louis Howe, one of
the secretaries to the President, had crossed my name off and said
that I was not to be invited—that the President would not have it.*
I thought I smelled a rat, right away—that they were trying to get
me mad—to get my goat. I said nothing. . . . It looked to me as if
they were trying to embarrass the administration in some way. . . .
So many queer people come to my house all the time and I like to
feel them all out.

Finally they said, "Now, we have arranged a way for you to
come to this convention."

I said, "How is that, without being invited?"

They said, "Well, you are to come as a delegate from Hawaii."

I said. "I do not live in Hawaii."

"Well, it does not make any difference. There is to be no delegate from one of the American Legion posts there in Honolulu,
and we have arranged to have you appointed by cable, by radio, to
represent them at the convention. You will be a delegate."

I said "No; I will not do this."

The substance of the second talk was this, that they had given up
this delegate idea, and I was to get two or three hundred legion-
naires from around that part of the country and bring them on a
special train to Chicago with me; that they would sit around in
the audience, be planted here and there, and I was to be nothing
but an ordinary legionnaire, going to my own convention as an
onlooker; not as a participant at all. I was to appear in the gallery.

These planted fellows were to begin to cheer and start a stampede and yell for a speech. Then I was to go to the platform and make a speech. I said, "Make a speech about what?"

"Oh," they said, "we have one here. . . ."

I said, "Listen. These friends of mine that I know around here, even if they wanted to go, could not afford to go. It would cost them a hundred to a hundred and fifty dollars to go out there and stay for 5 days and come back."

They said, "Well, we will pay that."

It was either then or the next time, or one of the times, they hauled out a bank-deposit book and showed me, I think it was $42,000 in deposits on that occasion, and on another occasion it was $64,000.

[I said] "Where did you get all this money? It cannot be yours."

He said that it was given to him by nine men, that the biggest contributor had given $9,000 and that the donations ran all the way from $2,500 to $9,000.

I said, "What is the object?"

He said the object was to take care of the rank and file of the soldiers, to get them their bonus and get them properly cared for.

Well, I knew that people who had $9,000 to give away were not in favor of the bonus. That looked fishy right away.

He gave me the names of two men; Colonel Murphy, Grayson M.-P. Murphy, for whom he worked, was one. He said, "I work for him. I am in his office"

I said, "What has Murphy got to do with this?"

"Well," he said "he is the man who underwrote the formation of the American Legion for $125,000. He underwrote it, paid for the field work of organizing it, and had not gotten all of it back yet."

"That is the reason he makes the kings, is it? He has still got a club over their heads."

"He is on our side, though. He wants to see the soldiers cared for."

"Is he responsible, too, for making the Legion a strike breaking outfit?"

"No, no. He does not control anything in the Legion now."

I said: "You know very well that it is nothing but a strike breaking outfit used by capital for that purpose and that is, the reason they have all those big club-houses and that is the reasons I pulled out from it. They have been using these dumb soldiers to break strikes."

He said: "Murphy hasn't anything to do with that. He is a very fine fellow."

I said, "I do not doubt that, but there is some reason for him putting $125,000 into this. . . ."

The next time I saw him was about the 1st of September, in a hotel in Newark.

I said, "You people are bluffing. You have not got any money." Whereupon he took out a big wallet; out of his hip pocket, and a great, big mass of thousand dollar bills and threw them out on the bed.

I said, "Don't you try to give me any thousand dollar bill. Remember, I was a cop once. Every one of the numbers on these bills has been taken. I know you people and what you are trying to do. You are just trying to get me by the neck. If I try to cash one of those thousand dollar bills, you would have me by the neck."

"Oh," he said, "we can change them into smaller denominations."

I said, "I know one thing. Somebody is using you. You are a wounded man. You are a bluejacket. You have got a silver plate in your head. I looked you up. You were wounded. You are being used by somebody, and I want to know the fellows who are using you."

He said, "I will send Mr. Clark. . . ."

I thought no more about it until the end of the week, when Clark called up and asked if he might spend Sunday with me. I said, "Yes."

He said, "You have got the speech?" I said, "Yes . . . They wrote a hell of a good speech, too." He laughed and said, "That speech cost a lot of money." *I got the impression that the speech had been written by John W. Davis—one or the other of them told me that.*

I said, "The speech has nothing to do with what I am going to Chicago for. The speech urges the convention to adopt the resolution that the United States shall return to the gold standard." MacGuire had said, "We want to see the soldiers' bonus paid in gold. We do not want the soldier to have rubber money or paper money. We want the gold. That is the reason for this speech."

"Yes" I said, "but it looks as if it were a big-business speech. There is something funny about that speech, Mr. Clark."

The conversations were almost the same with both of them.

Clark said, "You understand just how we are fixed. I have got $30,000,000. I do not want to lose it. I am willing to spend half of the $30,000,000 to save the other half."

"Well," I said, "I tell you very frankly, Mr. Clark, I have got one interest and that is the maintenance of a democracy. . . . What the hell does a soldier know about the gold standard? You are just working them, using them, just as they have been used right along."

He said, "Why do you want to be so stubborn? Why do you want to be different from other people? We can take care of you. You have got a mortgage on this house. . . . That can all be taken care of. It is perfectly legal, perfectly proper. . . ."

Finally I said, "You are trying to bribe me in my own house. You are very polite about it and I can hardly call it that, but it looks kind of funny to me, making that kind of proposition. You come out into the hall, I want to show you something."

We went out there. I have all the flags and banners and medals of honor. They have been given me by the Chinese and the Nicaraguans and the Haitians—by the poor people. I said to him, "You are trying to buy me away from my own kind. When you have made up your mind that I will not go with you, then you come on and tell me."

In a few minutes he came back to the back office and said, "Can I use your telephone?" "Yes." He called up Chicago . . . and he said to MacGuire, "General Butler is not coming to the convention. He has given me his reasons and they are excellent ones, and I apologize to him for my connection with it. I am not coming either. You can put this thing across. You have got $45,000. You can send those telegrams. You will have to do it in that way. The general is not coming. I can see why. I am going to Canada to rest. If you want me, you know where you can find me. You have got enough money to go through with it."

The convention came off and the gold standard was endorsed by the convention.

Then MacGuire stopped to see me on his way back from the convention . . . and told me that they had been successful in putting over their move.

I said, "Yes, but you did not endorse the soldiers' bonus."

He said, "Well, we have got to get sound currency before it is worth while to endorse a bonus."

I think there was one other visit to the house because he . . . proposed that I go to Boston to a soldiers' dinner to be given *by Governor Ely for the soldiers, and that I was to go with Al Smith*. He said, "We will have a private car for you on the end of the train *and have your picture taken with Governor Smith*. You will make a speech at this dinner and it will be worth a thousand dollars to you."

I said, "I do not want to have my picture taken with Governor Smith. I do not like him. . . . No, there is something wrong in this. There is no connection that I have with Al Smith that we should be riding along together to a soldiers' dinner. He is not for the soldiers either. . . ."

"Well" he said, "Al Smith is getting ready to assault the Administration in his magazine. It will appear in a month or so. He is going to take a shot at the money question. He has definitely broken with the President."

So I said at this time, "So I am going to be dragged in as a sort of publicity agent for Al Smith to get him to sell magazines by having our picture taken on the rear platform of a private car, is that the idea?"

"Well, you are to sit next to each other at dinner and you are both going to make speeches . . . and they will both be very much alike."

I said, "I am not going. You just cross that out. . . ."

He said, "I want to go around with you, around the country. I want to go around and talk to the soldiers in the background and see if we cannot get them to join a great big super organization to maintain the democracy. . . ."

I said, "If fiddling with this form of government is [your] business, I am out of it . . ."

"Oh." he said, "I would not disturb this form of government." I said, "You have got some reason for getting at these soldiers other than to maintain a democracy."

Then along in the latter part of August of this year . . . he called me on the telephone one day and said that he wanted to know if I could meet him in Philadelphia that afternoon. . . .

He said "The time has come now to get the soldiers together."

"Yes," I said, "I think so, too." He said. "I went abroad to study the part that the veteran plays in the various set-ups of the governments. . . . I went to Italy for 2 or 3 months and studied the position that the veterans of Italy occupy in the Fascist set-up of government, and I discovered that they are the background of Mussolini. They keep them on the pay rolls in various ways and keep them contented and happy; and they are his real backbone, the force on which he may depend, in case of trouble, to sustain him. But that set-up would not suit us at all. The soldiers of America would not like that. I then went to Germany to see what Hitler was doing, and his whole strength lies in organizations of soldiers, too. But that would not do. I looked into the Russian business. I found that the use of the soldiers over there would never appeal to our men. Then I went to France, and I found just exactly the organization we are going to have. It is an organization of supersoldiers." He gave me the French name for it. . . . It is a superorganization of members of all the other soldiers' organizations of France composed of . . . about 500,000, and that each one was a leader of 10 others, so that it gave them 5,000,000 votes. And he said, "Now, that is our idea here in America—to get up an organization of that kind."

I said, "What do you want to do with it when you get it up?"

"Well," he said, "we want to support the President."

I said, "Since when did you become a supporter of the President? The last time I talked to you you were against him."

He said. "Well, he is going to go along with us now."

"Is he?" . . .

He said. "Don't you understand the set-up has got to be changed a bit? . . . He has got to have more money. There is not any more money to give him. Eighty percent of the money now is in Government bonds, and he cannot keep this racket up much longer. . . . He has either got to get more money out of us or . . . change the method of financing the Government, and we are going to see to it that he does not change that method."

I said, "The idea of this great group of soldiers, then, is to sort of frighten him, is it?"

"No, no, no; not to frighten him. . . . Now, did it ever occur to you that the President is overworked? We might have an Assistant President, somebody to take the blame; and if things do not work out, he can drop him. . . . You know the American people will swallow that. We have got the newspaper. We will start a campaign that the President's health is failing. Everybody can tell that by looking at him, and the dumb American people will fall for it in a second. . . . Now about this superorganization—would you be interested in heading it?"

I said, "I am interested in it, but . . . you know, Jerry . . . my one hobby is maintaining a democracy. If you got these 500,000 soldiers advocating anything smelling of Fascism, 1 am going to get 500,000 more and lick the hell out of you, and we will have a real war right at home. You know that."

"Oh, no. We do not want that. We want to ease up on the President."

"Yes; and then you will put somebody in there you can run. . . . The President will go around and christen babies and dedicate bridges, and kiss children. Mr. Roosevelt will never agree to that himself."

"Oh, yes; he will. He will agree to that. . . . We have got $3,000,000 to start with, on the line, and we can get $300,000,000, if we need it. . . ."

He said, "I might as well tell you that our group is for you, for the head of this organization. Morgan and Hodges are against you. The Morgan interests say that you cannot be trusted, that you will be too radical. . . . *They are for Douglas MacArthur as the head of it. Douglas MacArthur's term expires in November, and if he is not reappointed it is to be presumed that he will be disappointed and sore and they are for getting him to head it. . . . They want either MacArthur or MacNider.* They do not want you. But our group tells them that you are the only fellow in America who can get the soldiers together. They say, 'Yes, but he will get them together and go in the wrong way.' . . ."

He said, "MacNider won't do either. He will not get the soldiers to follow him, because he has been opposed to the bonus. . . ."

I noticed that MacNider turned around for the bonus, and that there is a row over the reappointment of MacArthur. . . .

Now there is one point that I have forgotten which I think is the most important of all. I said, "What are you going to call this organization?" . . .

He did not give me the name of it, but he said that it would all be made public; a society to maintain the Constitution, and so forth, *and in about two weeks the American Liberty League appeared, which was just about what he described it to be.* . . .

They had a lot of talk this time about maintaining the Constitution. I said, "I do not see that the Constitution is in any danger," and I ask him again, "Why are you in this thing?" He said, "I am a business man. I have got a wife and children."

In other words, he had had a nice trip to Europe with his family, for 9 months, and he said that that cost plenty, too. . . .

CHAIRMAN. We thank you, General Butler, for coming here this morning.

INVESTIGATION OF UN-AMERICAN ACTIVITIES

[For release for morning papers, Nov. 20, 1934] . . .

This committee has had no evidence before it that would in the slightest degree warrant calling before it such men as John W. Davis, Gen. Hugh Johnson, General Harbord, Thomas W. Lamont, Admiral Sims, or Hanford MacNider.

The committee will not take cognizance of names brought into the testimony which constitute mere hearsay.

This committee is not concerned with premature newspaper accounts especially when given and published prior to the taking of the testimony.

As the result of information which has been in possession of this committee for some time, it was decided to hear the story of Maj. Gen. Smedley D. Butler and such others as might have knowledge germane to the issue.

In the course of his sworn testimony, General Butler testified that . . . one Gerald C. MacGuire, of New York, and William Doyle, of Boston, Mass, . . . suggested to him that he become a candidate for national commander of the American Legion at its convention at Chicago to be held in October 1933 and further stated that he told him that he was not interested and realized that he could not be elected commander. . . .

MacGuire returned on several other occasions and suggested to him that he go to the Legion convention at Chicago and make a speech urging a resolution . . . that the United States return to the gold standard. . . .

Butler further testified that on this occasion MacGuire showed him a bank book, the pages of which were flipped, indicating deposits of approximately $42,000. . . .

Butler then testified that he saw MacGuire again and that MacGuire appeared in his hotel room in Newark during the reunion of the Twenty-ninth Division in September 1933 and while in Butler's room took a wallet from his pocket, threw a bunch of $1,000 bills on the bed and that when Butler asked him, "How much money have you got there?" MacGuire is alleged to have replied, "$18,000," and on further questioning is alleged to have told Butler that he got the money from contributions the night before and has not had an opportunity to deposit them and wanted to give them to Butler for his help. . . .

Before MacGuire left Newark, according to Butler, he told the general that they were anxious "to see the soldiers' bonus paid in gold. We don't want the soldier to have rubber money."

Butler testified that during that week he had a telephone call from Clark and that he and his wife met Clark at the railroad station in Philadelphia the following Sunday. . . .

The American Legion convention in Chicago passed the resolution endorsing the gold standard; and according to Butler, after the convention MacGuire stopped by to see him and suggested that Butler go to Boston to attend a veterans' dinner again for the purpose of advocating the gold standard, which the general says he refused to do. . . .

MacGuire, according to Butler . . . had gone to Germany to see what Hitler was doing, and found that that situation would not do in the United States either, and that he had been in France, where he found just exactly the organization that we ought to have in this country and called it an organization of "super-soldiers", but that Butler did not remember the French name for that organization.

Butler further testified that MacGuire at that time told him that this French super organization was composed of about 500,000 men, and that each one of them was the leader of 10 others, and that that was the kind of an organization that we should have in the United States. . . .

I said, "The idea of this great group of soldiers, then, is to sort of frighten him [Roosevelt], is it?" "No, no, no; not to frighten him. This is to sustain him when others assault him." *He said, "You know, the President is weak. He will come right along with us. He was born in this class. He was raised in this class, and he will*

come back. He will run true to form. In the end he will come around.
But we have got to be prepared to sustain him when he does. . . ."

Butler claims that MacGuire then told him that the President was overworked, that he needed an assistant to take over the many heavy duties, and that such a position would be created and would probably be called "a secretary of general affairs", and that when all that was accomplished the President of the United States would be like the President of Finance. . . .

Butler testified that in the conversation MacGuire suggested that if necessary the Vice President and Secretary of State would resign and that this secretary of general affairs would become the Secretary of State and follow through to the Presidential succession.

Butler further stated that he discussed this entire matter with his confidant, Paul French, and that it was agreed between them that French should see MacGuire in New York.

Paul Comley French, a reporter for the *Philadelphia Record* and the *New York Evening Post*, followed the general on the witness stand, testified that General Butler had spoken to him about this matter, and that they agreed that French should go to New York to get the story.

French testified that he came to New York, September 13, 1934, and went to the offices of Grayson M.-P. Murphy & Co. on the twelfth floor of 52 Broadway and that MacGuire received him shortly after 1 o'clock in the afternoon and that they conducted their entire conversation in a small private office. . . .

French testified that MacGuire stated, "We need a fascist government in this country to save the Nation from the Communists who want to tear it down and wreck all that we have built in America. The only men who have patriotism to do it are the soldiers and Smedley Butler is the ideal leader. He could organize one million men over night."

Continuing, French stated that during the conversation MacGuire told him about his trip to Europe and of the studies that he had made of the Fascist, Nazi, and French movements and the parts that the veterans had played in them.

French further testified that MacGuire considered the movement entirely and tremendously patriotic and that any number of people with big names would be willing to help finance it. French stated that during the course of the conversation, MacGuire continually discussed "the need of a man on a white horse" and quoted MacGuire as having said "We might go along with Roosevelt" and then do with him "what Mussolini did with the King of Italy."

MacGuire, according to French, expressed the belief that half of the American Legion and the Veterans of Foreign Wars would follow General Butler if he would announce the plan that MacGuire had in mind. . . .

Gerald C. MacGuire was called to the stand late in the afternoon of Tuesday, November 20 and . . .

MacGuire in brief, claimed that the object of his visit was to induce Butler to run for commander of the American Legion and that he had also talked to General Butler about forming a committee for a sound dollar, and a sound currency.

MacGuire denied that he had in any way thought of unseating the royal family of the American Legion, but that he felt that if Butler could become a delegate at the Chicago convention, he might become commander.

MacGuire admitted that they did discuss the possibility of Butler becoming a delegate from Hawaii.

MacGuire claimed that he wanted to interest Butler in this Committee for a Sound Dollar, because, being a public man, he could go out and speak for the movement and that they wanted him to have an opportunity to make a little money.

MacGuire denied that he had at any time ever given Butler a prepared speech and claimed that he, MacGuire, was always for President Roosevelt.

At this point, MacGuire stated that he had met Butler on eight or nine different occasions, but that he had never talked to the general about taking 200 or 300 men to the Legion convention in Chicago, nor that he had ever shown Butler a bank book or that he had ever told Butler that he had large sums of money at his command.

MacGuire testified that he had been in Newark on the occasion of the reunion of the Twenty-ninth Division. That it was a Sunday and that all he had done was to hear Butler's speech and that he, MacGuire, then left.

To a question by chairman of the committee, MacGuire answered, "I never had any money and he (Butler) never asked me if I had any."

MacGuire acknowledged that he had mentioned the name of Robert Sterling Clark to Butler in connection with the Committee for a Sound Dollar and that he had told Butler that Clark would back up such a committee with money. . . .

MacGuire had a hazy recollection that Clark had talked to Butler, but denied emphatically that Clark had called him up while MacGuire was at the convention in Chicago, and that he did not make arrangements for Clark to meet Butler and did not know how the meeting was brought about. . . .

MacGuire denied telling Butler anything about any governmental set-ups in Europe, although he stated that he had told Butler that in his opinion, "Hitler would not last another year in Germany and that Mussolini was on the skids."

MacGuire again emphatically denied that he had said anything about the European veterans. Then MacGuire stated that Paul French had come to him and outlined a lot of things that Butler was trying to do with different veteran outfits in the country, and that he told French that Butler should not be mixed up with that kind of stuff. . . .

While being questioned by both Congressman McCormack and Dickstein, MacGuire suddenly remembered that Clark had given him some money in connection with some bond transactions and fixed the sum at $25,000, which he stated he placed on deposit with the Manufacturers Trust Co., in a "special account", and further stated that Clark had paid his expenses in going around the country looking over various municipalities in connection with the purchase of their bonds.

MacGuire testified that this $25,000 was to go back to Mr. Clark, and that he had repaid $20,000 of it to Mr. Albert G. Christmas and that Christmas again gave him another check for $20,000 which he redeposited in the Manufacturers Trust Co. in the special account.

It should be noted here that Albert G. Christmas, attorney, 160 Broadway, represents Mr. Clark.

MacGuire swore that this money was for the purpose of buying securities and that he had used the money to purchase letters of credit for that purpose. . . .

Continuing under oath MacGuire said that the $1,125 was drawn for expenses and that the $6,000 was tied up with other amounts, but that the cash was paid back to Christmas.

However, MacGuire testified he had no receipt from Christmas or anything else to show it. MacGuire admitted that he had bought and sold bonds to the value of approximately 9 million dollars for Clark, through the Murphy firm, but that this was the only time he had ever been handed any cash personally with which to buy them. . . .

He further claimed that he converted all of these letters of credit into cash at the First National Bank of Chicago and that he put the money into a safe deposit box in Chicago and that after the convention was over, he brought all of the cash back to Mr. Christmas, less expenses, because he had not purchased any bonds.

MacGuire could not explain why he had paid a premium of one-half of 1 percent, amounting to $150, on $30,300 worth of letters of credit only to cash them without having any purchases in mind and then bringing the currency back to New York.

Later in the questioning MacGuire admitted that he received $10,000 in currency from Christmas, while MacGuire, Christmas, and Clark were having luncheon at the Bankers Club, which had nothing whatever to do with these other funds.

MacGuire stated under oath, that he took this $10,000 and placed it in his safety deposit box at the Seaman's Savings Bank;

that it is no longer there; that he does not know when he took it out, nor does he remember what he did with it.

Again under questioning, MacGuire did not have any receipts for any of the sums of cash which he claims he repaid to Christmas as agent for Clark, in one case a sum of about $30,000. Note from the committee. Deposits in the Manufacturers Trust Co. special account which totaled $20,000 and the $10,000 which he admits he received in cash at the Bankers Club, are not part of the $31,000 which was used by the committee on sound money. . . .

Resuming his testimony on Friday, November 23, MacGuire failed to produce a book to which he had previously referred, in which he stated he had entered the moneys which he handled in connection with his trip to Chicago. . . .

The congressional committee then went into the carbons of reports presented by MacGuire which he had written while he was in Europe. Some were addressed merely "Gentlemen", others to Mr. Clark and one to Mr. Christmas. Mr. MacGuire had previously testified he had been sent to Europe by Mr. Clark to study economic conditions.

In his letter of April 6, 1934, which is headed "My dear sir", MacGuire writes as follows:

"There is no question but that another severe crisis is imminent. There have been various pieces of information given me to the effect that the Communists have been arming and are scattered in the outlying districts of Paris. However, this does not mean, to my mind, that there will be anything such as occurred in Vienna. If anything, it appears to me that the Communists may be used as a goat by the military, and that if this group should by any chance start demonstrations against the government, it may serve to call forth a "coup d'etat", which, it might be said, would be the use of the military.

"I had a very interesting talk last evening with a man who is quite well up on affairs here and he seems to be of the opinion that the Croix de Feu will be very patriotic during this crisis and will take the cuts or be the moving spirit in the veterans to accept the cuts. Therefore they will, in all probability, be in opposition to the Socialists and functionaries. The general spirit among the functionaries seems to be that the correct way to regain recovery is to spend more money and increase wages, rather than to put more people out of work and cut salaries."

In letter on March 6, 1934, addressed merely to "Gentlemen" MacGuire writes:

"The Croix de Feu is getting a great number of new recruits, and recently attended a meeting of this organization and was quite impressed with the type of men belonging. These fellows are interested only in the salvation of France, and I feel sure that the country could not be in better hands, because they are not politicians; they are a cross section of the best people of the country from all walks of life, people who gave their "all" between 1914 and 1918 that France might be safe, and I feel sure that if a crucial test ever comes to the Republic that those men will be the bulwark upon which France will be saved.

"There may be more uprisings, there may be more difficulties, but as is evidenced right now when the emergency arises party lines and party difficulties are forgotten as far as France is concerned, and all become united in the one desire and purpose to keep this country as it is, the most democratic, and the country of the greatest freedom in the European Continent."

MacGuire denied that he had spent a great deal of time going into veteran matters there, but he does use and gives a description of the Croix de Feu, which does compare with what Butler testified MacGuire had told him, and again MacGuire denied that he had told Butler about it.

In other parts of the correspondence what MacGuire wrote to Clark and Christmas about foreign veteran groups tallies with what Butler claims MacGuire told him, but which MacGuire denies he did.

In a letter dated April 24, 1934, addressed to "Gentlemen", MacGuire wrote:

"I just returned from a trip to Brussels, Rotterdam, Amsterdam, Hamburg, Copenhagen, Berlin, Prague, Leipzig, Vienna, Munich, Zurich, Basle, Geneva, and thence back to Paris.

"I was informed that there is a Fascist Party springing up in Holland under the leadership of a man named Mussait, who is an engineer by profession and who has approximately 50,000 followers at the present time ranging in age from 18 to 25 years. It is said that this man is in close touch with Berlin, and is modeling his entire program along the lines followed by Hitler in Germany. A number of people are quite alarmed because of the German influence and the probable financial support that this man is getting from Berlin. Generally speaking, trade conditions in Holland are extremely poor, the Germans have placed restrictions against the import of all foodstuffs from this country, and the large cotton mills that the Dutch have have been closed down for a considerable length of time, mainly because of our old friend Japanese competition in the Far East, particularly in the territories that the Dutch have as a market."

In another letter MacGuire said, "Everywhere you go you see men marching in groups and company formation."

MacGuire could not explain why he gave a check for $20,000 to Albert G. Christmas on September 15 and received a check back from Christmas 3 days later for the same amount. . . .

To all such questions MacGuire answered, "It is too far back" or "I don't recall."

Neither could MacGuire remember what the purpose of his trip was to Washington or whether he had given the Central Hanover bank thirteen $1,000 bills or that he had bought one of the letters of credit with a certified check drawn on the account of Mr. Christmas.

In the course of the questioning MacGuire could not remember whether he had ever handled thousand-dollar bills, and certainly could not remember producing 13 of them at one time in the bank. It must be remembered in this connection that the $13,000 purchase with $1,000 bills at the bank came just 6 days after Butler claims MacGuire showed him eighteen $1,000 bills in Newark.

From the foregoing it can readily be seen that in addition to the $30,000 which Clark gave MacGuire for the sound money committee that he produced approximately $75,000 more, which MacGuire reluctantly admitted on being confronted with the evidence.

This $75,000 is shown in the $26,000 that went into the Manufacturers' Trust account, $10,000 in currency at the luncheon, the purchase of letters of credit totaling $30,300, of which Christmas' certified check was represented as $15,000, expenses to Europe close to $8,000. This still stands unexplained.

Whether there was more and how much, the committee does not yet know.

The committee is awaiting the return to this country of both Mr. Clark and Mr. Christmas. As the evidence stands, it calls for an explanation that the committee has been unable to obtain from Mr. MacGuire.

25

Eisenhower, Farewell Address

President Dwight D. Eisenhower, elected in 1952 largely thanks to his legendary record as a general in the Second World War, delivered one of the most famous speeches in American history upon his departure from public life in January 1961. As a general, Eisenhower had personally witnessed the United States' surge to the position of a military superpower as had no other person, and his observations of the growing military-industrial complex were both keen and extremely well informed. After serving as Supreme Commander of Allied forces in Europe, General Eisenhower was president of Columbia University, maintained involvement in the Council on Foreign Relations, and served as NATO Supreme Commander before his election to the presidency. Eisenhower occupied the White House for eight years, and by the end of his terms, few people on the entire planet could speak on his chosen subject with more knowledge and firsthand experience.

Although the bulk of his speech focused on explaining the myriad and serious dangers facing American democracy and republicanism by virtue of its superpower status, the most powerful portions pleaded with fellow citizens to protect their libertarian inheritance. Aghast and no doubt truly terrified by the prospect of ever-increasing nuclear arsenals and the Cold War culture of "fearful hatred" between nations, Eisenhower seems almost desperate to warn his audience of the potentially hidden, sinister, and grave forces they face in the constant battle for a free society. With destruction of the species itself at stake, he implored citizens to tirelessly and virtuously strive for peace, prosperity, love, and mutual respect between all peoples: a harmonious world built on democratic goodwill toward all, the very antithesis of unipolar, technetronic imperialism.

President Dwight D. Eisenhower, "Farewell Address," 17 January, 1961[54]

Good evening, my fellow Americans.

First, I should like to express my gratitude to the radio and television networks for the opportunities they have given me over the years to bring reports and messages to our nation. My special thanks go to them for the opportunity of addressing you this evening.

Three days from now, after half century in the service of our country, I shall lay down the responsibilities of office as, in traditional and solemn ceremony, the authority of the Presidency is vested in my successor. This evening, I come to you with a message of leave-taking and farewell, and to share a few final thoughts with you, my countrymen.

Like every other citizen, I wish the new President, and all who will labor with him, Godspeed. I pray that the coming years will be blessed with peace and prosperity for all.

Our people expect their President and the Congress to find essential agreement on issues of great moment, the wise resolution of which will better shape the future of the nation. My own relations with the Congress, which began on a remote and tenuous basis when, long ago, a member of the Senate appointed me to West Point, have since ranged to the intimate during the war and immediate post-war period, and finally to the mutually interdependent during these past eight years. In this final relationship, the Congress and the Administration have, on most vital issues, cooperated well, to serve the national good, rather than mere partisanship, and so have assured that the business of the nation should go forward. So, my official relationship with the Congress ends in a feeling—on my part—of gratitude that we have been able to do so much together.

We now stand ten years past the midpoint of a century that has witnessed four major wars among great nations. Three of these involved our own country. Despite these holocausts, America is today the strongest, the most influential, and most productive nation in the world. Understandably proud of this pre-eminence, we yet realize that America's leadership and prestige depend, not merely upon our unmatched material progress, riches, and military strength, but on how we use our power in the interests of world peace and human betterment.

Throughout America's adventure in free government, our basic purposes have been to keep the peace, to foster progress in human achievement, and to enhance liberty, dignity, and integrity among peoples and among nations. To strive for less would be unworthy of a free and religious people. Any failure traceable to arrogance, or our lack of comprehension, or readiness to sacrifice would inflict upon us grievous hurt, both at home and abroad.

Progress toward these noble goals is persistently threatened by the conflict now engulfing the world. It commands our whole attention, absorbs our very beings. We face a hostile ideology global in scope, atheistic in character, ruthless in purpose, and insidious in method. Unhappily, the danger it poses promises to be of indefinite duration. To meet it successfully, there is called for, not so much the emotional and transitory sacrifices of crisis, but rather those which enable us to carry forward steadily, surely, and without complaint the burdens of a prolonged and complex struggle with liberty the stake. Only thus shall we remain, despite every provocation, on our charted course toward permanent peace and human betterment.

Crises there will continue to be. In meeting them, whether foreign or domestic, great or small, there is a recurring temptation to feel that some spectacular and costly action could become the miraculous solution to all current difficulties. A huge increase in newer elements of our defenses; development of unrealistic programs to cure every ill in agriculture; a dramatic expansion in basic and applied research—these and many other possibilities, each possibly promising in itself, may be suggested as the only way to the road we wish to travel.

But each proposal must be weighed in the light of a broader consideration: the need to maintain balance in and among national programs, balance between the private and the public economy, balance between the cost and hoped for advantages, balance between the clearly necessary and the comfortably desirable, balance between our essential requirements as a nation and the duties imposed by the nation upon the individual, balance between actions of the moment and the national welfare of the future. Good judgment seeks balance and progress. Lack of it eventually finds imbalance and frustration. The record of many decades stands as proof that our people and their Government have, in the main, understood these truths and have responded to them well, in the face of threat and stress.

But threats, new in kind or degree, constantly arise. Of these, I mention two only.

A vital element in keeping the peace is our military establishment. Our arms must be mighty, ready for instant action, so that no potential aggressor may be tempted to risk his own destruction. Our military organization today bears little relation to that known of any of my predecessors in peacetime, or, indeed, by the fighting men of World War II or Korea.

Until the latest of our world conflicts, the United States had no armaments industry. American makers of plowshares could, with time and as required, make swords as well. But we can no longer risk emergency improvisation of national defense. We have been compelled to create a permanent armaments industry of vast proportions. Added to this, three and a half million men and women are directly engaged in the defense establishment. We annually spend on military security alone more than the net income of all United States corporations.

Now this conjunction of an immense military establishment and a large arms industry is new in the American experience. The total influence—economic, political, even spiritual—is felt in every city, every Statehouse, every office of the Federal government. We recognize the imperative need for this development. Yet, we must not fail to comprehend its grave implications. Our toil, resources, and livelihood are all involved. So is the very structure of our society.

In the councils of government, we must guard against the acquisition of unwarranted influence, whether sought or unsought, by the military-industrial complex. The potential for the disastrous rise of misplaced power exists and will persist. We must never let the weight of this combination endanger our liberties or democratic processes. We should take nothing for granted. Only an alert and knowledgeable citizenry can compel the proper meshing of the huge industrial and military machinery of defense with our peaceful methods and goals, so that security and liberty may prosper together.

Akin to, and largely responsible for the sweeping changes in our industrial-military posture, has been the technological revolution during recent decades. In this revolution, research has become central; it also becomes more formalized, complex, and costly. A steadily increasing share is conducted for, by, or at the direction of, the Federal government.

Today, the solitary inventor, tinkering in his shop, has been overshadowed by task forces of scientists in laboratories and testing fields. In the same fashion, the free university, historically the fountainhead of free ideas and scientific discovery, has experienced a revolution in the conduct of research. Partly because of the huge costs involved, a government contract becomes virtually a substitute for intellectual curiosity. For every old blackboard there are now hundreds of new electronic computers. The prospect of domination of the nation's scholars by Federal employment, project allocations, and the power of money is ever present—and is gravely to be regarded.

Yet, in holding scientific research and discovery in respect, as we should, we must also be alert to the equal and opposite danger that public policy could itself become the captive of a scientific-technological elite.

It is the task of statesmanship to mold, to balance, and to integrate these and other forces, new and old, within the principles of our democratic system—ever aiming toward the supreme goals of our free society.

Another factor in maintaining balance involves the element of time. As we peer into society's future, we—you and I, and our government—must avoid the impulse to live only for today, plundering for our own ease and convenience the precious resources of tomorrow. We cannot mortgage the material assets of our grandchildren without risking the loss also of their political and spiritual heritage. We want democracy to survive for all generations to come, not to become the insolvent phantom of tomorrow.

Down the long lane of the history yet to be written, America knows that this world of ours, ever growing smaller, must avoid becoming a community of dreadful fear and hate, and be, instead, a proud confederation of mutual trust and respect. Such a confederation must be one of equals. The weakest must come to the conference table with the same confidence as do we, protected as we are by our moral, economic, and military strength. That table, though scarred by many past frustrations, cannot be abandoned for the certain agony of the battlefield.

Disarmament, with mutual honor and confidence, is a continuing imperative. Together we must learn how to compose differences, not with arms, but with intellect and decent purpose. Because this need is so sharp and apparent, I confess that I lay down my official responsibilities in this field with a definite sense of disappointment. As one who has witnessed the horror and the lingering sadness of war, as one who knows that another war could utterly destroy this civilization which has been so slowly and painfully built over thousands of years, I wish I could say tonight that a lasting peace is in sight.

Happily, I can say that war has been avoided. Steady progress toward our ultimate goal has been made. But so much remains to be done. As a private citizen, I shall never cease to do what little I can to help the world advance along that road.

So, in this, my last good night to you as your President, I thank you for the many opportunities you have given me for public service in war and in peace. I trust in that service you find some things worthy. As for the rest of it, I know you will find ways to improve performance in the future.

You and I, my fellow citizens, need to be strong in our faith that all nations, under God, will reach the goal of peace with justice. May we be ever unswerving in devotion to principle, confident but humble with power, diligent in pursuit of the Nations' great goals.

To all the peoples of the world, I once more give expression to America's prayerful and continuing aspiration: We pray that peoples of all faiths, all races, all nations, may have their great human needs satisfied; that those now denied opportunity shall come to enjoy it to the full; that all who yearn for freedom may experience its few spiritual blessings; that those who have freedom will understand, also, its heavy responsibility; that all who are insensitive to the needs of others will learn charity; that the scourges of poverty, disease, and ignorance will be made [to] disappear from the earth; and that in the goodness of time, all peoples will come to live together in a peace guaranteed by the binding force of mutual respect and love.

Now, on Friday noon, I am to become a private citizen. I am proud to do so. I look forward to it.

Thank you, and good night.

Barry Goldwater, Acceptance Speech (1964 Republican National Convention)

In mid-July 1964, the Republican Party descended upon the Cow Palace arena in Daly City, California. At the party's national convention, a clique of traditionalist-conservatives surrounding Senator Barry Goldwater fulfilled their long-laid plans to overtake the GOP. After Goldwater's surprisingly energizing campaign for the Senate in 1958 (a year of sweeping Democratic victories), conservative talk show host and activist Clarence Manion commissioned Leo Brent Bozell to author *The Conscience of a Conservative*. Manion and Bozell agreed with Goldwater to publish the small volume under the senator's name in 1960 during that year's Nixon convention. *The Conscience of a Conservative* launched a grassroots, ultra-conservative Goldwater movement culminating in the senator's primary victories in 1964. Through a difficult and often dirty primary season, Goldwater emerged with enough delegates to handily wrest the convention from Nelson Rockefeller's "liberal establishment" wing of the party. Goldwater delegates won their candidate and wrote the party's hard-line Cold Warrior platform. In his acceptance speech, Barry Goldwater echoed the ideas from his book and magnified his vision for the Republican Party's role in world history. His bold and enduring declaration on the virtues of extremism and the vices of moderation inspired generations of "conservative" advocates for American imperialism. Goldwater believed deeply that America was inherently virtuous and so thought it historically necessary that Americans act to defend liberty against the evils of communism. Goldwater temporarily conquered the GOP, but his loss to Lyndon Johnson was historical in its own right. Although scorned by history as an epic loser, in the decades since his convention speech, virtually no one has been more important to conservative ideas and activism than Barry Goldwater.

Senator Barry Goldwater, "Acceptance Speech, 1964 Republican National Convention."[55]

. . . From this moment, united and determined, we will go forward together, dedicated to the ultimate and undeniable greatness of the whole man. Together we will win.

I accept your nomination with a deep sense of humility. I accept, too, the responsibility that goes with it, and I seek your continued help and your continued guidance. My fellow Republicans, our cause is too great for any man to feel worthy of it. Our task would be too great for any man, did he not have with him the heart and the hands of this great Republican Party, and I promise you tonight that every fiber of my being is consecrated to our cause; that nothing shall be lacking from the struggle that can be brought to it by enthusiasm, by devotion, and plain hard work. In this world no person, no party can guarantee anything, but what we can do and what we shall do is to deserve victory, and victory will be ours.

The good Lord raised this mighty Republic to be a home for the brave and to flourish as the land of the free—not to stagnate in the swampland of collectivism, not to cringe before the bully of communism.

Now . . . the tide has been running against freedom. Our people have followed false prophets. We must, and we shall, return to proven ways—not because they are old, but because they are true. We must, and we shall, set the tide running again in the cause of freedom. And this party, with its every action, every word, every breath, and every heartbeat, has but a single resolve, and that is freedom—freedom made orderly for this nation by our constitutional government; freedom under a government limited by laws of nature and of nature's God; freedom—balanced so that liberty lacking order will not become the slavery of the prison cell; balanced so that liberty lacking order will not become the license of the mob and of the jungle.

Now, we Americans understand freedom. We have earned it, we have lived for it, and we have died for it. This Nation and its people are freedom's model in a searching world. We can be freedom's missionaries in a doubting world. But . . . first we must renew freedom's mission in our own hearts and in our own homes.

During four futile years, the administration which we shall replace has distorted and lost that faith. It has talked and talked and talked and talked the words of freedom. Now, failures cement the wall of shame in Berlin. Failures blot the sands of shame at the Bay of Pigs. Failures mark the slow death of freedom in Laos. Failures infest the jungles of Vietnam. And failures haunt the houses of our once great alliances and undermine the greatest bulwark ever erected by free nations—the NATO community. Failures proclaim lost leadership, obscure purpose, weakening wills, and the risk of inciting our sworn enemies to new aggressions and to new excesses. Because of this administration we are tonight a world divided—we are a Nation becalmed. We have lost the brisk pace of diversity and the genius of individual creativity. We are plodding at a pace set by centralized planning, red tape, rules without responsibility, and regimentation without recourse.

Rather than useful jobs in our country, people have been offered bureaucratic "make work," rather than moral leadership, they have been given bread and circuses, spectacles, and, yes, they have even been given scandals. Tonight there is violence in our streets, corruption in our highest offices, aimlessness among our youth, anxiety among our elders and there is a virtual despair among the many who look beyond material success for the inner meaning of their lives. Where examples of morality should be set, the opposite is seen. Small men, seeking great wealth or power, have too often and too long turned even the highest levels of public service into mere personal opportunity.

Now, certainly, simple honesty is not too much to demand of men in government. We find it in most. Republicans demand it from everyone. They demand it from everyone no matter how exalted or protected his position might be. The growing menace in our country tonight, to personal safety, to life, to limb and property, in homes, in churches, on the playgrounds, and places of business, particularly in our great cities, is the mounting concern, or should be, of every thoughtful citizen in the United States.

Security from domestic violence, no less than from foreign aggression, is the most elementary and fundamental purpose of any government, and a government that cannot fulfill that purpose is one that cannot long command the loyalty of its citizens. History shows us—demonstrates that nothing—nothing prepares the way for tyranny more than the failure of public officials to keep the streets from bullies and marauders.

Now, we Republicans see all this as more, much more, than the rest: of mere political differences or mere political mistakes. We see this as the result of a fundamentally and absolutely wrong view of man, his nature and his destiny. Those who seek to live your lives for you, to take your liberties in return for relieving you of yours, those who elevate the state and downgrade the citizen must see ultimately a world in which earthly power can be substituted for divine will, and this Nation was founded upon the rejection of that notion and upon the acceptance of God as the author of freedom.

Those who seek absolute power, even though they seek it to do what they regard as good, are simply demanding the right to enforce their own version of heaven on earth. And let me remind you, they are the very ones who always create the most hellish tyrannies. Absolute power does corrupt, and those who seek it must be suspect and must be opposed. Their mistaken course stems from false notions of equality, ladies and gentlemen. Equality, rightly understood, as our founding fathers understood it, leads to liberty and to the emancipation of creative differences. Wrongly understood, as it has been so tragically in our time, it leads first to conformity and then to despotism.

Fellow Republicans, it is the cause of Republicanism to resist concentrations of power, private or public, which enforce such conformity and inflict such despotism. It is the cause of Republicanism to ensure that power remains in the hands of the people. And, so help us God, that is exactly what a Republican president will do with the help of a Republican Congress.

It is further the cause of Republicanism to restore a clear understanding of the tyranny of man over man in the world at large. It is our cause to dispel the foggy thinking which avoids hard decisions in the illusion that a world of conflict will somehow mysteriously resolve itself into a world of harmony, if we just don't rock the boat or irritate the forces of aggression—and this is hogwash.

It is further the cause of Republicanism to remind ourselves, and the world, that only the strong can remain free, that only the strong can keep the peace.

Now, I needn't remind you . . . that Republicans have shouldered this hard responsibility and marched in this cause before. It was Republican leadership under Dwight Eisenhower that kept the peace, and passed along to this administration the mightiest arsenal for defense the world has ever known. And I needn't remind you that it was the strength and the unbelievable will of the Eisenhower years that kept the peace by using our strength, by using it in the Formosa Straits and in Lebanon and by showing it courageously at all times.

It was during those Republican years that the thrust of Communist imperialism was blunted. It was during those years of Republican leadership that this world moved closer, not to war, but closer to peace, than at any other time in the three decades just passed.

And I needn't remind you—but I will—that it's been during Democratic years that our strength to deter war has stood still, and even gone into a planned decline. It has been during Democratic years that we have weakly stumbled into conflict, timidly refusing to draw our own lines against aggression, deceitfully refusing to tell even our people of our full participation, and tragically, letting our finest men die on battlefields (unmarked by purpose, unmarked by pride or the prospect of victory).

Yesterday it was Korea. Tonight it is Vietnam. Make no bones of this. Don't try to sweep this under the rug. We are at war in Vietnam. And yet the President, who is Commander-in-Chief of our forces, refuses to say—refuses to say, mind you, whether or not the objective over there is victory. And his Secretary of Defense continues to mislead and misinform the American people, and enough of it has gone by.

And I needn't remind you, but I will; it has been during Democratic years that a billion persons were cast into Communist captivity and their fate cynically sealed.

Today in our beloved country we have an administration which seems eager to deal with communism in every coin known—from gold to wheat, from consulates to confidence, and even human freedom itself.

The Republican cause demands that we brand communism as a principal disturber of peace in the world today. Indeed, we should brand it as the only significant disturber of the peace, and we must make clear that until its goals of conquest are absolutely renounced and its rejections with all nations tempered, communism and the governments it now controls are enemies of every man on earth who is or wants to be free.

We here in America can keep the peace only if we remain vigilant and only if we remain strong. Only if we keep our eyes open and keep our guard up can we prevent war. And I want to make this abundantly clear—I don't intend to let peace or freedom be torn from our grasp because of lack of strength or lack of will—and that I promise you Americans.

I believe that we must look beyond the defense of freedom today to its extension tomorrow. I believe that the communism which boasts it will bury us will, instead, give way to the forces of freedom. And I can see in the distant and yet recognizable future the outlines of a world worthy [of] our dedication, our every risk, our every effort, our every sacrifice along the way. Yes, a world that will redeem the suffering of those who will be liberated from tyranny. I can see and I suggest that all thoughtful men must contemplate the flowering of an Atlantic civilization, the whole world of Europe unified and free, trading openly across its borders, communicating openly across the world. This is a goal far, far more meaningful than a moon shot.

It's a truly inspiring goal for all free men to set for themselves during the latter half of the twentieth century. I can also see—and all free men must thrill to—the events of this Atlantic civilization joined by its great ocean highway to the United States. What a destiny, what a destiny can be ours to stand as a great central pillar linking Europe, the Americans and the venerable and vital peoples and cultures of the Pacific. I can see a day when all the Americas, North and South, will be linked in a mighty system, a system in which the errors and misunderstandings of the past will be submerged one by one in a rising tide of prosperity and interdependence. We know that the misunderstandings of centuries are not to be wiped away in a day or wiped away in an hour. But we pledge—we pledge that human sympathy—what our neighbors to the South call that attitude of "simpatico"—no less than enlightened self-interest will be our guide.

I can see this Atlantic civilization galvanizing and guiding emergent nations everywhere.

I know this freedom is not the fruit of every soil. I know that our own freedom was achieved through centuries, by unremitting efforts by brave and wise men. I know that the road to freedom is a long and a challenging road. I know also that some men may walk away from it, that some men resist challenge, accepting the false security of governmental paternalism.

And I pledge that the America I envision in the years ahead will extend its hand in health, in teaching and in cultivation, so that all new nations will be at least encouraged to go our way, so that they will not wander down the dark alleys of tyranny or to the dead-end streets of collectivism. My fellow Republicans, we do no man a service by hiding freedom's light under a bushel of mistaken humility.

I seek an America proud of its past, proud of its ways, proud of its dreams, and determined actively to proclaim them. But our example to the world must, like charity, begin at home.

In our vision of a good and decent future, free and peaceful, there must be room for deliberation of the energy and talent of the individual—otherwise our vision is blind at the outset.

We must assure a society here which, while never abandoning the needy or forsaking the helpless, nurtures incentives and opportunity for the creative and the productive. We must know the whole good is the product of many single contributions.

I cherish a day when our children once again will restore as heroes the sort of men and women who—unafraid and undaunted—pursue the truth, strive to cure disease, subdue and make fruitful our natural environment and produce the inventive engines of production, science, and technology.

This Nation, whose creative people have enhanced this entire span of history, should again thrive upon the greatness of all those things which we, as individual citizens, can and should do. During Republican years, this again will be a nation of men and women, of families proud of their role, jealous of their responsibilities, unlimited in their aspirations—a Nation where all who can will be self-reliant.

We Republicans see in our constitutional form of government the great framework which assures the orderly but dynamic fulfillment of the whole man, and we see the whole man as the great reason for instituting orderly government in the first place.

We see, in private property and in economy based upon and fostering private property, the one way to make government a durable ally of the whole man, rather than his determined enemy. We see in the sanctity of private property the only durable foundation for constitutional government in a free society. And beyond that, we see, in cherished diversity of ways, diversity of thoughts, of motives and accomplishments. We do not seek to lead anyone's life for him—we seek only to secure his rights and to guarantee him opportunity to strive, with government performing only those needed and constitutionally sanctioned tasks which cannot otherwise be performed.

We Republicans seek a government that attends to its inherent responsibilities of maintaining a stable monetary and fiscal climate, encouraging a free and a competitive economy and enforcing law and order. Thus do we seek inventiveness, diversity, and creativity within a stable order, for we Republicans define government's role where needed at many, many levels, preferably through the one closest to the people involved.

Our towns and our cities, then our counties, then our states, then our regional contacts—and only then, the national government. That, let me remind you, is the ladder of liberty, built by decentralized power. On it also we must have balance between the branches of government at every level.

Balance, diversity, creativity—these are the elements of Republican equation. Republicans agree, Republicans agree heartily to disagree on many, many of their applications, but we have never disagreed on the basic fundamental issues of why you and I are Republicans.

This is a party, this Republican Party, a Party for free men, not for blind followers, and not for conformists.

Back in 1858 Abraham Lincoln said this of the Republican party—and I quote him, because he probably could have said it during the last week or so: "It was composed of strained, discordant, and even hostile elements" in 1858. Yet all of these elements agreed on one paramount objective: To arrest the progress of slavery, and place it in the course of ultimate extinction.

Today, as then, but more urgently and more broadly than then, the task of preserving and enlarging freedom at home and safeguarding it from the forces of tyranny abroad is great enough to challenge all our resources and to require all our strength. Anyone who joins us in all sincerity, we welcome. Those who do not care for our cause, we don't expect to enter our ranks in any case. And let our Republicanism, so focused and so dedicated, not be made fuzzy and futile by unthinking and stupid labels.

I would remind you that extremism in the defense of liberty is no vice. And let me remind you also that moderation in the pursuit of justice is no virtue.

The beauty of the very system we Republicans are pledged to restore and revitalize, the beauty of this Federal system of ours is in its reconciliation of diversity with unity. We must not see malice in honest differences of opinion, and no matter how great, so long as they are not inconsistent with the pledges we have given to each other in and through our Constitution. Our Republican cause is not to level out the world or make its people conform in computer regimented sameness. Our Republican cause is to free our people and light the way for liberty throughout the world.

Ours is a very human cause for very humane goals.

This Party, its good people, and its unquestionable devotion to freedom, will not fulfill the purposes of this campaign which we launch here now until our cause has won the day, inspired the world, and shown the way to a tomorrow worthy of all our yesteryears.

I repeat, I accept your nomination with humbleness, with pride, and you and I are going to fight for the goodness of our land. Thank you.

Conclusion

The New Necromancers: Technology, Democracy, and Individualism

Although little discussed today, William Godwin remains one of the most brilliant radical liberal writers of his age. He is considered by many the first modern anarchist, and his writings earned him renown and great respect in his day. A true and shining example of Enlightenment-era skepticism, Godwin devoted much of his career to dispelling ignorance, myths, half-truths, and lies. His 1834 *Lives of the Necromancers* is an especially important foray into philosophy, cosmology, and psychology. Throughout the volume, Godwin investigates examples of supernatural beliefs throughout world history. His purpose was "to exhibit a fair delineation of the credulity of the human mind": an intellectual inoculation for his popular audience against poisonously bad ideas. He would write a history of exploitative elites (the perspective *from above*) by deconstructing their activities *from below*.

413

Across the Atlantic, Edgar Allan Poe reviewed *Lives of the Necromancers*, remarking that Godwin's writing exhibited "an air of mature thought—of deliberate premeditation pervading, in a remarkable degree, even his most common-place observations." In Godwin's hands, the most banal cultural myths, legends, and institutions became outright lies and well-orchestrated aristocratic deceptions. Poe commented that "No English writer . . . with the single exception of Coleridge, has a fuller appreciation of the value of words." The American *literatus* continued: "His compilation is an invaluable work, evincing much labor and research, and full of absorbing interest." "The only drawback," Poe concluded with mournful respect, "is found in the author's unwelcome announcement in the Preface, that for the present he winds up his literary labors with the production of this book." Godwin's most insightful pen, he declared, "should never for a moment be idle."

To begin the volume, our learned, enlightened author introduces his empiricist, rationalist attack on all things supernatural. Godwin believed that nature, properly conceived, encompasses all things, and through man's unique powers of reason we can divine nature's laws. Throughout the ages and into the very mists of human existence, however, there have been those who seek to obfuscate and obscure from individuals the power to reason. The charismatic, the cunning, and the immoral seekers after power have, from time immemorial, organized themselves into classes of conspirators against the liberties and wisdom of the common people. Godwin's *Lives of the Necromancers* was an attempt to disarm those classes of priests, magicians, fortune-tellers, divine-right monarchs, and lickspittle court devotionists and their narratives from above; to dispel the mysticisms that clouded common people's minds, from astrology and physiognomy to the psychology of dreams and cold-reading hucksterism. Behind it all, sadly and unfortunately, lay the "boundless ambition" of even the most average of people. Because practically everyone can be swept away with grandiose dreams and visions of the supernatural and the real blending together, practically everyone falls prey to those who would lie, cheat, and worse to dominate their fellow beings. The role of the educator, then, is to dispel the myths that accumulate like so many cobwebs in the corners of the mind, steadily shrinking the bounds of mental life. Godwin begins his encyclopedic spring cleaning by detailing humanity's desire to attain evergreater power and knowledge, so much so that they may even predict and control the future.

The necromancer's dark disturbance of the deceased violated the broadly accepted laws of ethics and religious sentiment. Only those individuals motivated by the most wicked and horrifying lusts would resort to such unnatural means of acquiring power. No less batty—although decidedly more benign—were the alchemists, Rosicrucians, Magi, and a variety of other Egyptian and Middle Eastern priesthoods. The alchemist promised both unending wealth and immortality, and in search of those grandiose dreams the Rosicrucians seem to have indulged in hallucinogenic communications with elemental creatures. Godwin writes that the priests would attempt to purge "the organs of human sight" with a "universal medicine, and that certain glass globes should be chemically prepared with one or other of the four elements."

On completion of the ritual, "the initiated immediately had a sight of innumerable beings of a luminous substance, but of thin and evanescent structure, that people the elements on all sides of us." Because leading initiates claimed the ability to control those fearsome beings, they commanded the full loyalty of their subordinate priests. From further east and of far more ancient origins, the Magi reportedly engaged in similarly cultish communications with the gods to enforce the priestly hierarchy. Godwin explains that phenomenon by noting that before the dawn of modernity, scientific knowledge was reserved exclusively for the elite few and a very small number of specialists. In this atmosphere of monopolized knowledge about science and technology, the cunning clerisy sharply separated and insulated themselves from the vast herd of common laborers and even those of middling status within the ruling class itself. The divisions between the ruling, exploitative few and the ruled, exploited many were so stark that conquerors such as Alexander lived on after death, venerated as gods incarnate.

Godwin begins his discussion on ancient Greek mysticism by restating his basic argument: "to the eye of uninstructed ignorance every thing is astonishing, every thing is unexpected." Until one interrogates the world from below, one cannot hope to uncover narratives hidden by the perfumed clouds from above. Although legend might hold that Amphion could arrange stones on command with his lyre, the truth is probably far more mundane. Like the geometer and philosopher Pythagoras, Amphion was in all likelihood merely one of the few existing truly skilled engineers or architects in the Greek world. Pythagoras, in fact, was so brilliant

that Godwin laments his rather bizarre pretensions to divin-
ity. The great thinker commanded the worship of his followers,
who gladly (for Godwin: ignorantly) followed his will. Between
Pythagoras and his students, the master's word was unquestioned
law. Thus did the master ensure that no students could ever
take his place or surpass his grandeur. His student Epimenides,
however, seems to have learned much. A man of apparently few
scruples, Epimenides claimed to be in contact with invisible entities ("nymphs") and spirits that accorded him unique powers and
abilities in our world. He was supposed to have practiced a sort of
remote viewing or astral projection and seems to have supported
himself by performing exorcisms throughout the countryside,
restoring ruined farms to prosperousness. But perhaps the most
powerful of all ancient Greek cultists were the Oracles at Delphi.
With precision, empiricism, and rationalism and a desire to
investigate Greek mysticism from below, Godwin identifies the
oracular operation as a natural gas-induced fever dream dressed
with various theatricals and filtered entirely through the secretive,
exclusionary priestesses. The combined influence of the Oracles'
abilities to deceive and the Greeks' penchant to believe such non-
sense affected the histories of entire states, societies, and western
civilization itself. Events always turn, after all, at the intersection
of interests and ideas.

The eighth century BCE remains famous for both Greek and
Roman history—for Greece, it was the period in which the polis
proliferated and replaced Dark Age kings; for Rome, it was the
traditional era of its foundation by Romulus and Remus. Then,
Rome existed at the fringes of the civilized world, barely over the

edge of barbarism. The ignorant early Romans stood in religious and civic awe of their new kings. Legend held that Romulus was swept by a spontaneous storm into the heavens. Following such an unexpected turn of events, an influential senator assured the populace that their king had been summoned to live among the gods. Rome's second king, Numa, built upon Romulus's elaborate example in showmanship by disappearing into a cave to commune with the goddess Egeria. He emerged from the cave with new legal codes and institutional arrangements that his subjects accepted as the divine will. Not quite so lucky in his attempts at political performance art, Tullus Hostilius attempted to conjure the god Jupiter Elicius but invoked the god's lightning against himself. He died in a house fire, the true causes of which, one can only guess.

In his discussion of the Christian era in Roman history, our author juxtaposes the spiritual magic of the apostles and even Christ himself to the more physical and sensational magic of the pagans. Although Jesus clearly claimed the ability to cast out demons, the career of Simon Magus, for example, is far more magical. Yes, yes, Jesus may have offered the only real salvation from sin, Godwin hints, but Magus could reportedly fly through the air, pass through miles of matter at a time, make himself invisible; he could shape shift, transfigure matter, bring statues to life, and bid defiance to all locks. He was also apparently fireproof. Not all proper magicians of the period were simple fraudsters, however, nor idealistic carpenters, for that matter. Apollonius of Tyana was a rough contemporary of Jesus born in Asia Minor. After spending years in the Pythagorean cult, he researched a trail across the world, all the way to India. He learned everything he could about the variety of magical traditions each culture offered, eventually synthesizing his knowledge into good deeds for the people of Tyana. Whether magician or mere philosopher, the word "fraudster" simply does not fit well with such a beneficent figure. In fact, as the odd case of the writer Apuleius shows, the individual often has little to do with his or her own legend. In Apuleius's case, his transcendental literature was mistaken for literal, magical manipulations of nature. Godwin corrects the record, rescuing Apuleius from the condemnation of the ages.

Eastern priests and magicians were little different from the westerners—they practiced transfiguration to mystify audiences with visual fantasies; they built intricate fooling machines to convince marks of their supernatural authority; they produced convenient sorcerous excuses for distasteful personal behavior. Regardless of one's culture, necromancy, alchemy, sorcery, and magical showmanship of all kinds provided clever and remorseless individuals a host of sociopolitical and economic advantages. The Zoroastrian Magi claimed the power to influence natural phenomena and produce miracles. Godwin notes that easterners, whether Magi, yogis, or independent practitioners, were especially skilled at their craft. Rocail seems to have invented a mechanical automaton disguised as a magically living statue. Hakem acquired fame and infamy through the use of luminescence—probably chemical—supposedly serving to hide his ugliness as well as dazzle and bewilder commoners into a state of deference. Godwin's "Story of a Goule" seems to suggest that a husband took advantage of occultist beliefs to dispose of a troublesome wife.

Each of those stories and the many more that have existed throughout the history of eastern civilizations are most noteworthy to Godwin, however, for their consistency with western myths. Our author concludes that mystical beliefs serve very particular and powerful functions for human beings. The particular details of how individuals across cultures use mysticism vary, but within the sociological functions of the beliefs lie timeless truths about both the necromancers and their societies. Occultism was certainly not something merely imposed "from above"; rather, it represented a core set of beliefs and a worldview held by vast numbers of the population. Godwin is adamant that education alone could finally expel belief in witchcraft, and he carefully notes that the powers accumulated by elite occultists depend almost entirely on credulity and deference "from below."

Early medieval Europe was a world flush with supernatural entities and powerful individuals who could access such otherworldly power through highly specialized occultic learning. Angels flitted hither and thither through the skies to influence human affairs, demons haunted every crack and crevice in the earth while God's saints endlessly battled them, witches and sorcerers spun their mysterious spells and practiced their magical crafts for both benevolent and malevolent purposes, and alchemists and necromancers desperately searched for an existence extending well beyond the tragically short confines of a natural lifespan. Fraudsters and fanatics of every sort crowded into European monasteries, feudal courts, and dupable villages. They ruthlessly and skillfully exploited the mystical foolishness implanted in medieval minds, and some of them became so famous that their legacies survived in popular culture for centuries—even to the present day. In his discussion of Europe's Dark Age depths, Godwin pays particular attention to the stories of Merlin and St. Dunstan, both immensely important in folklore and popular culture.

In the crusading era (ca. 1090s–early 1500s), many western-ers wholeheartedly embraced the knowledge and technology open to them through sustained networks with the Near, Middle, and Far East. Even a century before the Crusades, "The more curi-ous and inquisitive spirits of Europe," including Pope Silvester II, "by degrees adopted the practice of resorting to Spain for the purpose of enlarging their sphere of observation and knowledge." Godwin's selections on three popes illustrate well a larger shift in his treatment of occultism throughout the book. Silvester II seems to have studiously learned science and technology in the nonwestern world and translated his knowledge into a reputation for mystical power. What seemed supernatural was in fact tech-nological power. Benedict IX supposedly engaged in witchcraft as part of his overall lifestyle of debauchery, reaping the very worldly pleasures of sorcery. Pope Gregory VII, whose pontificate was consumed by the Investiture Crisis, was posthumously charged by his enemies with a variety of necromantic activities. Interesting to note, however, Godwin believes Gregory's relentless pursuit of papal power reflected "genuine enthusiasm," rather than mere huckstering or trickery.

Magic could serve many different social purposes, not all of which were the result of ill will toward others. One particu-larly interesting section relays the Muslim tale of a miraculous tub of water. When a man plunges his face into the water, he is transported to an entirely new life, which he then lives day after day, struggle after struggle, joy after joy, to the end of his days. When the lifetime-long vision abruptly ends, the protagonist emerges from the water tub mere moments later. During the late Medieval period, elite and learned Europeans became increasingly aware that knowledge and technology represented the power to transform the world according to one's own visions. Through exceeding cleverness, ingenuity, inventiveness, scrupulousness, and mechanical skill, men of cunning (such as Silvester) and vision (such as Gregory) were often able to become men of power—and we all know what they say about power.

In Europe's High Middle Ages, knowledge of and participation in the occult broadened well beyond the realm of highly educated popes, secluded monks, and traveling hucksters. A seemingly endless array of friars, philosophers, scientists, alchemists, and educators joined the magical fray to advance their own power, influence, and visions. Unlike their cloistered cousins in the monasteries, friars lived and preached among the people. The friars "were distinguished by a fervor of devotion," essentially independent of the church hierarchy, and they possessed a distinctly ferocious commitment to charity and science, which made them both rare and indispensable to their world. The friars largely divided over time into sects of Dominicans and Franciscans, "And all that was most illustrious in intellect at this period belonged either to the one or the other." Those new men of learning who proliferated across a more and more commercially prosperous Europe constructed grand machines, such as Albertus Magnus's automatons; they discovered powerful and mysterious new substances, such as Roger Bacon's gunpowder; they supposedly communicated with the devil, receiving the inspiration for inventions such as artificial intelligence; they performed incredible feats of transfiguration on themselves, the bodies of others, and all sorts of physical material; and generations of alchemists tinkered away, either hopelessly attempting to turn lesser metals into gold, struggling to create the elixir of life, or cleverly devising ways to fool royals into giving them more money.

Thanks to figures such as Petrarch, however, "the energies of the human mind were to loosen its shackles, and its independence was ultimately to extinguish those delusions and that superstition which had so long enslaved it." Through an ironic twist of history, the enlightened and educated no longer practiced witchcraft, but they would have defended to the death one's right to do so. From the Renaissance onward, Godwin takes a much more conciliatory and pitying tone toward his subject witches and necromancers. Europeans became more and more keenly aware of the physical laws governing natural phenomena. In the process, they learned a sharp lesson about human credulity and the limits of actual occultist practice. As scientists uncovered the facts of nature, they left firmly behind them the superstitions of early ages. Science helped to demystify witchcraft and expose it as a sociological, not supernatural, phenomenon. Political institutions, however, lagged cutting-edge learning by several centuries, and witches continued to suffer at the hands of persecutionists. Although the period ca. 1300–1650 witnessed an explosion of scientific and technological learning, Europeans also dug themselves into deep and violently antagonistic religious and political positions. Marginalized and powerless individuals often made easy targets both for angry mobs and for political or religious leaders in desperate need of a scapegoat. Among those marginalized groups sacrificed to violent forces in European history were Godwin's necromancers, sorcerers, alchemists, and all the rest. To illustrate the point, Godwin details the famous story of Joan of Arc, followed by a long string of tales from centuries of witch trials, torture, and executions.

Joan of Arc was executed for fear of her communications with demons, and witch trials proliferated throughout Europe during the late Medieval period, but Godwin takes great care to steadily remind us that those people were not actually necromancers. They were quacks—cold-blooded quacks with ill will in many cases—but mere quacks nonetheless. Many of them, such as Joan, were genuine enthusiasts who truly believed in mystical power. Others simply sought to get a piece of the church and state's action by exploiting public ignorance for personal gain. As two case studies in the latter form of mere hucksterism, Godwin offers Benvenuto Cellini's story of a priest and his "magic lantern," followed by a short biography of John Dee. Cellini's Sicilian priest seems to have filled the same niche that modern New Orleans tourist voodoo shops occupy—he essentially offered an elaborate and ceremonial show that seemed sufficiently authentic and complex to convince Cellini that the causes were mystical rather than technological. John Dee was a mathematician and Queen Elizabeth I's court astrologer before he was a degenerating traveling salesman of useless philosopher's stones. His rise to the heights of power and influence and consequent decline to the depths of failure and despair is in many ways emblematic of the

Faustian bargain's usual outcome: those who grasp endlessly after power place themselves in the positions most vulnerable to the avarice of other powerful people. In John Dee's case, his entire career was built on astrological and alchemical promises, which he constantly failed to deliver, leaving him entirely at the mercy of those still more powerful than he. By placing their entire ethics, their senses of personal identity, and the bulk of their natural lives under the command of power's dictates, such people condemned themselves to be the victims of power's demands. Joan of Arc and John Dee may both have been quacks, but who can deny that there is greater dignity and respect in Joan's genuine enthusiasm than in John's mere hucksterism?

During the Renaissance, intellectuals discovered and widely publicized the natural, mechanical, and technological sources of previously mysterious phenomena by interrogating the historical record and subjecting it to the light of reason. The Scientific Revolution and the Enlightenment continued that process, severing the once-strong link between the practice of witchcraft and the actual wielding of political power. As the politically and economically powerful ceased to be terrified, impressed, or inspired by occultist ravings, the magicians receded in social, academic, and political status to the position of an extremely lonesome minority of religious believers and peripatetic con men. As magic lost its power in European courts, it retained command of the average person's worldview. For the uneducated, the world still abounded with spirits, strange energies, and endless signs of Satan's battle against God. In the transitional Early Modern period, monarchs such as James VI of Scotland (later James I of England) could exploit the marginality of witches for their own political purposes. A particularly literary monarch, James wrote his own *Demonology* and orchestrated show trials for accused witches who he perceived to have wronged him in some way or another. Individuals such as Agnes Sampson and John Fian stood accused of causing a storm to delay the king's travel to Norway (where he was betrothed to marry). For their crimes, they suffered horrifying torture and execution.

Although James seems to have had a sort of empiricist change of heart by the end of his life, the backward example of his administration and "scholarship" were invaluable to future bad actors, such as the witch-hunter Matthew Hopkins. Throughout his bloody career (which flourished in the early days of England's Civil War), Hopkins traveled through England convincing localities that witch training grounds existed in their midst, and Satan was actively attempting to invade the village. Hopkins' solution was for the towns to hire his hunters to murder more than 300 women accused of making satanic pacts. His reign of terror over just two years exterminated more marginalized people than had the previous two centuries of witch hunting in England. Having built a dandy career out of the horrible affair, Hopkins published his manual *The Discovery of Witches* in 1647. Within a few decades, the practice spread across the Atlantic to yet another Puritan society that seemed to have gone insane.

For his conclusions, Godwin takes us from Sweden in 1670 to Puritan New England a generation later. In our detour to Sweden, Godwin details the history of County Dalecarlia, which today borders Norway in the central part of the country. Godwin assures us that the locals were a perfectly average sort of common folk, minding their own affairs, living and letting live. When a small coven of "witches" began expanding their numbers in the town of Mohra in 1670, however, it sent the locals into a frenzy. The obviously troubled witches supposedly engaged in a variety of satanic festivities, dining with the devil himself on occasion. The devil commanded his witch envoys at Mohra to confiscate children from the village to expand the ranks of his followers. Hundreds of children fell ill with similar symptoms, and "The whole town of Mohra became subject to the infection." The town petitioned the king for powers of inquiry into the matter, and Charles XI established the necessary court. Godwin reports that the number of witches in Mohra rose from the original "two or three witches existing in some of the obscure quarters of this place" to 70 now tried by the court. Every single witch—including those who confessed and begged mercy—was executed. The court then turned on the children who confessed involvement in the witches' plot: Swedish authorities executed 15 children and condemned 56 others to torture as retribution.

From Sweden, we shift to the infamous witch trials in Salem, Massachusetts, in 1692. Godwin's theory of the Salem trials is representative of scholarly thought for quite some time: they were largely the result of a combination of personal animus, avarice, and cruelty within a deeply occultist culture. The Puritans were terribly fussy and moralizing people, by and large, and their history of Indian extermination and the destruction of alternative cultures in New England reflects their mystical worldview. True-believer Puritans saw Satan and his minions behind every tree and in the eyes of every person not Elect. They preached a creed of humility and righteousness so self-assured that it easily translated into frenzied witch hunting. In fact, many copies of Matthew Hopkins' *The Discovery of Witches* rested (no doubt with well-worn pages) on saints' bookshelves. Once the first baseless accusations flew, the flood was unstoppable. As Godwin writes, "The accusations were of the most vulgar and contemptible sort, invisible pinchings and blows, fits, with the blastings and mortality of cattle, and wains stuck fast in the ground, or losing their wheels." The supposed victims claimed that spectral forces that only the accuser could see terrorized them and vandalized their property. On the basis of such outlandish testimony, New England courts executed 19 witches and subjected many repented convicts to purifying torture. One thing only ended the feverish trials: accusers gradually turned on the affluent and influential after using up the easier targets of marginalized and poor women. Once the Massachusetts Bay elite felt their interests were also seriously threatened by the hysterical outbreak, they reasserted control over the courts and ended the trials.

Finally, our author concludes that enough is enough with the witches already!—We are so fortunate to live in an age in which necromancers possess no supernatural powers nor do they have the ability to exploit significant portions of the population. Rather, knowledge and science have advanced so far that we see through any potential threat those individuals pose and, indeed, have even come to pity the occultist and his or her decidedly strange persona. Therefore, Godwin finishes, let us bask in the learning of our age, never forgetting the ignorant depths to which humans can plunge, forever "harassed with imaginary terrors, and haunted by suggestions." Despite Godwin's optimism, though, modern readers may leave this volume uncomfortably aware that we, too, have our true believers, necromancers, and persecutionists—they are the technocrats, the statist-futurists, the millennial and post-millennial pietists, the delusional post-Soviet socialists, the corporatists, professional academia (itself a monopolistic and calcifying living fossil from the Medieval period); they are the constant doomsayers, the hordes of political hucksters worshipping at the altar of Keynesian calculationism, the protectionists, and the cultural mytho-nationalists (to name a few). Humanity's raw intelligence has indeed increased dramatically from the ancient era to the present—especially so in the years since Godwin's death—but true progress remains unevenly distributed. With almost two centuries of horrifying hindsight, we know better and cannot afford to have so hopeful an outlook as Godwin's. Our true believers, hucksters, and technocrats all have access to technologies that, if reserved to the private playgrounds of a privileged few, could dramatically hamper human beings' prospects for the future on a scale never before imagined.

Summoning demons would be as nothing compared with the ability to command murderous swarms of microdrones. None of the disasters caused throughout Godwin's volume would stand in comparison to the destruction unleashed by a single hydrogen bomb—and a small handful of chief executives throughout the world command thousands of those weapons. Perhaps even more bizarre to conceive of is the idea of a real philosopher's stone—unlimited, infinitely reproducible material wealth and unlimited life, both provided technologically through means only dreamed of in the most feverish of medieval minds—hoarded by a single individual. Yet today, those things are closer than ever before—and they are *real*. Technology virtually indistinguishable from magic operates all around us every day, and we rarely think twice about it.

If Ray Kurzweil, Google's director of engineering and one of the world's leading futurist thinkers, is to be believed, we are literally a few decades from entering not only "The Age of Intelligent Machines," but also "The Age of Spiritual Machines." Kurzweil has built a fabulously successful career as an inventor and researcher by studying pattern recognition—his technical field—and the implications of important computing concepts, such as Moore's Law and the Turing test, and by introducing challenging innovations of his own. Economist James D. Miller writes that Moore's Law (named after Gordon Moore, a cofounder of Intel) "has an excellent track record of predicting increases in computer power and performance." Although it is more of an observation of technological performance than a physical law of computation, the concept "implies that the quantity of computing power you could buy for a given amount of money would double about every year. Repeated doubling makes things very big, very fast. Twenty doublings yields about a millionfold increase."

Should Moore's Law hold, Kurzweil predicts that computers will soon be able to pass the famous Turing test, in which artificial intelligences can convince us bio-intellects that they, too, are human. And "Once a computer achieves a level of intelligence comparable to human intelligence," Kurzweil assures us, "it will necessarily soar past it." With superhuman artificial intelligence (AI) improving and replicating itself at superhuman speed, the resulting "intelligence explosion" would alter human life in entirely unforeseen ways comparable only to relatively more minor events, such as the Neolithic and Industrial Revolutions. AIs capable of communicating with nanobots embedded in our brains could interpret our thoughts faster even than we can and break the central planner's information dilemma. With economic superabundance approximating the end of physical scarcity, universal free energy would likely become the only valuable resource. Should we produce friendly AIs, humanity would have its greatest ally ever in the quest for knowledge, longevity, and happiness. Should we produce unfriendly or indifferent AIs, we would likely find ourselves immediately exterminated as wasters of free energy. Because the possibility of human- and superhuman-level intelligence would introduce such intense change into human society, the past offers no reliable guide to the future. We cannot, as it were, see beyond the point of singularity to predict future events.

Although there is evidence that Moore's Law is reaching the limits of current technology, Kurzweil and his fellow "singularitarians" largely rest assured that (as has happened with some frequency in the past) new technologies will continue the exponential pace of computing power. "By 2019," he wrote in 2012, "a $1,000 computer will match the processing power of the human brain—about 20 million billion calculations per second." And although the exact timing of Kurzweilian predictions may change from year to year, the trend toward superhuman artificial intelligence is almost inevitable. Economist James Miller writes, "Imagine . . . that Kurzweil underestimates by a factor of a thousand how much computing power will be needed to take us to a Singularity. Because of Moore's Law yearly doubling of the amount of computing power you can buy per dollar, such a thousandfold error would cause Kurzweil's predictions to be off by only a decade." Although it is in no way the intention of this essay—much less this volume—to confirm or deny Kurzweil's hypotheses, premises, or conclusions, it *is* my contention that futurist technologies offer a new class of thoroughly modern necromancers, alchemists, and witches opportunities to achieve the power-mad dreams of their historic forebears.[56]

Godwin was fortunate enough to see witchcraft disappear into a world of mechanical technologies and education. In our own age, technology has become intensely and amazingly more miraculous than anything the most talented of historical magicians could have ever pulled off, and although we no longer think these miracles have mystical origins, they do offer societies' wealthiest and most powerful few a unique historical opportunity to determine the fate of the entire human population. The difference between a dystopian hellscape, in which humanity is exterminated by robot overlords, and a technological millennium, in which the mind finally escapes its bodily prison, may well depend on our popular (and elite) conceptions of history and economics. When $1,000 can purchase the computing power of the entire human species' brains (Kurzweil predicts this will be sometime between roughly 2045 and 2060), our notions about whether societies are sculpted from below, through peaceful interaction and trade, or from above, through the imposition of force in interpersonal affairs, will undoubtedly affect the sorts of AI we produce and the uses to which their "masters" may put them.

Lives of the Necromancers is so interesting precisely because it takes those relatively few people in society who used widespread beliefs in the supernatural off their perch at the tip of the social hierarchy. Viewing them and their activities from below, as it were, and through their own actual daily lived experience, Godwin dispels the mystique and lays bare the true evil of their deeds. Necromancers and witches were not evil for pretending to contact demons and dead people; their evil arose from their exploitation of less intelligent or more gullible people. Yet Godwin believed that knowledge increasingly distinguished mere hucksters from true believers. There were those who believed in mysticism and magic out of genuine and even good-natured faith that occult practice benefited humanity. Then there were those gradually exposed as a class of mere exploiters who, cumulatively, hoarded information and technology from the population so that the few lords and priests might better shear their human sheep. So, once again, although Godwin ended his volume on a hopeful note, we must conclude this one with an admittedly strange and perhaps pessimistic question: *Is Ray Kurzweil a necromancer?*—and, if so, is he a Joan of Arc–style true believer or a mere huckster? When those brave, brilliant, and enterprising great men and women and the powerful nation-states of the modern day strike out into the unknown wilds of superhuman artificial intelligence, will they emulate Early Modern corporations and Modern constitutional nation-states by hoarding the future's benefits and powers for themselves? Or will we be able to fulfill Thomas Paine's desire that government be rebuilt from the right end?

Decision theorist, founder of the Singularity Institute, researcher at the Machine Intelligence Research Institute, and "very small-l libertarian"[57] Eliezer Yudkowsky is among those most concerned about the implications of an unfriendly AI-induced singularity. To ensure that any superhuman AI humans created would be friendly, Yudkowsky has solicited funding for a seed AI from billionaire investor Peter Thiel (among others). Having properly ensured the seed AI would indeed be friendly, Yudkowsky intends to switch it on and watch the "utopian Singularity" unfold. "One approach" to implementing the future tech utopia, James Miller writes, "would be to have an AI function as an ideal libertarian government." Because Miller takes the libertarian ideal to be "1. Enforcing property rights, and 2. Providing for the common defense against external and internal enemies," it should not be surprising that creating a libertarian "ultra-intelligent ruler" would require less programming skill than creating a hyper-interventionist one. Programmers and researchers such as Yudkowsky and Kurzweil "creating libertarian ultra-intelligence could take advantage of all the brainpower libertarians have directed toward figuring out how a libertarian government would operate." Essentially, of course, the AI would have only to leave us alone unless we desired peaceful interactions with it. Miller continues, "A libertarian ultra-AI ruler would essentially turn itself into an operating system for the universe, in which it sets the very basic rules—don't kill, steal, or renege on promises—and lets people do whatever else they want."[58]

Yudkowsky himself once wanted exactly that. Now he considers the idea "simple but wrong" and favors what Miller calls "extrapolation," in which the AI makes its decisions not according to your expressed preference but rather your real and true preference, of which even you may not be aware. As Miller explains the view, when the Greek goddess Eos asked Zeus to immortalize her lover, Zeus granted her wish, although the immortal lover continued to age forever. The fate is eventually worse than death. Had Zeus cleverly (and reasonably, even humanely) extrapolated that in fact what Eos wanted was an immortal lover whose condition never depreciated, the results would have pleased everyone involved much more. Thus, although we very often have clear visions of a better world we would much prefer to inhabit, a wide variety of inhibitions rise up to prevent positive action. Extrapolative AIs could cut through such inaction, coordinate huge amounts of conflicting preferences in the human mind, and alter our world accordingly despite our individual inabilities or unwillingness to carry out our own preferences. Smithian economics requires trade to produce new value from the same materials; AI economics may not even require consumers to express their preferences to themselves. The shift would require entirely new thinking in the social sciences.

Yet observers of contemporary society may with much justification believe that most of the population—including the political class—is doggedly committed to very old thinking. Miller and Kurzweil feel quite comfortable in asserting that our beneficence outweighs our villainy, and Miller goes so far as to apply Ricardo's law of comparative advantage to exchanges between superintelligent AIs and human beings. Although we may be inferior in every regard, it would still be in the self-interest of a benevolent AI to cooperate peacefully with other species. Similarly, we are told to rest assured that "If the affluent make wide-scale use of intelligence-enhancing genetics for their children, Americans across the political spectrum would almost certainly support governments making the services available to the poor." Miller continues, assuming (naively?) that "Liberals profess a desire for equality of outcome, whereas conservatives claim to believe in equality of opportunity—both of which would become impossible if only the rich, or everyone but the poor, used genetic enhancements to create smarter children." Because African Americans, for example, are the poorest group in America, and because sub-Saharan Africa is the poorest region in the world, Miller reasons that if the rich enjoyed sole access to advanced technologies, individuals with whiter skin would disproportionately soar above their darker-complected fellows. The racial disparity in access to future technologies "would so horrify liberals that providing intelligence enhancements to the poor would likely become their top priority."[59] Although it is not my intention to suggest a 21st-century Luddism, nor do I believe that elites are likely to be able to monopolize the benefits of powerful new technologies, I do harbor deep suspicions that much of modern-day benevolence is merely social signaling fueled by the power of constant networking. Without genuine intellectual, ideological, and moral convictions that individuals are important *as such*, our societies are likely condemned to repeat history's train of horrors. Although it certainly serves a variety of political purposes when liberals preach universal charity and conservatives preach universal virtue, I suspect that without political battles to fight, much of the concern would evaporate into indifference.

But, fear not!—in a scenario that feels very much as if it could have been written in a modernized version of *Lives of the Necromancers*, Miller offers readers the following:

> While walking down the street, you feel a cold hand on your shoulders and turn around to see a strange-looking man touching you. He mumbles, "Here is your destiny" and hands you a scroll that contains fifty predictions for the next year and one prophecy that will supposedly unfold in 2045.

> A year later you realize that every single one of the scroll's predictions for the year has come true. The accuracy of the scroll convinces you that its 2045 prophecy will also come to pass. The prophecy reads:

> The year 2045 will bring the world one of three possible fates:

> 1. Total annihilation—everyone dies.
> 2. Immense wealth—everyone becomes rich.
> 3. Unimaginable change—everyone's past wealth and material possessions no longer have value . . .

> As you might have figured out, I'm the strange-looking man, and this book is your scroll.[60]

Miller's point is the same as that of all those who have sought to divine the future and exercise control over events—knowledge of the future could position those in the present to do extraordinarily well as time goes on. Should you accept his and Ray Kurzweil's (and many others') arguments, which place the singularity between 2045 and 2060, surviving to that time frame should be among your top priorities. And maybe it already is. Once again, it is not my intention to affect the technical discussions surrounding modern computing and philosophy of mind, but rather to suggest that if indeed we do want a world in which technology benefits all human beings, we must not maintain a calcified worldview from above. We must reorient our understandings of human history—and probably all of the social sciences—to account for the different ways in which billions of human beings experience the world. No single narrative will do; no teleological tales in which nation-states and political organizations are the highest forms of human action. Rather, the histories informing our present and future should reflect the reality of human life as closely as possible by constructing it both from the bottom up and the top down. Somewhere in between, with a little luck, we can all find space to move forward into a new era of technological magic together. With a better, demystified, and sympathetic understanding of how we got here, we can enter into the construction of (another) new world in genuine good faith.

Informed by history from above, the current and future generations of intelligence pioneers may well seek to create a new privileged class of rulers over a distinctly new sort of human society, in which industrial workers and capitalists are replaced by liquidated populations and elite-robot superbeings. Armed with vigorous, passionate, and sympathetic history from below, however, we may well just succeed in sorting out the saints from the demons after all, before they've had their way with us.

Notes

Introduction

1. Anthony Comegna, ed., *Liberty and Power: A Reader* (Washington: Cato Institute, 2017).

2. Ludwig von Mises, "Psychology and Thymology," chap. 12 in *Theory and History: An Interpretation of Social and Economic Evolution*, 2nd ed. (Auburn, AL: Ludwig von Mises Institute, 2007), pp. 264–84. Originally published in 1957.

3. For American and Atlantic history from above by method—that is, using aggregated data, sources produced by elites, or writing about the elite perspective—see the following: Bernard Bailyn, *The New England Merchants in the Seventeenth Century* (New York: Harper & Row, 1955); Bernard Bailyn, *The Ideological Origins of the American Revolution* (Cambridge, MA: Belknap Press, 1967); Bernard Bailyn, *Atlantic History: Concept and Contours* (Cambridge, MA: Harvard University Press, 2005); Lance Banning, *The Jeffersonian Persuasion: Evolution of a Party Ideology* (Ithaca, NY: Cornell University Press, 1978); Henry Steele Commager, *Jefferson, Nationalism, and the Enlightenment* (New York: George Braziller, 1975); Paul Conkin, *Prophets of Prosperity: America's First Political Economists* (Bloomington: Indiana University Press, 1980); Edwin Merrick Dodd, *American Business Corporations until 1860, with Special Reference to Massachusetts* (Cambridge, MA: Harvard University Press, 1954); Paul Finkelman, *Proslavery Thought, Ideology, and Politics* (New York: Garland Publishing, 1989); Robert William Fogel and Stanley L. Engerman, *Time on the Cross: The Economics of American Negro Slavery* (Boston: Little, Brown, 1974); Paul Gilroy, *The Black Atlantic: Modernity and Double Consciousness* (Cambridge, MA: Harvard University Press, 1993); Carter Goodrich, *Government Promotion of American Canals and Railroads, 1800–1890*

(Westport, CT: Greenwood Press, 1960); Jack P. Greene and Philip D. Morgan, eds., *Atlantic History: A Critical Appraisal* (Oxford, UK: Oxford University Press, 2009); Gwendolyn Midlo Hall, *Slavery and African Ethnicities in the Americas* (Chapel Hill: University of North Carolina Press, 2005); Bray Hammond, *Banks and Politics in America: From the Revolution to the Civil War* (Princeton, NJ: Princeton University Press, 1957); Louis Hartz, *The Liberal Tradition in America: An Interpretation of American Political Thought Since the Revolution* (New York: Harcourt, Brace & World, 1955); Michael Holt, *The Fate of Their Country: Politicians, Slavery Extension, and the Coming of the Civil War* (New York: Hill & Wang, 2004); James Willard Hurst, *The Legitimacy of the Business Corporation in the Law of the United States, 1780–1970* (Charlottesville: University of Virginia Press, 1970); Henry Farnham May, *The Enlightenment in America* (Oxford, UK: Oxford University Press, 1976); Edmund Morgan, *The Birth of the Republic, 1763–1789* (Chicago: University of Chicago Press, 1956); Douglass North, *The Economic Growth of the United States, 1790–1860,* (New York: W. W. Norton, 1966); Peter Onuf, *The Mind of Thomas Jefferson* (Charlottesville: University of Virginia Press, 2007); Vernon Louis Parrington, *Main Currents in American Thought: An Interpretation of American Literature from the Beginnings to 1920, Vols. 1–3* (New York: Harcourt, Brace & World, 1958; original printing 1927); David Pletcher, *The Awkward Years: American Foreign Policy under Garfield and Arthur* (Columbia: University of Missouri Press, 1962); Carroll Quigley, *The Anglo-American Establishment: From Rhodes to Cliveden* (New York: Books in Focus, 1981; originally published 1949); Joel Silbey, *The Shrine of Party: Congressional Voting Behavior, 1841–1852* (Pittsburgh: University of Pittsburgh Press, 1967); J. Mills Thornton, *Politics and Power in a Slave Society: Alabama, 1800–1860* (Baton Rouge: Louisiana State University Press, 1978); Glyndon Van Deusen, *The Jacksonian Era, 1828–1848* (New York: Harper & Brothers, 1959).

4. For American and Atlantic history from above by methodology, see the following: John Ashworth, *"Agrarians & Aristocrats": Party Political Ideology in the United States, 1837–1846* (London: Royal Historical Society, 1983); C. A. Bayly, *The Birth of the Modern World, 1780–1914* (Malden, MA: Blackwell Publishing, 2004); Thomas Bender, *A Nation among Nations: America's Place in World History* (New York: Hill & Wang, 2006); Christopher Clark, *Social Change in America: From the Revolution through the Civil War* (Chicago: Ivan R. Dee Publisher, 2006); David Eltis, *Economic Growth and the Ending of the Transatlantic Slave Trade* (New York: Oxford University Press, 1987); Tony Freyer, *Producers versus Capitalists: Constitutional Conflict in Antebellum America* (Charlottesville: University of Virginia Press, 1994); Daniel Gaido, *The Formative Period of American Capitalism: A Materialist Interpretation* (London: Routledge, 2006);

Gary W. Gallagher and Rachel A. Shelden, eds., *A Political Nation: New Directions in Mid-Nineteenth-Century American Political History* (Charlottesville: University of Virginia Press, 2012); Daniel Walker Howe, *What Hath God Wrought: The Transformation of America, 1815–1848* (Oxford, UK: Oxford University Press, 2007); Walter Hugins, *Jacksonian Democracy and the Working Class: A Study of the New York Workingmen's Movement, 1829–1837* (Stanford, CA: Stanford University Press, 1960); Paul Johnson, *A Shopkeeper's Millennium: Society and Revivals in Rochester, New York, 1815–1837*, 25th anniversary ed. (New York: Hill & Wang, 2004); Lawrence Kohl, *The Politics of Individualism: Parties and the American Character in the Jacksonian Era* (New York: Oxford University Press, 1989); Wim Klooster, *Revolutions in the Atlantic World: A Comparative History* (New York: New York University Press, 2009); Scott Martin, *Cultural Change and the Market Revolution in America, 1789–1860* (Lanham, MD: Rowman & Littlefield, 2005); Marvin Meyers, *The Jacksonian Persuasion* (Stanford, CA: Stanford University Press, 1957); R. R. Palmer, *The Age of Democratic Revolution: A Political History of Europe and America, 1760–1800*, Vol. 1, *The Struggle* (Princeton, NJ: Princeton University Press, 1959); Edward Pessen, *Jacksonian America: Society, Personality, and Politics* (Homewood, IL: Dorsey Press, 1969); Charles Sellers, *The Market Revolution: Jacksonian America, 1815–1846* (New York: Oxford University Press, 1991); Melvin Stokes and Stephen Conway, eds., *The Market Revolution in America: Social, Political, and Religious Expressions, 1800–1880* (Charlottesville, VA: University of Virginia Press, 1996); William Strauss and Neil Howe, *Generations: The History of America's Future, 1584 to 2069* (New York: William Morrow, 1991); William Strauss and Neil Howe, *The Fourth Turning: An American Prophecy—What the Cycles of History Tell Us about America's Next Rendezvous with Destiny* (New York: Broadway Books, 1997); Neil Howe, William Strauss, and R. J. Matson, *Millennials Rising: The Next Great Generation* (New York: Vintage Books, 2000); John Thornton, *Africa and Africans in the Making of the Atlantic World, 1400–1680* (Cambridge, UK: Cambridge University Press, 1992); Rush Welter, *The Mind of America: 1820–1860* (New York: Columbia University Press, 1975); Sean Wilentz, *Chants Democratic: New York City and the Rise of the American Working Class, 1768–1850* (New York: Oxford University Press, 1984); Sean Wilentz, *The Rise of American Democracy: Jefferson to Lincoln* (New York: W. W. Norton & Company, 2005); Eric Williams, *Capitalism and Slavery* (New York: Russell & Russell, 1961; originally published 1944).

5. For examples of history from below on the early modern and revolutionary periods in Western and Atlantic history, see the following: Juliana Barr, *Peace Came in the Form of a Woman: Indians and Spaniards in the Texas Borderlands* (Chapel Hill: University of North Carolina Press, 2007); Robert Baum, *Shrines of the Slave Trade: Diola Religion*

and Society in Precolonial Senegambia (New York: Oxford University Press, 1999); Robin Blackburn, *The Making of New World Slavery: From the Baroque to the Modern* (London: Verso, 1997); A. Adu Boahen, *African Perspectives on Colonialism* (Baltimore: Johns Hopkins University Press, 1998); Russell Bourne, *The Red King's Rebellion: Racial Politics in New England, 1675–1678* (New York: Oxford University Press, 1990); T. H. Breen, *The Marketplace of Revolution: How Consumer Politics Shaped American Independence* (Oxford, UK: Oxford University Press, 2004); Vincent Carretta, *Equiano, the African: Biography of a Self-Made Man* (London: Penguin Books, 2005); Ross Cordy, *A Study of Prehistoric Social Change: The Development of Complex Societies in the Hawaiian Islands* (New York: Academic Press, 1981); Bayo Holsey, *Routes of Remembrance: Refashioning the Slave Trade in Ghana* (Chicago: University of Chicago Press, 2008); C. L. R. James, *The Black Jacobins: Toussaint L'Ouverture and the San Domingo Revolution* (New York: Vintage, 1989); Robin Law, *The Slave Coast of West Africa, 1550–1750: The Impact of the Atlantic Slave Trade on an African Society* (Oxford, UK: Clarendon Press, 1991); Peter Linebaugh and Marcus Rediker, *Many-Headed Hydra: The Hidden History of the Revolutionary Atlantic* (Boston: Beacon Press, 2000); Sidney Mintz, *Sweetness and Power: The Place of Sugar in Modern History* (New York: Penguin Books, 1985); Jennifer Morgan, *Laboring Women: Reproduction and Gender in New World Slavery* (Philadelphia: University of Pennsylvania Press, 2004); Philip Morgan, *Slave Counterpoint: Black Culture in the Eighteenth-Century Chesapeake & Lowcountry* (Chapel Hill: University of North Carolina Press, 1998); Gary Nash, *Red, White, and Black: The People of Early North America*, 5th ed. (Upper Saddle River, NJ: Prentice-Hall, 2006); Pablo Perez-Mallaina, *Spain's Men of the Sea: Life on the Indies Fleets in the Sixteenth Century* (Baltimore: Johns Hopkins University Press, 1998); Marcus Rediker, *Villains of All Nations: Atlantic Pirates in the Golden Age* (Boston: Beacon Press, 2004); Marcus Rediker, *The Slave Ship: A Human History* (London: Penguin Books, 2007); Murray Rothbard, *Conceived in Liberty*, 4 vols. (Auburn, AL: Mises Institute, 1999); Julius Sheppard Scott, "The Common Wind: Currents of Afro-American Communication in the Era of the Haitian Revolution" (PhD diss., Duke University, 1986); Rosalind Shaw, *Memories of the Slave Trade: Ritual and the Historical Imagination in Sierra Leone* (Chicago: University of Chicago Press, 2002); Stephanie Smallwood, *Saltwater Slavery: A Middle Passage from Africa to American Diaspora* (Cambridge, MA: Harvard University Press, 2007); Barbara Clark Smith, *The Freedoms We Lost: Consent and Resistance in Revolutionary America* (New York: New Press, 2010); David Stannard, *Before the Horror: The Population of Hawaii on the Eve of Western Contact* (Honolulu: Social Science Research Institute, 1989); Megan Vaughan, *Creating the Creole Island: Slavery in Eighteenth-Century Mauritius*

(Durham, NC: Duke University Press, 2003); Eric Wolf, *Peasants* (Englewood Cliffs, NJ: Prentice-Hall, 1966); Eric Wolf, *Europe and the People Without History* (Berkeley: University of California Press, 1982).

6. For 19th-century history from below, see the following: Herbert Aptheker, *American Negro Slave Revolts*, 5th ed. (New York: International Publishers, 1983; original printing 1943); Stuart Banner, *Possessing the Pacific: Land, Settlers, and Indigenous People from Australia to Alaska* (Cambridge, MA: Harvard University Press, 2007); Nina Baym, *American Women Writers and the Work of History, 1790–1860* (New Brunswick, NJ: Rutgers University Press, 1995); Ira Berlin, Joseph Patrick Reidy, and Leslie S. Rowland, eds., *Freedom's Soldiers: The Black Military Experience in the Civil War* (New York: Cambridge University Press, 1998); John F. Burns and Richard J. Orsi, eds., *Taming the Elephant: Politics, Government, and Law in Pioneer California* (Berkeley: University of California Press, 2003); Jack Cahill, *Forgotten Patriots: Canadian Rebels on Australia's Convict Shores* (Toronto: Robin Brass Studio, 1998); Craig Calhoun, *The Roots of Radicalism: Tradition, the Public Sphere, and Early Nineteenth-Century Social Movements* (Chicago: University of Chicago Press, 2012); Joan Cashin, *A Family Venture: Men and Women on the Southern Frontier* (Baltimore: Johns Hopkins University Press, 1991); Erik Chaput, *The People's Martyr: Thomas Wilson Dorr and His 1842 Rhode Island Rebellion* (Lawrence: University of Kansas Press, 2013); Edward P. Cheney, *The Anti-rent Agitation in the State of New York, 1839–1846* (Philadelphia: University of Pennsylvania, 1887); Christopher Clark, *Social Change in America: From the Revolution through the Civil War* (Chicago: Ivan R. Dee, 2006); George M. Dennison, *The Dorr War: Republicanism on Trial, 1831–1861* (Lexington: University of Kentucky Press, 1976); Ruth Dunley, "A.D. Smith: Knight-Errant of Radical Democracy," (PhD diss., University of Ottawa, 2008); Eric Foner, *Reconstruction: America's Unfinished Revolution, 1863–1877* (New York: HarperCollins, 2002; originally published 1988); Eric Foner, *Free Soil, Free Labor, Free Men: The Ideology of the Republican Party before the Civil War* (Oxford, UK: Oxford University Press, 1995); Eugene D. Genovese, *Roll, Jordan, Roll: The World the Slaves Made* (New York: Pantheon Books, 1972); Eugene D. Genovese, *The Political Economy of Slavery: Studies in the Economy and Society of the Slave South*, 2nd ed. (Middletown, CT: Wesleyan University Press, 1989; originally published 1965); Marvin Gettleman, *The Dorr Rebellion: A Study in American Radicalism: 1833–1849* (New York: Random House, 1973); Jonathan Glickstein, *Concepts of Free Labor in Antebellum America* (New Haven, CT: Yale University Press, 1991); Elliott Gorn, *The Manly Art: Bare-Knuckle Prize Fighting in America* (Ithaca, NY: Cornell University Press, 1986); David Grimstead, *American Mobbing, 1828–1861: Toward Civil War* (New York: Oxford University Press, 1998);

Herbert G. Gutman, *Slavery and the Numbers Game: A Critique of Time on the Cross* (Urbana and Chicago: University of Illinois Press, 1975); Herbert G. Gutman, *The Black Family in Slavery and Freedom, 1750–1925* (New York: Vintage Books, 1976); Reeve Huston, *Land and Freedom: Rural Society, Popular Protest, and Party Politics in Antebellum New York* (Oxford, UK: Oxford University Press, 2000); Randall Jimerson, *The Private Civil War: Popular Thought during the Sectional Conflict* (Baton Rouge: Louisiana State University Press, 1988); Mary Kelley, *Learning to Stand and Speak: Women, Education, and Public Life in America's Republic* (Chapel Hill: University of North Carolina Press, 2006); Oscar Kinchen, *The Rise and Fall of the Patriot Hunters* (New York: Bookman Associates, 1956); Naomi Lamoreaux, *Insider Lending: Banks, Personal Connections, and Economic Development in Industrial New England* (Cambridge, UK: Cambridge University Press, 1994); Kathy Peiss, *Cheap Amusements: Working Women and Leisure in Turn-of-the-Century New York* (Philadelphia: Temple University Press, 1986); Lewis Perry, *Radical Abolitionism: Anarchy and the Government of God in Antislavery Thought* (Ithaca, NY: Cornell University Press, 1973); Marcus Rediker, *The Amistad Rebellion: An Atlantic Odyssey of Slavery and Freedom* (London: Penguin, 2013); W. J. Rorabaugh, *The Alcoholic Republic: An American Tradition* (Oxford, UK: Oxford University Press, 1979); Mary P. Ryan, *Civic Wars: Democracy and Public Life in the American City during the Nineteenth Century* (Berkeley: University of California Press, 1997); Rosemarie Zagarri, *Revolutionary Backlash: Women and Politics in the Early American Republic* (Philadelphia: University of Pennsylvania Press, 2007); Ronald and Mary Zboray, *Voices without Votes: Women and Politics in Antebellum New England* (Durham: University of New Hampshire Press, 2010).

7. For more explicitly theoretical or historiographical discussions of history from below and its applications compared with history from above, see the following: Daniel Gaido, *The Formative Period of American Capitalism: A Materialist Interpretation* (London: Routledge, 2006); Ernest Gellner, *Plough, Sword and Book: The Structure of Human History* (Chicago: University of Chicago Press, 1988); Eric Hobsbawm, *On History* (New York: New Press, 1997); Marnie Hughes-Warrington, *Revisionist Histories* (London: Routledge, 2013); Marnie Hughes-Warrington, ed., *World Histories* (New York: Palgrave MacMillan, 2005); Rose Wilder Lane, *The Discovery of Freedom: Man's Struggle against Authority* (San Francisco: Fox & Wilkes, 1993; original printing 1943); Sidney Lens, *Radicalism in America: Great Rebels and the Causes for Which They Fought from 1620 to the Present* (New York: Thomas Crowley, 1969); Staughton Lynd, *Intellectual Origins of American Radicalism* (New York: Pantheon Books, 1968); Albert Memmi, *The Colonizer and the Colonized*, expanded ed. (Boston: Beacon Press, 1991; originally

published 1968); Alun Munslow, *A History of History* (London: Routledge, 2012); Walter Nugent, *Structures of American Social History* (Bloomington: Indiana University Press, 1981); Matt Perry, *Marxism and History* (New York: Palgrave, 2002); Bernard Sternsher, *Consensus, Conflict, and American Historians* (Bloomington: Indiana University Press, 1975); A. A. M. Van Der Linden, *A Revolt against Liberalism: American Radical Historians, 1959–1976* (Amsterdam: Rodopi, 1996).

Chapter 3

8. Peter Linebaugh, *The Incomplete, True, Authentic, and Wonderful History of May Day* (Oakland, CA: PM Press, 2016), p. 15.

9. Nathaniel Hawthorne, "The May-Pole of Merry Mount," in *Twice-Told Tales* (Boston: John B. Russell, 1837), pp. 87–93; see also Jack Dempsey, ed., *New English Canaan, by Thomas Morton of "Merrymount:" Text, Notes, Biography & Criticism* (Stoneham, MA: Jack Dempsey, 2000). For a broad and powerful overview of popular rebellions in the Early Modern period, see Peter Linebaugh and Marcus Rediker, *The Many-Headed Hydra: Sailors, Slaves, Commoners, and the Hidden History of the Revolutionary Atlantic* (Boston: Beacon Press, 2013).

10. Thomas Morton, *New English Canaan; or New Canaan: Containing an Abstract of New England* (Amsterdam: Jacob Frederick Stam, 1637), https://www.libertarianism .org/publications/essays/new-english-canaan-part-i.

Chapter 4

11. Daniel Defoe, *An Account of the Conduct and Proceedings of the late John Gow alias Smith, Captain of the late Pirates, Executed for Murder and Piracy* (London, 1725), https://www .libertarianism.org/publications/essays/saga-john-gow-part-i; https://www.libertarianism .org/publications/essays/saga-john-gow-part-ii.

Chapter 5

12. William Snelgrave, *A New Account of Some Parts of Guinea, and the Slave-Trade* (London: Printed for James, John, and Paul Knapton, 1734).

13. Robin Law, *The Slave Coast of West Africa, 1550–1750: The Impact of the Atlantic Slave Trade on an African Society* (Oxford: Clarendon Press, 1991), p. 348.

Chapter 6

14. Snelgrave, *A New Account.*

Chapter 7

15. For more on the tortured lives of sailors, see Marcus Rediker, *Villains of All Nations: Atlantic Pirates in the Golden Age* (Boston: Beacon Press, 2004).

Chapter 8

16. David Walker, *Walker's Appeal, in Four Articles, Together with a Preamble to the Colored Citizens of the World, but in Particular and Very Expressly to Those of the United States of America* (Excerpts) (Boston: Printed for the author, 1829).

Chapter 9

17. This document has been reproduced from Fitzwilliam Byrdsall, *The History of the Loco-Foco or Equal Rights Party, Its Movements, Conventions and Proceedings, with Short Characteristic Sketches of Its Prominent Men* (New York: Clement & Packard, 1842), pp. 39–42.

Chapter 10

18. Theodore Sedgwick III, "Monarchy vs. Democracy," *New York Evening Post*, January 4, 1836, https://www.libertarianism.org/publications/essays/monarchy-vs-democracy.

Chapter 11

19. William Leggett, "The Restraining Law and Its Abominations," *New York Evening Post*, August 31, 1836, https://www.libertarianism.org/publications/essays/wall-street-palaces.

20. William Leggett, "The Street of the Palaces," *New York Plaindealer*, December 10, 1836.

Chapter 12

21. John L. O'Sullivan, "Introduction: The Democratic Principle, the Importance of Its Assertion, and Application to Our Political System and Literature," *U.S. Magazine & Democratic Review* 1, no. 1 (1837), https://www.libertarianism.org/publications/essays/problematic-triad-democracy-liberty-nationalism?.

Chapter 13

22. William Leggett, "Abolition Insolence," *New York Plaindealer*, July 29, 1837, https://www.libertarianism.org/publications/essays/leggett-spooner-abolishing-slavery-without-state.

23. Lysander Spooner, *A Plan for the Abolition of Slavery* (1858).

Chapter 14

24. "Autobiography of Ferret Snapp Newcraft, Esq., Being a Full Exposition and Exemplification of 'The Credit System,'" *U.S. Magazine & Democratic Review* 2, no. 6 (May 1838): 167–87, http://www.yamaguchy.com/library/gouge/ferret.html.

Chapter 15

25. Unsigned Author, "Extracts from the Private Diary of a Certain Bank Director," *US Magazine & Democratic Review* 2, no. 8 (July 1838), https://www.libertarianism .org/publications/essays/extracts-private-diary-certain-bank-director-part-i.

Chapter 16

26. Robert J. Scholnick, "Extermination and Democracy: O'Sullivan, the Democratic Review, and Empire, 1837–1840," *American Periodicals* 15, no. 2 (2005): 123–41; Edward Widmer, *Young America: The Flowering of Democracy in New York City* (New York: Oxford University Press, 1999); Perry Miller, *The Raven and the Whale: The War of Words and Wits in the Era of Poe and Melville* (New York: Harcourt, Brace & World, 1956); Mark Lause, *Young America: Land, Labor, and the Republican Community* (Chicago: University of Illinois Press, 2005); Yonatan Eyal, *The Young America Movement and the Transformation of the Democratic Party, 1828–1861* (Cambridge, UK: Cambridge University Press, 2007).

27. John L. O'Sullivan, "The Great Nation of Futurity," *U.S. Magazine & Democratic Review* 16, no. 23 (November 1839): 426–30, https://www.libertarianism.org/media /classics-liberty/john-l-osullivan-great-nation-futurity.

Chapter 17

28. Sarah O'Dowd, *A Rhode Island Original: Frances Harriet Whipple Green McDougall* (Lebanon, NH: University Press of New England, 2004); Frances Harriet Whipple, *Memoirs of Elleanor Eldridge*, ed. Joycelyn Moody (Morgantown: West Virginia University Press, 2014); Frances H. Green, *Elleanor's Second Book* (Providence, RI: B. T. Albro, 1842); Frances H. Green, *The Mechanic* (Providence, RI: Burnett & King, 1842); Frances Harriet Green, *The Housekeeper's Book* (Philadelphia: William Marshall, 1837); Sidney S. Rider, "Bibliographical Memoir of Frances H. McDougall, Born Whipple," in *Bibliographical Memoirs of Three Rhode Island Authors: Joseph K. Angell, Frances H. (Whipple) McDougall, Catharine R. Williams* (Providence, RI: Sidney S. Rider, 1880).

29. Frances Whipple, *Memoirs of Elleanor Eldridge*, Excerpts (Providence, RI: B. T. Albro, 1841), https://www.libertarianism.org/publications/essays/elleanor-eldridge-folk -hero-african-american-feminism.

Chapter 18

30. James Gemmel (One of the Captives), "Two Years in Van Dieman's Land," *New York Daily Plebeian* 1, no. 5, July 1, 1842.

Chapter 19

31. Erik Chaput, *The People's Martyr: Thomas Wilson Dorr and His 1842 Rhode Island Rebellion* (Lawrence: University of Kansas Press, 2013); Russell J. DeSimone, "Lewis and Ann Parlin," issue 6 of *Rhode Island's Rebellion: A Look at Some Aspects of the Dorr War* (Middletown, RI: Bartlett Press, 2009); Marvin Gettleman, *The Dorr Rebellion: A Study in American Radicalism: 1833–1849* (New York: Random House, 1973); Ronald and Mary Zboray, *Voices without Votes: Women and Politics in Antebellum New England* (Durham: University of New Hampshire Press, 2010); George M. Dennison, *The Dorr War: Republicanism on Trial, 1831–1861* (Lexington: University of Kentucky Press, 1976); Patrick T. Conley, *Democracy in Decline: Rhode Island's Constitutional Development, 1776–1841* (Providence: Rhode Island Historical Society, 1977).

32. "Great Meeting in Relation to Rhode Island," New York *Daily Plebeian* 1, no. 110, November 1842, https://www.libertarianism.org/publications/essays/woman-spunk-ann-parlins-vision-revolution.

Chapter 20

33. Levi D. Slamm, "Oppression vs. Freedom," *New York Daily Plebeian*, September 21, 1842, https://www.libertarianism.org/publications/essays/battling-empire-part-i.

34. "Emmett," "Ireland and her Wrongs," *Daily Plebeian*, June 12, 1843.

35. Levi D. Slamm, "Opposition to the British Empire," *Daily Plebeian*, June 23, 1843.

36. Levi D. Slamm, "British Honor at Cabul," *Daily Plebeian*, February 25, 1843.

37. "Correspondence of the *Plebeian*," *Daily Plebeian*, May 26, 1843.

38 Levi D. Slamm, "British Usurpation of the Sandwich Islands," *Daily Plebeian*, June 8, 1843.

39. Unsigned Correspondent, "From the Cincinnati Gazette: India," *Daily Plebeian*, July 19, 1843.

Chapter 21

40. Luther S. Dixon, ed., *Reports of Cases Argued and Determined in the Supreme Court of the State of Wisconsin, with Tables of the Cases and Principal Matters. Abram D. Smith, Official Reporter. Vol. III, Containing Cases Decided at the June and December Terms, 1854*

(Chicago: Callaghan & Company, Law Publishers, 1875), 13–134. See also Ruth Dunley, "A.D. Smith: Knight-Errant of Radical Democracy" (PhD diss., University of Ottawa, 2008).

41. Abram D. Smith, In re Booth, 1854, https://www.libertarianism.org/media/classics-liberty/abram-d-smith-re-booth-part-1.

42. Abram D. Smith, In re Booth oral remarks, 1854, https://www.libertarianism.org/media/classics-liberty/abram-d-smith-nullification-part-2.

Chapter 22

43. Lysander Spooner, "Abolition Plan, To the Non-Slaveholders of the South," 1858, https://www.libertarianinstitute.org/libertarianism/plan-abolition-slavery-non-slaveholders-south-1858/.

Chapter 23

44. "Fascisti Idea to Spread—Exiled Russians Would Adopt Plan in Own Country—One Million Men in Italy Are Banded Together to Advance Nationalism and War on Socialists and Communists," *Kansas City Star*, August 9, 1922. https://www.libertarianism.org/publications/essays/fascism-american-reactions-1922.

45. United News, "'Discipline—and Work' Aim of Italy's Man of Hour and Fascisti Head," *Dallas Morning News*, August 21, 1922.

46. Paul Scott Mowrer, "Fascisti Leader Backed by 1,000,000 Armed Men Is Now Unchallenged Ruler of Italy," *Fort Worth Star-Telegram*, October 30, 1922.

47. "Men and Affairs," *Fort Worth Star-Telegram*, November 5, 1922.

48. "Revolt Against Socialism," *Portland Morning Oregonian*, November 6, 1922.

49. J. W. T. Mason, "Middle Class Takes Fascism to Gain Rights—Revolt in Italy Projected by Underpaid 'White Collar' Folk, Says Writer," *Duluth News Tribune*, November 12, 1922.

50. "The Cure for Bolshevism," *San Jose (CA) Mercury Herald*, November 25, 1922.

51. "Letter Tells of Conditions Now in Italy," *Grand Forks (ND) Herald*, December 31, 1922.

Chapter 24

52. *Investigation of Nazi Propaganda Activities and Investigation of Certain Other Propaganda Activities, Public Statement of Special Committee on Un-American Activities, House of Representatives, Seventy-Third Congress, Second Session,* Released to the Press

Representatives by Hon. John W. McCormack and Hon. Samuel Dickstein, who were sitting as a Subcommittee, Released in New York City, NY, November 24, 1934 (Washington, DC: United States Government Printing Office, 1934); See also John L. Spivak, *A Man in His Time* (New York: Horizon Press, 1967), pp. 311, 322–25; Antony Sutton, "FDR: Man on the White Horse," chap. 10 in *Wall Street and FDR* (New York: Arlington House Publishers, 1975).

53. Ibid. See also: Testimony before Congress of Maj. Gen. S. D. Butler (Retired), Excerpts, https://www.libertarianism.org/publications/essays/smedley-butler-business-plot-part-i.

Chapter 25

54. Dwight D. Eisenhower, "Farewell Address," January 17, 1961, http://www.americanrhetoric.com/speeches/dwightdeisenhowerfarewell.html.

Chapter 26

55. Barry Goldwater, Acceptance Speech, 1964 Republican National Convention, https://www.washingtonpost.com/wp-srv/politics/daily/may98/goldwaterspeech.htm.

Conclusion

56. James D. Miller, *Singularity Rising: Surviving and Thriving in a Smarter, Richer, and More Dangerous World*, (Dallas: BenBella Books, 2012), pp. iv–9; Jay W. Richards, *Are We Spiritual Machines? Ray Kurzweil vs. the Critics of Strong A.I.* (Seattle: Discovery Institute, 2002), pp. 12–13; Bruce Schneier, *Data and Goliath: The Hidden Battles to Collect Your Data and Control Your World* (New York: W. W. Norton & Company, 2015).

57. Eliezer Yudkowsky, "Is That Your True Rejection?," *Cato Unbound: A Journal of Debate*, September 7, 2011, https://www.cato-unbound.org/2011/09/07/eliezer-yudkowsky/true-rejection.

58. Miller, *Singularity Rising*, pp. 35–42.

59. Ibid., pp. 172–73.

60. Ibid., pp. 175–76.

Index

Ableman, Stephen V. R., 318–34

Ableman v. Booth, 317

"Abolition Insolence" (Leggett), 207–9

abolitionist movement
  free African Americans and, 149–65
  growth of, 205–6
  Leggett's support for, 175–76, 205–9
  Smith and, 316–18
  Spooner's support for, 210–14, 335–45
  Whipple's contributions to, 264–74

"Abolition Plan, To the Non-Slaveholders of the South" (Spooner), 335–45

"Acceptance Speech, 1964 Republican National Convention" (Goldwater), 400–411

An Account of the Conduct and Proceedings of the late John Gow alias Smith, Captain of the late Pirates, Executed for Murder and Piracy (Defoe), 95–109

Afghanistan, British imperialism in, 297–98, 306–7

African Americans (free)
  abolitionist movement and, 149–65
  feminist movement and, 264–74
  resistance by, 12
  Special Field Order No. 15 land grants to, 318

aggregated data, history and, 6–7

Albertus Magnus, 422–23

alchemists, 415

Alliance Mutual Assurance, 178–79

American culture and institutions

O'Sullivan's promotion of, 191–203, 255–62

Young America movement and, 215–17

American exceptionalism

Jacksonian vision of, 183

liberal historical theory and, 8–9

Americanism, fascism and, 349–50

American Legion, 364–71, 378–80

American Liberty League, 376

American Revolution, from-above and from-below perspectives on, 10–13

Amphion, 416–17

ancient history, Morton's references to, 47

Antebellum era, 205–6

anti-British movement

Slamm's discussion of, 309–14

spread in Western frontier of, 295–98, 303–5

antinomianism, 10, 52, 315

Apollonius of Tyana, 418–19

Apuleius, 419

Arthur, Sir George, 280, 282–83

Articles of Confederation, 11

artificial intelligence, 430–39

artificial rights, locofocism and, 12

"Autobiography of Ferret Snapp Newcraft, Esq., Being a Full Exposition and Exemplification of 'The Credit System,'" 217–33

"Bacchanale Triumphe" (Morton), 48, 50, 73–76

Bacon, Roger, 423

banking system, satirical and critical analysis of, 215–33, 235–54

Bank of the United States, Jacksonian opposition to, 233–34

Becker, Carl, 10–11

Beemer, Jacob, 278

Benedict IX (Pope), 421

benevolence, artificial intelligence and, 435–39

Bonighton, Richard, 20–23

Booth, Sherman, 316, 318–34

Bozell, Leo Brent, 399

"British Honor at Cabul"
(Slamm), 306–7

British imperialism
American rivalry with, 276–84
Canadian rebellion and, 14,
275–84
colonialism and, 45–46
corporate charters and, 19–21
growth of, 295–98
Ireland and, 296, 301–3
Slamm's essays on, 295–314

"British Usurpation of the Sandwich Islands" (Slamm), 309–11

Brown, John, 206

Bryant, William Cullen, 175, 191

"Business Plot," 15, 363–88

Butler, Gen. Smedley D., 15
"Business Plot" and, 363–88
Congressional testimony by,
365–76
Senate report on investigation
of, 376–88

Canadian rebellion, 13, 275,
280–84, 295–96, 315–16

capitalism
mercantilism and, 29–31
monarchy and, 20–21

Caribbean, slavery in, 150

Castelli, Gerda Hellberg, 360–62

Catholicism, Puritanism and, 52

Cellini, Benvenuto, 424

Charles I (King of England), 20

Charles II (King of England),
286

Charles XI (King of Sweden),
426–27

Charter government in Rhode
Island, 285–86

Charter of Privileges and
Exemptions of the Dutch
West India Company; June 7,
1629, 34–43

China, British imperialism and,
296–98, 307–9

Christianity
Godwin's discussion of, 418–19
slavery and, 150, 158–60

Christmas, Albert G., 382–88

citizens' rights, Smith's advocacy
for, 316–17

Clark, Robert Sterling, 370–71,
378, 381–88

Clay, Henry, 151, 161–62

Cleveland Female Seminary, 316

colonialism
from-above perspective on,
9–10
from-below perspective on, 7–9

land enclosure in England and, 45–46

piracy and, 138

Walker's abolitionist appeal against, 151–53, 160–65

Commission to Sir Ferdinando Gorges as Governor of New England by Charles; July 23, 1637, 26–28

Committee for a Sound Dollar, 381

Conscience of a Conservative, The (Goldwater), 399–400

Constitution
British imperialism and, 303–4
consensus concerning, 11–12
corporate charters and, 10
history and role of, 4–5
Jacksonian banking reform and, 235–36
Leggett's discussion of, 183–84
Locofoco Declaration of Principles and, 168–73
ratification of, 11–12
Smith's discussion of, 315–16, 327–34
Walker's discussion of, 150

corporate charters. See also *specific charters by name*
colonialism and, 7–10
history of, 19–21

Leggett's criticism of, 184–90

mercantilism and, 29–31

revolt against, 13–14

Sedgwick's campaign against, 176–77

corporatism, democracy and, 14–16

"Correspondence of the *Plebeian*" *(Daily Plebeian)*, 307–9

Cotton, Charles O., 319

Council for New England, 20, 23–26

County Anti-Slavery Society, 316

"Cure for Bolshevism, The" 359–60

Dahomey, empire of, 111–21

Davis, John W., 370, 376

Declaration for Resignation of the Charter by the Council for New England; April 25, 1635, 23–26

Declaration of Principles (Locofoco Party), 168–73

Dee, John, 424–25

Defoe, Daniel, 95–109

democracy
Leggett's discussion of, 177–90
O'Sullivan's vision of, 191–203

Sedgwick's discussion of, 177–82

Democratic Party
  banking system and, 235–36
  Canadian revolution attempt and, 275
  expulsion of Leggett from, 175–76, 206
  Locofocos and, 167–73
  O'Sullivan's vision for, 13, 191–203
  Smith and, 315–17

democratic republicanism
  British imperialism and, 295–98
  O'Sullivan's concept of, 193–203

Democratic Review, 13

Demonology (James I), 426

Dickstein, Samuel, 382. *See also* McCormack-Dickstein Committee

Direct Tax Act, 318

Direct Tax Commission, 318

"'Discipline—and Work' Aim of Italy's Man of Hour and Fascisti Head," 352–53

Discovery of Witches, The (Hopkins), 426, 428

Dominicans, Godwin's discussion of, 422–23

Dorr, Thomas Wilson, 285–86

Dorrites, 285–86

"Dorr War," 285–86

Doyle, William, 366, 377

Dred Scott decision, 206

Durham Report on the Canadian Rebellion, 295–96

Dutch West India Company, charter of, 30–31, 34–43

Early Modern era
  Godwin's discussion of, 425–26
  Marymount settlement and, 49–52

Eastern priests and magicians, Godwin's discussion of, 419–20

Egeria (goddess), 418

Eisenhower, Dwight D., 15, 389–97

Eldridge, Elleanor, 264–74

Eldridge, George, 266

Elizabeth I (Queen of England), 20

Elleanor's Second Book (Whipple), 264

Enlightenment, 425

Eos (Greek goddess), 435

Epimenides, 417

"Equal Rights" Democrats, 167–68

Equal Rights Party. *See* Locofoco Party

European slave trade, West African kings and, 111–21

"Extracts from the Private Diary of a Certain Bank Director" *(U.S. Magazine and Democratic Review),* 237–54

"Farewell Address," 17 January 1961 (Eisenhower), 390–97

fascism, American reactions to, 349–62

"Fascisti Leader Backed by 1,000,000 Armed Men is Now Unchallenged Ruler of Italy" (Mowrer), 353–55

feminism
  of Ann Parlin, 286–94
  Whipple's contributions to, 264–74

feudalism, corporate charters and, 29–31

Fian, John, 426

First National Bank of Chicago, 383

First World War, 15

Fort Worth *Star-Telegram,* 350

Franciscans, Godwin's discussion of, 422–23

Franklin, Sir John, 277–80

free African Americans. *See* African Americans; slavery

freedom, Goldwater's discussion of, 401

free settlers, colonialism and, 46

French, Paul Comley, 379, 382

French Revolution, 295

from-above perspective in history, 1–6, 10–16

from-below perspective in history, 7–16

"From the Cincinnati Gazette: India" *(Daily Plebeian),* 311–14

Fugitive Slave Act, 14, 316, 325–34

Gardiner, Sir Christopher, 86–89

Garland, Benammi S., 319

Gemmel, James, 13, 275–84

General Charter for Those who Discover Any New Passages, Havens, Countries, or Places; March 27, 1614, 32–34

Glover, Joshua, 316–34

Godwin, William, 413–39

Goldwater, Barry, 15, 399–411

Gorges, Sir Ferdinando, 20–21, 26–28, 46, 53–54

Gorges, Robert, 21, 26–28

government

  Eisenhower's discussion of, 390–97

  Goldwater's discussion of, 400–411

  O'Sullivan's discussion of, 196–203, 257–62

Gow, John, 10, 93–109

Grant of Land North of the Saco River to Thomas Lewis and Richard Bonighton by the Council for New England; February 12, 1629, 21–23

"Great Clam Bakes," 285–86

"Great Meeting in Relation to Rhode Island" (Parlin), 287–94

"Great Nation of Futurity, The" (O'Sullivan), 256–62

Greek mysticism, Godwin's discussion of, 416–17

Gregory VII (Pope), 421

"gun-slave cycle," 117

Hakem, 419

Hamilton, Alexander, 175

Harbord (General), 376

Harper's Ferry, Brown's raid on, 206

Hawthorne, Nathaniel, 49, 191, 256

High Church Anglicanism, Puritanism and, 45–46

history

  artificial intelligence and, 438–39

  from-above and from-below perspectives in, 1–16

Hitler, Adolf, 373

Holy Roman Empire, slavery and, 150, 158–60

Hopkins, Matthew, 426–28

Hutchinson, Anne, 10, 52

ignorance, Walker on slavery and, 156–58

imperialism

  American conservative advocacy for, 400–411

  British-American rivalry and, 276–84

  from-above perspective on, 9–10

  from-below perspective on, 7–9

  land enclosure in England and, 45–46

  piracy and, 138

indentured servants, colonialism
and, 46
India, British imperialism in,
297–98, 311–14
In re Booth, 317–34
"Introduction: The Democratic
Principle, the Importance of
Its Assertion, and Applica-
tion to Our Political System
and Literature" (O'Sullivan),
192–203
Investiture Crisis, 421
Ireland, British imperialism in,
296, 301–3
"Ireland and Her Wrongs"
("Emmett" (Slamm)), 301–3

Jacksonian era
abolitionism and, 205–6
American exceptionalism and,
183
banking system during,
215–33, 235–54
British imperialism and,
295–98
Locofoco and Dorrite activism
during, 285–86
slavery during, 175
Young America movement and,
191, 256, 275

James I (King of England), 20,
425–26
James VI (King of Scotland) 425
Jefferson, Thomas, 151, 156,
169, 171
Joan of Arc, Godwin's discussion
of, 424–25
Johnson, Gen. Hugh, 376
Johnson, Lyndon Baines, 400
Jonson, Ben, 45, 50
Jupiter Elicius, 418

Kansas City *Star*, 349–50
Khan, Mahomed Akber, 306–7
Kurzweil, Ray, 430–36, 438

Lamont, Thomas W., 376
land enclosure, colonialism and,
45–46
Las Casas, Bartholomew,
158–60
Law, Robin, 114
Leggett, William, 12
abolitionist movement and,
175–76, 205–9
on law and democracy, 183–90
Monarchy and Democracy by,
177–82
on New York Restraining Law,
184–87

"Letter Tells of Conditions Now in Italy" (Castelli), 360–62

Lewis, Thomas, 20–23

liberal historical theory, from-below perspective and, 8–9

Lincoln, Abraham, 410

Linebaugh, Peter, 48–50

Lives of the Necromancers (Godwin), 413–39

lobbying, politics and, 216

Locke, John, 125, 336

Locofoco Party
  corporate charters and, 14
  formation of, 167–73, 175
  Jacksonian banking reforms and, 216–17
  O'Sullivan and, 237
  political activism of, 285–86
  rivalry with Britain and, 276
  slavery and, 12
  Smith and, 315–16

logrolling, political practice of, 216

MacArthur, Gen. Douglas, 364, 366, 375

MacGuire, Gerald, 366–67, 371–72, 377–88

Machine Intelligence Research Institute, 434

Mackenzie, William Lyon, 275, 283

Macnaghten, Sir William, 306–7

MacNider, Hanford, 375–76

magic, Godwin's discussion of, 421–22

Magi priesthood, Godwin's discussion of, 415–16, 419–20

Magus, Simon, 418

Manifest Destiny, 13, 183, 256–62, 298, 316

Manion, Clarence, 399

Manufacturers Trust Co., 382–84

Marxist historical theory, 8–9

Marymount settlement, 9–10, 46–92

Mason, J. W. T., 357–59

Massachusetts Bay Colony, antinomianism and, 52

Maypole celebration by Native Americans, Morton's description of, 48–50, 63–68

McCormack, John W., 382

McCormack-Dickstein Committee, 363–65, 382–84

medieval Europe, Godwin's discussion of, 420–24

Melville, Herman, 191

Memoirs of Elleanor Eldridge, The
(Whipple), 264–74

"Men and Affairs" *(Fort Worth
Star-Telegram)*, 355–56

mercantilism
corporate charters and, 29–31
piracy and, 138

methodological collectivism, 5–6

"Middle Class Takes Fascism
to Gain Rights—Revolt in
Italy Projected by Underpaid
'White Collar' Folk, Says
Writer" (Mason), 357–59

military establishment, Eisenhower's discussion of, 393–97

Miller, James D., 430, 432,
434–39

Miller, Linus Wilson, 277, 281

Milwaukee Daily Free Democrat,
316–18

Mises, Ludwig von, 1–2

monarchy
capitalism and, 20–21
mercantilism and, 29–31
Sedgwick's discussion of,
177–82

Monarchy v. Democracy
(Sedgwick), 177–82

Moore, Gordon, 430

Moore's Law, 430–32

Morton, Thomas, 9–10, 15,
45–52

Mowrer, Paul Scott, 353–55

Murphy, Grayson M.-P.,
368–69, 379

mushroom aristocracy, 7–8

Mussolini, Benito, 15, 349–62,
373

mutual assurance associations,
Sedgwick's discussion of,
178–82

Napoleonic Wars, 295–96

national culture. *See* American
culture and institutions

national literature. *See also* American culture and institutions
O'Sullivan's promotion of,
201–3, 255–62
Young America movement and,
215–17

national security, Goldwater's
discussion of, 403–11

Native Americans
in Marymount settlement,
48–52
Morton's discussion of, 46–47,
53–63

Puritan extermination of, 427–28

Netherlands, corporate charters and colonialism in, 30–31

New Account of Some Parts of Guinea, and the Slave-Trade, A (Snelgrave)
defense of slavery in, 123–32
piracy and slavery in, 133–45
West African slave trade discussed in, 111–21

New English Canaan; or New Canaan: Containing an, Abstract of New England (Morton), 46–92

New Masses magazine, 363–64

New York Daily Plebeian, 276, 296–98

New York Evening Post, 175–76, 184–87, 379

New York Plaindealer, 187–90

occultism, Godwin's discussion of, 420–23

Opium Wars (China), British imperialism and, 296–98, 307–9

"Opposition to the British Empire" (Slamm), 303–5

"Oppression vs. Freedom" (Slamm), 298–300

Oracles at Delphi, 417

Oregon Committee of Ohio, 296, 303–5

Original literary magazine, 264

O'Sullivan, John Lewis, 12–13, 191–203, 215, 237, 255–62

Paine, Byron, 316

Parlin, Ann, 13–14, 285–94

Pequot War, 52

Petrarch, 423

Philadelphia Record, 379

piracy
Defoe's account of, 95–109
"Golden Age" of, 93–95, 137–38
slavery and, 133–45
Snelgrave on ideology of, 137–38

Plan for the Abolition of Slavery, A (Spooner), 210–14

Poe, Edgar Allan, 414

power
corporate charters and, 29–31
historical role of, 6–7
Leggett's discussion of, 184–90
Smith's discussion of, 319–34

Preamble & Resolutions of the Equal Rights Party Convention, 170–73

Puritanism. *See also* Separatists
corporate charter and, 9–10
cultural influence of, 255–56
High Church Anglicanism and, 45–46
Marymount settlement and, 9–10, 47–52
Morton's critique of, 51–52
witch trials and, 426–28

Pythagoras, 416–18

quantitative history, 6

race
as sociopolitical construction, 131
technology and, 436
Whipple's writing on, 264–74

Randolph, John, 151

Rediker, Marcus, 137–38

"relief captives," 279–80

Remus, 417

Renaissance, Godwin's discussion of, 423–25

Republican Party, 399–411

"Restraining Law" (New York), 184–87

"Restraining Law and Its Abominations, The" (Leggett), 184–87

"Revolt Against Socialism" *(Portland Morning Oregonian)*, 356–57

Rhode Island
"Door War" in, 285–86
racism and sexism in, 264–74
Suffragist movement in, 286–94

Ricardo's law of comparative advantage, 435–36

Rocail, 419

Rockefeller, Nelson, 400

Roman history, Godwin's discussion of, 417–18

Romulus, 417–18

Roosevelt, Franklin D., 15, 363–65, 373–75, 378–81

Rosicrucians, 415

Russell, John (Lord), 280–81

Salem witch trials, 427–28

Sampson, Agnes, 426

Sandwich Islands, British imperialism in, 309–11

Scientific Revolution, 425

Second World War, 389, 393

"Secret Six" group, 206

Sedgwick, Theodore, III, 12, 176–82

Separatists. *See also* Puritanism
destruction of Marymount by, 67–73
justice policies of, 83–84
Morton's critique of, 51–52, 63–67, 83–92
religious hierarchy and practices of, 79–83

sexism, Whipple's writing on, 264–74

Shakespeare, William, 45

Sherman, Gen. William Tecumseh, 318

Shrimp (Captain). *See* Standish, Miles

Silvester II (Pope), 421

Sims (Adm.), 376

Singularity Institute, 434

Slamm, Levi, 14, 276
"British Honor at Cabul," 306–7
on British imperialism, 296–314
"British Usurpation of the Sandwich Islands," 309–11
"Correspondence of the *Plebeian*," 307–9

"From the Cincinnati Gazette: India," 311–14

"Ireland and Her Wrongs" essay, 296, 301–3

"Opposition to the British Empire," 303–5

"Oppression vs. Freedom" essay, 298–300

slavery. *See also* abolitionist movement; African Americans (free)
history of, 10, 155–60
Leggett's discussion of, 175–76, 205–9
Locofoco and, 12
piracy and, 133–45
slave ship mutinies, 126–32
Snelgrave's defense of, 123–32
Spooner's discussion of, 11–12, 14, 205–6, 210–14, 335–45
Walker's abolitionist pleas against, 149–65
in West Africa, 111–21

Smith, Abram D., 14, 315–34
corruption scandal involving, 317
Direct Tax Act and, 318
oral remarks made by, 327–34
In re Booth case and, 318–34

Smith, Al, 372

Snelgrave, William, 10
    capture by pirates, 133–45
    defense of slavery by, 123–32
    on West African slave trade,
        111–21
sovereignty of states, Smith's
    discussion of, 322–34
Spanish colonialism, slavery and,
    150
Special Committee Un-American
    Activities, report by, 376–88
Special Field Order No. 15, land
    grants to freed slaves under,
    318
Spivak, John L., 363–64
Spooner, Lysander, "Abolition
    Plan, To the Non-Slavehold-
    ers of the South," 11–12, 14,
    205–6, 210–14, 335–45
Standish, Miles, 48, 51, 76–79
states' rights, Smith's discussion
    of, 322–34
"Story of a Goule" (Godwin), 419
"Street of the Palaces, The"
    (Leggett), 187–90
structural unemployment, colo-
    nialism and, 45–46
Stuart monarchy, corporate char-
    ters and, 20–21

Suffragist movement, 285–94
Sweden, Godwin's discussion of,
    426–27

Tammany Hall, 167–68
Taney, Roger B. (Chief Justice),
    317
technology, Eisenhower's discus-
    sion of, 394–97
terrorism, piracy as dialectic of,
    138
Thiel, Peter, 434
Thirty Years War, 20
"thymology," 1–2
Tudor monarchy, 20–21
Tullus Hostilius, 418
Turing test, 430
Turner, Nat, 12, 151
"Two Years in Von Dieman's
    Land" (Gemmel), 276–84
Tyler, John, 282–83, 292

"Unconstitutionality of Slavery,
    The" (Spooner), 336
*United States Magazine & Demo-
    cratic Review*, 191–203, 215,
    236–37, 255–56
Van Buren, Martin, 275
Veterans of Foreign Wars, 380

Victor Emmanuel III (King of Italy), 349

Victoria (Queen of England), Slamm's criticism of, 298–314

Vietnam War, Goldwater's discussion of, 405–6

"Voluntary Principle," O'Sullivan's concept of, 192

Walker, David, 12, 149–65

Walker's Appeal, in Four Articles, Together with a Preamble to the Colored Citizens of the World, but in Particular and Very Expressly to Those of, the United States of America (Excerpts) (Walker), 151–65

Washington Globe, 176, 207

West African kings, European slave trade and, 111–21

Whig party, banking system and, 215–16, 236

Whipple, Abraham, 263

Whipple, Frances (Frances Harriet Whipple Green McDougall), 13, 263–74

Whitman, Walt, 191, 256

Whittier, John Greenleaf, 191

Whydah, kingdom of, Dahomey militarism and destruction of, 111–21

Williams, Roger, 52, 263

witchcraft, Godwin's discussion of, 419–28, 432–33

Woodman, Elijah, 278, 282

Young America movement
American culture and, 191, 215–17, 256
British imperialism and, 296–98
Canadian rebellion and, 275
exceptionalism and, 183

Yudkowsky, Eliezer, 434–35

Zeus (Greek god), 435

Zoroastrian Magi, Godwin's discussion of, 419–20

Libertarianism.org

Liberty. It's a simple idea and the linchpin of a complex system of values and practices: justice, prosperity, responsibility, toleration, cooperation, and peace. Many people believe that liberty is the core political value of modern civilization itself, the one that gives substance and form to all the other values of social life. They're called libertarians.

Libertarianism.org is the Cato Institute's treasury of resources about the theory and history of liberty. The book you're holding is a small part of what Libertarianism.org has to offer. In addition to hosting classic texts by historical libertarian figures and original articles from modern-day thinkers, Libertarianism.org publishes podcasts, videos, online introductory courses, and books on a variety of topics within the libertarian tradition.

Cato Institute

Founded in 1977, the Cato Institute is a public policy research foundation dedicated to broadening the parameters of policy debate to allow consideration of more options that are consistent with the principles of limited government, individual liberty, and peace. To that end, the Institute strives to achieve greater involvement of the intelligent, concerned lay public in questions of policy and the proper role of government.

The Institute is named for *Cato's Letters*, libertarian pamphlets that were widely read in the American Colonies in the early 18th century and played a major role in laying the philosophical foundation for the American Revolution.

Despite the achievement of the nation's Founders, today virtually no aspect of life is free from government encroachment. A pervasive intolerance for individual rights is shown by government's arbitrary intrusions into private economic transactions and its disregard for civil liberties. And while freedom around the globe has notably increased in the past several decades, many countries have moved in the opposite direction, and most governments still do not respect or safeguard the wide range of civil and economic liberties.

To address those issues, the Cato Institute undertakes an extensive publications program on the complete spectrum of policy issues. Books, monographs, and shorter studies are commissioned to examine the federal budget, Social Security, regulation, military spending, international trade, and myriad other issues. Major policy conferences are held throughout the year, from which papers are published thrice yearly in the *Cato Journal*. The Institute also publishes the quarterly magazine *Regulation*.

In order to maintain its independence, the Cato Institute accepts no government funding. Contributions are received from foundations, corporations, and individuals, and other revenue is generated from the sale of publications. The Institute is a nonprofit, tax-exempt, educational foundation under Section 501(c)3 of the Internal Revenue Code.

CATO INSTITUTE
1000 Massachusetts Ave., N.W.
Washington, D.C. 20001
www.cato.org